ACCLAIM FOR *The Billionaire's Vinegar*

"Captivating."
— *New York Times Book Review*

"*The Billionaire's Vinegar* is full of detail that will delight wine lovers. It will also appeal to anyone who merely savors a great tale well told. Unlike Monsieur Yquem's dodgy plonk, this book is the genuine article."
— *The Economist*

"Detailed, vibrant, and narratively gripping . . . It reads like a mystery novel set in the exclusive world of vintage and rare wine auctioneering."
— *Chicago Reader*

"For anyone with at least a curiosity about precious old wines and the love of a good story, this well-crafted piece of journalism may prove as intriguing and enjoyable as a fine old Bordeaux."
— *Seattle Times*

"This book has no right to be as exciting as it is."
— *Good Morning America*

"It is the fine details—the bouquet, the body, the notes, the finish— that make this book such a lasting pleasure, to be savored and remembered long after the last page is turned. Ben Wallace has told a splendid story just wonderfully, his touch light and deft, his instinct pitch-perfect. Of all the marvelous legends of the wine trade, this curiously unforgettable saga most amply deserves the appellation: a classic."
— SIMON WINCHESTER, author of *The Professor and the Madman* and *A Crack in the Edge of the World*

"An old bottle of wine is rare, but a ripping good mystery about one is rarer still. . . . Wallace has a great story to tell, and he builds the tension clue by clue. . . . What *The Billionaire's Vinegar* is really about, though, is desire more than wine: the desire of con artists to get what they can and the desire of the victims to believe what they wish. Desire runs through this book like wine sediment: shifting, murky, and tinged with bitterness."
        —*Globe and Mail*

"Engaging and vivid, Wallace's prose is supremely well composed and turns a complex web of commercial transactions—albeit an intriguing one—into a mystery of Hitchcockian proportions."
        —*Decanter*

"Wallace sips the story slowly, taking leisurely digressions into techniques for faking wine and detecting same with everything from Monticello scholarship to nuclear physics. He paints a colorful backdrop of eccentric oenophiles, decadent tastings, and overripe flavor rhetoric. . . . Investigating wines so old and rare they could taste like anything, he playfully questions the very foundations of connoisseurship."
        —*Publishers Weekly*

"Truly riveting . . . For anyone familiar with the wine world, the book will provide extraordinary enjoyment, more or less as beach material. But this book has great potential to cross over to a mainstream audience. . . . In some ways, the most interesting aspect of the story is how people want so much to believe in things, and so, they do. That is really the take-away message of the book, and Wallace has done a lovely job of presenting it."
        —*Barron's*

"I thoroughly enjoyed the book."
—ROBERT M. PARKER JR.

"*The Billionaire's Vinegar* is the ultimate page-turner. Written with literary intelligence, it has a cast of characters like something out of *Fawlty Towers* meets *The Departed*. It takes you into a subculture so deep and delicious, you can almost taste the wine that turns so many seemingly rational people into madmen. It is superb nonfiction."
—BUZZ BISSINGER, author of *Friday Night Lights*

"Call it wine noir: this nonfiction exposé shows a counterfeiter defrauding a well-heeled handful of oenophiles. . . . Read it with a glass of 2005 Catena Malbec . . . as a reminder that great wine should be consumed, not just collected."
—*Men's Health*

"A gem of a book . . . Mr. Wallace answers questions raised about Rodenstock and his remarkable find with a narrative that moves slowly and gracefully through lively and interesting information. Mr. Wallace seems to consciously take his time revealing what he knows, much like someone tasting a fine wine. There is no rush or urgency. Just a tale that oenophiles, history buffs, and ordinary wine lovers alike will savor."
—*Washington Times*

"Terrific."
—*Slate*

"It's a story that brings together the disparate themes of wealth, greed, narcissism, ego, and fraud, with a dollop of history and some nifty detective work thrown in for good pleasure—and it's a compelling read. . . . What makes this such a good read is that it is as much about people as it is about wine."
—*The World of Fine Wine*

The Billionaire's Vinegar

THE MYSTERY OF THE WORLD'S
MOST EXPENSIVE BOTTLE OF WINE

BENJAMIN WALLACE

THREE RIVERS PRESS
NEW YORK

Originally published in hardcover in slightly different form in the United States
by Crown Publishers, an imprint of the Crown Publishing Group, a division
of Random House, Inc., New York, in 2008.

Library of Congress Cataloging-in-Publication Data

Wallace, Benjamin, 1968–
The Billionaire's vinegar : the mystery of the world's most
expensive bottle of wine / Benjamin Wallace.
Includes bibliographical references.
1. Wine and wine making—Miscellanea.   I. Title.
TP548.W2945 2008
641.2'223—dc22   2007031645

ISBN 978-0-307-33878-5

Printed in the United States of America

Design by Lauren Dong

10   9   8   7

First Paperback Edition

To my parents,
and in memory of Claire Wickham Woodroffe

CONTENTS

The

Billionaire's Vinegar

CHAPTER 1

LOT 337

A HUSH HAD COME OVER THE WEST ROOM. PHOTOG-
raphers' flashes strobed the standing-room-only crowd
silently, and the lone sound was the crisp voice of the auctioneer. To the world, Michael Broadbent projected a central-
casting British cool, but under the bespoke suit, he was practicing a
kind of mind control that calmed him in these situations. The trick
was to focus narrowly, almost autistically, on numbers: lot number,
number of bidders, paddle numbers, bid steps.

Even after all these years, he still found it bracingly creative to
conjure excitement out of a heap of dirty old bottles. No matter
how many of them the fifty-eight-year-old Broadbent might see, he
retained his boyish sense of marvel at the longevity of wine. Inert
antiques were all very well, but there was magic in old wine—a
mysterious and wonderful alchemy in something that could live and
change for two hundred years and still be *drinkable*.

Auctioneer was Broadbent's most public role, but it was only
one of his distinctions in the wine world. In London he cut a familiar figure, pedaling to work each day on his Dutch ladies' bicycle

with basket, legs gunning furiously, a trilby hat perched on his head. Often he was elsewhere, and he kept up a brutal schedule. As founding director of the Christie's wine department, he had spent the last two decades crisscrossing the planet, cataloging the dank and dusty contents of rich men's cellars, tasting tens of thousands of fine wines, and jotting his impressions in slender red hardcover notebooks. Those unassuming scribblings amounted to the most comprehensive diary of wine ever recorded. That diary now consisted of sixty of the Ideal notebooks, and he had collected them in a published tome that was the standard reference on old wines. Under Broadbent's direction, Christie's had largely invented and come to dominate the global market in old and rare wines. While Christie's as a whole was smaller than its great rival, Sotheby's, its wine department was more than twice as big, bringing in £7.3 million the previous season.

Broadbent's peers in the trade acknowledged that his palate was the most experienced in the world. His pocket textbook on wine tasting, the definitive work of its kind, was in its eleventh edition, having sold more than 160,000 copies, and had been translated into eight languages. Any collector hosting an event that aspired to any seriousness made sure to invite Broadbent and his famously sensitive nose. When he arrived at a wine gathering, if so much as a trace of woodsmoke or the merest whiff of cigarette ash besmirched the air, Broadbent would scrunch up his nose, and everything would come to a halt while windows and doors were flung open.

A lean six feet tall, Broadbent had a fringy sweep of whitening hair, and his smile, distinctly hail-fellow-well-met, was tempered by the cocked eyebrow of a worldly man. He looked more aristocratic than many of the dukes and princes alongside whom he sat on Christie's board of directors.

When Broadbent tasted, he would lay his wristwatch next to his little red notebook, so that he could time the wine's changes in the glass. During lulls, if a piano was on hand, he might charm guests with some Brahms, or he might go off by himself to sketch the local scenery.

He was happy to opine, at these tastings, on the wines under consideration. He had a knack for putting wine into memorable words. Sometimes he borrowed from literature, describing one wine as "black as Egypt's night." More often, he minted his own rakish descriptions, seeing a woman in every wine. A '79 Pétrus reminded him of Sophia Loren: "You can admire them, but you don't want to go to bed with them." A double magnum of '47 Cantenac-Brown evoked chocolate and "schoolgirls' uniforms."

THE TASTE OF the wine he was selling right now in London, just past 2:30 p.m. on Thursday, December 5, 1985, was impossible to know. December 5 had special meaning for Broadbent; it was the same date that James Christie, in 1766, had held the auction house's very first sale. Moments earlier, Broadbent had stepped up to the rostrum in a three-piece suit with a pocket square, and peered out at the room through his eyeglasses.

Lot 337 was the first item of the afternoon session and had been carefully removed from its green felt berth in a glass case nearby. Lucy Godsal, a secretary in Broadbent's office, held the bottle aloft for the room to see. She looked very Christie's—blond, headband, pearl necklace—and Broadbent liked her; she was smart, hardworking, and pretty.

Broadbent had never sold anything quite like this before. A Château Lafite from 1787, it was the oldest authenticated vintage red wine ever to come up for auction at Christie's. And that was the least of its merits. The bottle was engraved with the initials "Th.J." As Broadbent had described it in the auction catalog, "Th.J. are the initials of Thomas Jefferson." Almost miraculously, the bottle was full of wine and appeared to have survived two centuries intact. The container itself was beautiful and distinctive. "This is one time,"

Broadbent quipped to the crowd, "when the buyer will get something back on the bottle."

The admittedly fragmentary tale of how the bottle had been found only added to its mystique. According to Hardy Rodenstock, the German collector who had consigned the bottle to Christie's, in the spring of 1985 workers tearing down a house in Paris had broken through a false wall in the basement and happened upon a hidden cache of extremely old wines. The Lafite, inscribed with the initials of the Founding Father, who had lived in Paris from 1784 to 1789 and was the foremost American wine connoisseur of his day, had been among them.

The integrity of the seals, and the high fill levels, Rodenstock had told Broadbent, were remarkable for their age. The cellar had been almost hermetically preserved, its steady temperature in the sweet spot of 50 to 57 degrees Fahrenheit. Rodenstock theorized that the bottles had been walled up to protect them during the chaos of the French Revolution, and had lain undisturbed for two hundred years.

Not surprisingly, Rodenstock refused to divulge the precise location, the exact number of bottles, or anything else about the discovery, despite Broadbent's entreaties. Rodenstock was the leading private collector in Europe, and he had already made a name for himself in rare-wine circles as an unusually skilled bottle hunter. Though he was a longtime customer of Christie's, Rodenstock was a competitor when it came to obtaining private cellars. Private-cellar purchases were often cash deals that went unreported to tax authorities. A certain reticence about his sources was to be expected.

Broadbent felt there were a couple of possibilities. One was that the bottle had indeed been discovered during the excavations of the old Marais district in Paris, much of which had recently been torn up and redeveloped. A rumor less credited by Broadbent, and which he had no intention of putting in the catalog copy, was that the bottle had been part of some sort of Nazi cellar.

Broadbent knew Rodenstock well, trusted him, and would not normally be too concerned with how he had obtained the bottle. But to Broadbent's annoyance, a historical researcher in America had recently been making noises in the press, questioning whether the bottle was in fact Jefferson's. Broadbent had conducted his own research and was satisfied that the circumstantial evidence argued overwhelmingly in favor of the attribution. He couldn't prove it, but on balance, the inducements to proceed outweighed any risk of embarrassment.

The auctioneer's delight in an object that would sell itself accounted for only half of Broadbent's excitement. There was also the oenophile's anticipation, for Lafite was Broadbent's favorite wine. He loved the way it developed in the glass, revealing new depths and facets as it breathed. He thought Lafite the acme of elegance, a racehorse beside the show horse of Mouton and the cart horse of Latour. But to open a bottle as old as this was to play roulette; Broadbent couldn't help wondering what it might taste like. And how to price such an object? When cataloging it for auction, Broadbent gave the estimate as "inestimable." He was rather pleased with his pun.

A number of commission bids—those placed in advance by bidders who could not, or didn't want to, attend—had come in. Château Lafite-Rothschild, modern successor to the eighteenth-century vineyard, had placed a £5,000 bid; this had been so eclipsed by other advance bids that the Château was out of the running before the session even began. Broadbent could feel confident that a new single-bottle price record was about to be set.

In the West Room, he opened the bidding at £10,000. At first the bids came slowly, moving in £2,000 increments. A paddle would rise here. Another would bob up there. But things quickly heated up, and soon several people were raising paddles at every step.

Broadbent knew everyone in the London trade, and many of them were here in this room, but he reserved his greatest expectations for the Americans. The Jefferson connection, the strength of the dollar (it had hit a historic high earlier in the year), recent auction history—all these factors would surely tempt a deep-pocketed Yank to repatriate the bottle. Marvin Shanken, publisher of the magazine *Wine Spectator,* was here today, but Broadbent's highest hopes were aimed at the fellow who sat left of the center aisle from where Broadbent stood: Christoper "Kip" Forbes, the thirty-five-year-old son of publisher Malcolm Forbes.

Broadbent didn't think much of Malcolm Forbes, finding him to be "a mean sort of chap." He knew that the American publisher collected first growths, the top-ranked Bordeaux reds, though only in lousy vintages. But it was undeniable that Forbes had money and would spend it for something he wanted, and Kip soon entered the bidding.

The price volleyed remorselessly to £20,000, then £30,000. At £40,000, it seemed, fleetingly, that a cap might have been reached, but the bidding resurged. Only after Kip Forbes bid £50,000—$75,000—did all the other paddles stay down. This was a new record for a bottle of wine, by a wide margin. The previous record, set the year before at an auction in Dallas, was $38,000 for a Jéroboam (equivalent to six bottles) of 1870 Mouton-Rothschild; the record for a normal-size bottle was $31,000, paid in 1980 for an 1822 Lafite. Today's price now far exceeded Broadbent's most wishful imaginings. He felt vindicated by his decision to go ahead with the sale.

He began the ritual countdown. "Any more?"

He scanned the crowd for takers. "Any more?"

Again Broadbent looked around the room, daring the bidders with his eyes to outdo Forbes. Nothing.

Then, at the rear of the room, he saw a movement.

CHAPTER 2

INCOGNITO

O N FEBRUARY 22, 1788, WRITING FROM PARIS, THOMAS Jefferson placed an order for 250 bottles of Lafite. In the past he would have sent the letter to one of the merchants through whom he had previously made his wine requests. But on this occasion he wrote directly to the owner of the property, having recently become wise to the dangers of doing otherwise.

Now forty-four years old, Jefferson was an especially tall man by eighteenth-century standards, topping six foot two, with an erect posture, a ruddy, freckled face, and fair, reddish hair. He had spent the last four years as American commissioner, and then minister, to France. Faint tremors of class struggle had become the insistent rumblings of the early French Revolution, and Jefferson was torn. The author of the Declaration of Independence sympathized with the poor and oppressed, while the gourmand and the architect of Monticello was drawn to the refinements of salon culture.

He had welcomed the chance to come to Europe. Jefferson's beloved wife, Martha, had died when he was just thirty-nine, leaving him a grieving widower and single father. And Jefferson had dreamed of coming to France since he was a young man. The diversions of Paris were exactly what he needed to lift him out of his depression. In contrast to his earthier fellow minister, Ben Franklin, who was legendary in the City of Light for wearing a beaver hat and biting the heads off asparagus, Jefferson fit right in.

Though he called himself "a savage of the mountains of America," in France Jefferson took to wearing a powdered wig and a topaz ring. His mansion on the Champs-Élysées was a place of blue silk damask curtains, crystal decanters, a well-stocked wine cellar, and a household staff that included a *frotteur,* whose sole function was to clean the parquet floors by spinning around with brushes strapped to his feet. Intoxicated with the French high life, Jefferson hosted frequent dinner parties, serving some of the best wines of France.

Jefferson was not the only Founding Father who was fond of wine. Franklin, for one, kept a substantial cellar in Paris and called wine "proof that God loves us and that he likes to see us happy." But Jefferson, who had been ordering wine for many years, had recently acquired an unmatched breadth and depth of knowledge about the subject.

Not only had he learned which were the best wines, but he had also become savvy about the mischief to which an unwary consumer might fall prey. In his 1788 letter to the owner of Lafite, Jefferson spelled out his concern directly: "If it would be possible to have them bottled and packed at your estate, it would doubtless be a guarantee that the wine was genuine, and the drawing-off and so forth well done." Jefferson owed his newfound wine sophistication to a life-changing trip he had made the year before.

THE TIME WAS ripe for an escape from Paris. He had become infatuated with a married English-Italian woman, Maria Cosway, but by early 1787 the romance seemed to have fizzled. In February, with his daughter Patsy safely cloistered in a convent school and his official duties in the hands of William Short, his trusted personal secretary, Jefferson embarked on a tour of France and northern Italy. He had dislocated his right wrist in a mysterious accident—historians have speculated that he was trying to jump over a fence to impress Cosway—and he justified the trip as being curative.

His itinerary also happened to take him through all of the country's major wine regions. In view of Jefferson's personal debts, which were already substantial, and the momentous challenges facing the struggling young country that was paying his way in Europe, the decision to take a three-and-a-half-month vacation could be seen as almost comically self-indulgent. Patsy Jefferson noted rather freshly, in a letter to her father a week after he left Paris, that she was "inclined to think that your voyage is rather for your pleasure than for your health."

Jefferson had been keen on wine for a long time. When he began building Monticello in 1769, at the age of twenty-six, the first part constructed was the wine cellar. As the second governor of Virginia, Jefferson gained access to an official stock of Bordeaux, Burgundy, German Rieslings, and Champagne. One story, passed down among Jefferson's slaves, held that his Virginia cellar had been emptied three years before he left for France, when British troops, commanded by the reviled Banastre "The Butcher" Tarleton, destroyed Jefferson's casks and smashed his bottles with their swords, flooding the dirt floor.

It wasn't just drinking wine that interested Jefferson. True independence, he was sure, meant agricultural self-sufficiency. Americans would have to make their own wine if they didn't want to rely on imports. Jefferson had first planted vines at Monticello in 1771, and a few years before his trip to Europe, he had encouraged an Italian immigrant named Filippo Mazzei to grow European wine-grape varieties by giving him 193 acres in Monticello's backyard. Both efforts failed, but Jefferson remained hopeful for American wine.

Now, as his horse-drawn carriage clattered along the post roads of France, he at last had a chance to see the most fabled vineyards in the world. He traveled light, bringing only a single trunk with him. Wanting to experience the real France, unfiltered by preferential treatment and unburdened by diplomatic obligations, he traveled incognito, the plan being to hire a different valet in each town, so that no one would find out who he was.

Jefferson drank France in with guzzling intemperance. Aesthete and classicist, he basked in the scattered ruins of the Roman Empire. Social observer, he talked his way into people's homes to see how they lived, ate their bread, and lay on their beds as if to rest but really to feel their softness. Farmer and wine aficionado, he moved from Burgundy to the Rhône Valley to Bordeaux; in each of these wine-growing areas, he closely studied the grapes grown, the composition of the soil, and the techniques of winemaking. He scrutinized the training of vines and the disparate blending methods. He obsessed over the production capacities of each château and the prices charged for each wine.

Jefferson was compulsively inquisitive, and he spoke French well enough to grill laborers and cellarmasters alike. How many years before a vine started to yield good fruit? Twenty-five. Did the winemakers dung their soil? A little. Did the vineyard overseer's pay include board? No, just room and drink. Jefferson's interest was more than pedantic; he was devouring all information that might help his young country to make its own wine.

At Aix-en-Provence, he luxuriated in the southern sun and soaked his aching wrist ten times a day in the spa town's mineral-rich waters. At Agen, he ate the tiny thrushes called ortolans. For nine days, Jefferson left the road altogether, barging two hundred miles from the Mediterranean coast up the canal of Languedoc to Toulouse, serenaded by trees full of nightingales. He loved traveling this way, and divided his time between walking on the bank alongside the slow-moving boat and sitting in his coach, which rested wheelless atop the barge. Away from the crush of duty and unknown to those around him, he was able to relax and reflect— and perhaps get Maria Cosway out of his mind. During the entire 3,000-mile trip, he wouldn't write a single letter to her.

Back on the road, he made the remaining journey to Bordeaux in three days. Along the way, he passed through rich farmland planted with corn, rye, and beans. As soon as he ferried west across the Garonne, just south of Bordeaux proper, the picture changed. On May 24, as he rolled through the district of Sauternes and entered Bordeaux, he looked out through the glass windows of his carriage and saw nothing but grapevines. An ocean away, the next day, the Constitutional Convention opened in Philadelphia.

In Bordeaux, Jefferson lingered. Though Burgundy's reputation as a wine region was older, a combination of circumstances had led to Bordeaux's greater fame abroad. Burgundy, being farther inland, had less access to export channels, and the complex ownership structure of the vineyards made the region hard to understand. The wine itself was unreliable; the region's northern position meant more underripe vintages, and the fickleness of the thin-skinned pinot noir, the grape used to make Burgundy's reds, only aggravated the problem.

Jefferson had told a colleague that he wanted to visit Bordeaux because it was one "of those seaports with which we trade." The most important port in France, it served as the main staging area for trade with its West Indian colonies, a funnel for the bounty of southern France. But its role as a commercial hub was probably the least of the city's attractions for Jefferson. Wine accounted for a full third of the cargo leaving Bordeaux, and some two-thirds of the region's inhabitants were involved in some way in the business. Although in the course of his life Jefferson was a serial monogamist when it came to his favorite wines, regularly announcing some new one as supreme in his affections, his high esteem for Bordeaux would remain constant.

The place was booming. White stone mansions for the ascendant class of lawyers and merchants were going up in the commercial core; along its fringe the city was sprouting fresh streets. Bordeaux was now among the loveliest and most prosperous of European cities—with none of the wretched hunger and social turmoil rampant in other parts of France. Seven years before Jefferson arrived, Europe's grandest new theater had been erected here, a neoclassical edifice fronted by a majestic portico with twelve soaring Corinthian columns.

Jefferson checked into the Hôtel de Richlieu in the city center and, over the next four days, divided his time between attending to business and being a tourist. A packet of letters and books, forwarded from Paris, awaited him here. Keeping up with correspondence was not, for Jefferson, simply a matter of putting pen to paper. He carried with him a portable copying press, and made duplicates of every letter he sent. In a separate journal he kept a record of every letter written and received. Now, writing with the special ink required to make copies, Jefferson spent a morning replying to correspondence. He also came to the aid of Thomas Barclay, the former American consul, who had recently traveled to North Africa to negotiate a peace with the Barbary pirates. Barclay had been released from debtor's prison in Bordeaux a few days before, and Jefferson lent him 1,000 livres, fudging the expense to the United States as being "on acct. of [Mr. Barclay's] Marocco [sic] mission." Barclay was about to return to Paris, and Jefferson bet him a bottle of Burgundy that he would beat him there.

Not one to let nation-building get in the way of a little sightseeing, Jefferson visited the ruins of a third-century Roman arena and, given as he was to making constant comparisons, measured the height, width, and thickness of the bricks. He made a day trip southwest to Château Haut-Brion, in Graves, where the vines were just beginning their annual flowering. Haut-Brion was likely the only leading Bordeaux château Jefferson had time to visit.

On his third night in the city, Jefferson saw a play at the Grand Théâtre, which was only a few minutes' walk from his hotel. The girls who danced and sang there, according to the city's "scandalous chronicle," were kept, at lofty salaries, by Bordeaux merchants. Jefferson enjoyed meals featuring the season's produce of peas, cherries, and strawberries, and he admired the procession of elms along the Quai des Chartrons, an arcing strand that followed the curve of the Garonne River as it cut through the middle of the city.

The quay—ugly, muddy, stone-pocked, and only sporadically paved—was alive with the stir of commerce. It was the center of Bordeaux's wine trade. Wagons drawn by cream-colored oxen wheeled past, and ocean-bound schooners heaped with barrels plied the broad waterway. The merchants had their offices here, and at the shore, barges took on and put off their quietly sloshing freight. Increasingly the wine was going to England, which had recently concluded a low-tariff trade pact with France, and where the upper and middle classes were developing a taste for better wines.

The first modern wine brands, with special status accorded to particular estates and vintages, were just then coming to prominence. The recent reinvention of the cork and the glass bottle, pioneered by the ancient Romans but long forgotten, had renewed the idea of deliberately aging wine. And the idea was now made practicable by the development of cylindrical bottles, which could be laid down horizontally, efficiently stacked en masse, and left to mature in the damp and darkness of a personal wine cellar. It was the finest wines, those with the greatest capacity to improve with age, that were set aside rather than consumed immediately. And the French wines that turned out to be best suited for aging were the reds of Bordeaux.

If the building boom in the city center was fairly recent, for nearly a century a "fury of planting" had been transforming the marshy terrain in the surrounding countryside, traditionally sown with grain, into a sprawling quality-wine district. Wine had been made here in smaller quantities for much longer. The climate, tempered by breezes off the Atlantic and its estuaries, was hospitable to the grape, and through centuries of trial and error, the Bordelais had learned much about vine-growing and vinification. They had found and demarcated the best sites—with the optimal exposure to sun, drainage, and gravelly soil—and had begun to identify the grapes most suited to the area: cabernet sauvignon, merlot, cabernet franc, petit verdot, and malbec.

Claret, as the English called the light, blended style of red wine particular to Bordeaux, was well established by now, as were the top vineyards; a specific hierarchy had been generally acknowledged since at least 1730, when Bordeaux brokers divided the vineyards into three classes. The ranking mirrored the prices different wines fetched on the market and had been consistent for more than fifty years.

Until now, when Jefferson had ordered wine from Bordeaux, he had done so through an agent, and his requests had been generic. Just a year earlier he had asked John Bondfield, America's consul in Bordeaux who had supplied Ben Franklin with wine, to arrange a shipment of twelve dozen bottles of red Bordeaux and twelve dozen of white, "of fine quality," in either bottles or casks, as Bondfield saw fit. For these bottles, Jefferson paid two livres each. Now that he was in Bordeaux, Jefferson could see the quality pyramid for himself. He learned that the best white Bordeaux came from the Sauternes district, and that the best of these was a sweet wine called Yquem, which sold the equivalent of 150,000 bottles annually. And he learned that four red wines, from vineyards planted in the seventeenth century, fetched the highest prices of all.

Haut-Brion, variously spelled by English writers as Ho Bryan, Oberon, and Obrian, had been the first of the Bordeaux wines to be specifically sought after in England. In 1663 the diarist Samuel Pepys noted that he drank "a sort of French wine called Ho Bryan that hath a good and most particular taste that I ever met with," and fourteen years later the political philosopher John Locke visited the estate. By around 1700, the *London Gazette* was announcing coffee-house auctions of "Lafitte, Margouze and La Tour," all located on the tongue of land northwest of the city known as the Médoc. The Duc de Richelieu, a libertine exiled to Bordeaux in the middle of the century, held all-night orgies and developed a taste for the wines of the region, in particular Lafite. Upon his return to the Versailles court of Louis XV, the duke spread the Lafite gospel, telling the king it was "the secret of eternal youth," and it became a fashionable wine. By the time of Jefferson's visit in 1787, the privileged quartet that would subsequently be known as the *premiers crus,* or first growths, sold for up to two and a half times the price of the next-best wines. Haut-Brion sold the equivalent of 75,000 bottles a year, Latour 125,000, Margaux 150,000, and Lafite 175,000.

Jefferson recorded all this, as well as the names of several second- and third-tier wines, among the latter a wine called Mouton. He also learned about Bordeaux vintages. The rule of vintage variation was ancient: If a crop's quality fluctuates with annual weather, so must anything made from that crop. The most famous wine in ancient Rome was called Falernian, and its 121 BC vintage was legendary. AD 1540 was a storied vintage for Steinwein, a white wine favored by King Ludwig II of Bavaria.

In Bordeaux's off years, vintage purity fell by the wayside, and vintages would be blended; in good years, the wines were made separately. When Jefferson visited the region, the finest available year was 1784, "the best vintage which has happened in nine years," as Jefferson wrote to a friend. "I may safely assure you therefore that, according to the taste of this country and of England there cannot be a bottle of better Bordeaux produced in France."

Before sailing north from the Quai on May 29, five days after his arrival, Jefferson put his new knowledge to use, ordering 252 bottles of 1784 Haut-Brion from a local merchant, including seventy-two bottles to be sent directly to his brother-in-law Francis Eppes in Virginia. "I cannot deny myself the pleasure of asking you to participate of a small parcel of wine I have been chusing for myself," he wrote to Eppes. "I do it the rather as it will furnish you a specimen of what is the very best Bourdeaux wine." Instead of Haut-Brion, however, the merchant filled the order with 1784 Margaux.

Jefferson got back to Paris on June 10, 1787, refreshed and perhaps ready for another romantic attachment. The next month his younger daughter, Polly, arrived from America, attended by a light-skinned, fourteen-year-old slave girl named Sally Hemings.

Despite his three-and-a-half-month trip, Jefferson's connoisseurship was in one respect still a blunt instrument. His personal taxonomy of wine was divided into a mere five categories: sweet, acid, dry, silky, and astringent. The characteristics he was most concerned about were rudimentary things like hardiness, since the wine needed to survive long, bumpy journeys. In his letters he would enthuse about a particular wine's "strength" or "flavor," or speak of "the best vintage" of a wine or of "the most celebrated" producers. That was about as precise as he got.

But in a number of important ways, Jefferson's 1787 trip had made him the greatest wine connoisseur writing in any language at the time. Learning the best vineyards and vintages was part of it, but two shifts in Jefferson's behavior hinted at a deeper, more hard-won sophistication. He was no longer asking someone else which wines to buy, instead deciding for himself. And he was becoming skeptical about the integrity of the wines, an issue seemingly as old as wine itself. He now resolved to make it his standard practice to order wine straight from the châteaux. That September he told a friend that, when it came to buying direct, he could "assure you that it is from them alone that genuine wine is to be got, and not from any wine merchant whatever."

There were all sorts of reasons and ways to fiddle with the product. Some meddling was customary "improvement," and some was the work of charlatans. Dutch merchants dosed claret with brandy to help it survive rugged journeys to distant markets, and added sugar and spices to bring it in line with the Low Country taste for sweeter, more resinous wine. The Bordeaux negociants who sold to the English market tailored the wine to that nation's gin-and-Port-benumbed palates by spiking it with stronger Spanish or French wine as well as distilled spirits. Newer wine might be mixed with old to extend its shelf life; water, or inferior wine, might be mixed with good stuff in order to stretch it; less appealing vintages were worked on to make them taste better.

None of this was new. In the *Canterbury Tales,* the Pardoner warned his listeners to avoid "mysteriously" mixed wines. Much earlier, Pliny bemoaned the problem of doctored wine: "Now not even the greatest can enjoy pure wines anywhere. . . . Trade morality has come to such a pass that only labels and cellar names are sold, and the must is adulterated while it is still in the press. And the result is a strange paradox; the wine of least repute is least sophisticated and most wholesome." The Romans were so liberal in their manipulations—using smoke, fire, and seawater to accelerate the aging process—that British writer H. Warner Allen would later describe their era as "the Golden Age of Wine Faking."

It remained a problem in Thomas Jefferson's day. An early-nineteenth-century recipe called for a "very inferior French wine sold to the adulterators" to be "mixed with rough cider, and coloured to resemble claret" by adding cochineal and vegetable dye. Just seven years after Jefferson's visit to Bordeaux, Paris officials analyzed wine samples from sixty-eight merchants and declared that only eight of them could be legitimately called wine. During his Bordeaux visit, Jefferson spoke with a broker named Desgrands, who said he and his peers never mixed the best wines, but only the lesser ones, and then to improve them.

Upon his return to Paris, Jefferson was duly skeptical. "I would prefer to receive it directly from your hands," he wrote from Paris to Monsieur d'Yquem in December of 1787, requesting 250 bottles of 1784 Yquem, "because I would be sure that it is genuine, good and sound." The following year, he placed his order with the owner of Lafite.

ON SEPTEMBER 17, 1789, Jefferson hosted a dinner party in Paris. Among the guests were Gouverneur Morris—a high-born, peg-legged New York lawyer and politician who kept the same mistress as the bishop of Autun, also known as Talleyrand; the Marquis de Lafayette, the red-haired, thirty-two-year-old aristocrat-revolutionary; the Duc de La Rochefoucauld, with whom Jefferson liked to discuss farming experiments, and who a few years later would be stoned to death and disemboweled by a mob in front of his wife and mother; and the Marquis de Condorcet, the vaunted mathematician and *philosophe* who had a bleached pallor and was given to biting his nails.

It was chilly out, and a fire crackled in the drawing room. The house, at the intersection of the Champs-Élysées and the rue de Berri on the western edge of the city, had a spare, half-empty look; much of the contents had already been crated for shipment to Monticello, since Jefferson was soon to quit Paris for what he thought would be a six-month leave in America. Two months earlier, a mob had overrun the Bastille. Paris was in tumult, and Jefferson had requested that guards be posted outside; his house had been robbed three times recently, the candlesticks taken from his dining table, and he had put bars and bells on the windows.

The group sat down to eat at four-thirty in the afternoon, and they discussed rumors that Louis XVI was plotting an escape from France. Paris was suffering a bread shortage, but the repast was almost certainly accompanied by fine wines. Jefferson's slave James Hemings had learned French cooking through several apprenticeships and now ran Jefferson's Paris kitchen. While recognizing that he had more to learn from Europeans about the pleasures of the table than they from him, Jefferson was not strictly deferential. During his stay in Paris, he pressed pecans on the French, served corn on the cob grown in his Paris garden, and accompanied it with Virginia ham.

Nine days later, Jefferson departed overland for Le Havre, from which he crossed the English Channel and boarded a ship bound for the infant United States. Among the eighty-six packing cases of European finery that he had bought and shipped back to America were hampers full of various wines, including two containers earmarked for John Jay and George Washington.

Jefferson intended to return to Paris, but Gouverneur Morris bet William Short, Jefferson's secretary, a beaver hat that Jefferson would not. As it turned out, Morris won the bet: Jefferson was appointed secretary of state. His majordomo was left to dismantle the Paris household. He sold his master's horses, chariot, cabriolet, and paper press, and packed up the rest of his furniture for shipment to Philadelphia, swaddling each box in oilcloth. Each of Jefferson's books he wrapped in paper.

Amid the growing chaos of Revolutionary France, a silver-plated harness for Jefferson's horses, as well as his coach cushions, was stolen. Some wine, too, remained unaccounted for. One hundred twenty-five bottles of 1784 Haut-Brion that Jefferson had ordered in May 1788 never arrived. And a batch of provisions that arrived at Monticello just before Christmas of 1789 was short one box of assorted wines.

CHAPTER 3

TOMB RAIDER

W̲HEN MICHAEL BROADBENT ARRIVED AT HOPE-
toun House, after negotiating the long driveway in the
dark, it was clear that he had interrupted Lord Linlithgow, who opened the door wearing crimson suspenders. The butler
arrived at the door at the same time, still pulling on his black jacket.
The marquis and his servant had both been watching the Miss World
competition on TV, and were now trading opinions about the con-
testants.

It was October 1966. A senior partner at Christie's had introduced Broadbent to his friend "Charlie," the Marquis of Linlithgow,
who mentioned that he and his brother were growing rather weary of
their hit-or-miss collection of eighteenth-century Madeira. Broadbent had asked whether he might come up from London to see
the cellar, and now here he was, in a mansion on the outskirts of
Edinburgh. Broadbent chatted briefly with His Lordship over a glass
of whiskey by the fireplace, then went to bed.

He was new to his job as head of Christie's fledgling wine

department, and nervous. He couldn't sleep, so he opened *My Life and Loves,* the sexually explicit memoirs of Frank Harris, a turn-of-the-twentieth-century womanizer and magazine editor.

When the sun came up, Broadbent descended to the cellars. They were directly beneath the flagstones of the main hall, and organized into bins, columbarium-like walls of stone niches containing not ashes but wine. Everything was covered in dust, but it didn't matter. In houses like this, the bottles didn't have labels; you knew what was in them through a combination of bin labels and cellar books. One wall at a time, moving top to bottom, left to right, Broadbent wrote down the inventory: the Madeiras, claret, Port, Champagne, and some weird old liqueurs.

As he was leaving, Lord Linlithgow mentioned that his neighbor Harry, sixth Earl of Rosebery, was "getting on" and had a cellar full of old claret he might be happy to unload. The marquis handed Broadbent a scrap of paper with a list of wines. It was impressive. Lord Rosebery was the son of Hannah de Rothschild, and his cellar consisted mainly of pre-phylloxera Lafite. Phylloxera was the yellow root louse that devastated Bordeaux's vineyards in the late 1870s. Eventually, winemakers survived the epidemic by grafting French vines onto American rootstocks, which were immune to the pest. (The susceptibility of ungrafted European vines, on the other hand, explained in part why Jefferson's and Filippo Mazzei's 1770s experiments with them in the United States had failed.) Many connoisseurs believed that the wines of Bordeaux had never again attained their earlier level of quality and ageability. For such collectors, a trove of pre-phylloxera first growths was the Grail.

Soon after his visit with Lord Linlithgow, Broadbent returned to Scotland to visit Lord Rosebery's pile there. This one, Dalmeny, had its own golf course. The butler led Broadbent to the cellar, a stone room with a gravel floor and slate bins. There were rows upon rows of double magnums of 1865 Lafite, enormous bottles that put Broadbent in mind of the howitzer shells he had seen during his stint in the Royal Artillery. He packed what he could fit into his car and hurtled down the A1 motorway to London. Next he visited Mentmore, Lord Rosebery's home in Buckinghamshire, where the front hall contained an enormous table displaying Lord Rosebery's many hats and walking sticks, all neatly arrayed. The cellars here were much larger than those at Dalmeny, and Broadbent spent a full day cataloging the contents. He took a break only to have lunch with Lord Rosebery and his wife, who bickered as if he weren't there.

On Thursday, May 31, 1967, in the Great Rooms at its King Street headquarters in London, Christie's held its first "Finest and Rarest Wines" sale. The selection, which, besides the cellars of Linlithgow and Rosebery, included lots from "Amiya, Dowager Countess of Sandwich" and "the Right Honourable the Lord Bruntisfield," was a dream for collectors. There were quaint, lopsided, mouth-blown bottles of oddities like eighteenth-century Milk Punch, extract of absinthe, 1830 Tokay, and Sandeman's 1911 Coronation Vintage Port, as well as several nineteenth-century bottles of a strange, flat Champagne called Sillery that was once popular with the British upper class. Most coveted was the collection of pre-phylloxera Bordeaux, 164 of the best wines in the best vintages, in the most desirable bottle sizes.

In Bordeaux, big bottles could range from magnum (the equivalent of two bottles) to Marie-Jeanne (three bottles) to double magnum (four bottles) to Jéroboam (six bottles) to Impériale (eight bottles). In Burgundy and Champagne, older Jéroboams were called Rehoboams, an Impériale was called a Methuselah, and even bigger bottles existed, including a Salmanazar (twelve bottles), a Balthazar (sixteen bottles), and a Nebuchadnezzar (twenty bottles). Collectors loved these—for their rarity, for their drama, and for the fact that wine aged more slowly in them. In the Rosebery sale, the Lafites alone included nineteen magnums of 1858, a magnum of 1864, two Jéroboams of 1865, and forty-four magnums and seventy bottles of 1874. The sale, in a single stroke, established

Christie's wine department as a seller of rarities, ushered in a new age of wine collecting, and positioned Michael Broadbent as its public face.

TRADITIONALLY, WINE HAD left France for foreign markets in sixty-three-gallon casks known as hogsheads. British gentlemen would store these casks and drink their way through one before ordering another of its kind. Sir Robert Walpole, the eighteenth-century prime minister, had a cellar full of them; he particularly liked Margaux and Lafite.

It was during the quarter-century preceding Thomas Jefferson's visit to Bordeaux—the same period when the cylindrical, cork-stoppered, easily stacked glass bottle became common and opened the way to long-term storage and maturation of claret—that the English adopted the custom of laying down bottles to drink years later. English gentlemen subdivided their cellars into bins, each big enough for three hundred bottles (the equivalent of a hogshead). They labeled the bins with château name and vintage, and filled them with bottles that were motley in appearance. These were un-labeled bottles filled from casks by a gentleman, or more likely his butler. (After 1850, they would be joined by labeled bottles filled by middlemen such as Bordeaux or London merchants, and, less fre-quently—until the 1920s—labeled bottles filled at the châteaux themselves.)

Inevitably, cellaring of wine trickled down to the middle classes. The practice was popular enough by the 1760s that the same Pall Mall bookseller who had published Samuel Johnson's *Dictionary* came out with a book for recording wine purchases. *The Cellar-Book, or Butler's Assistant, in keeping a Regular Account of his Liquors* sold well enough to generate several editions.

Exactly which wines the English laid down stayed remarkably constant. The passion they and the Scottish nobility shared for first-growth claret approached an addiction. Lafite, in particular, enjoyed a special status both in Bordeaux, where in all the early classifications it was ranked first among firsts, and in Britain, where it was the preferred wine of the peerage. Below these four was a broader, increasingly articulated hierarchy of growths. In 1787, Jefferson mentioned three tiers, around 1800 a fourth tier was named, and around 1820 a fifth.

This unofficial five-tier stratification of Bordeaux's wines would be codified thirty-five years later. With the Paris Universal Exposition approaching, Napoleon III charged the Bordeaux Chamber of Commerce with drawing up a list of the best. The chamber turned this over to the region's brokers, who, to avoid the indelicacy of picking favorites, instead drew up a list merely of the most expensive wines, and arranged them by price. The resulting Classification of 1855 formalized a numerical ranking of sixty-one of the most sought-after reds. Below the four first growths were fifteen second growths, fourteen third growths, ten fourth growths, and eighteen fifth growths. All of the wines came from the so-called left bank, west of the Garonne River. The predominantly merlot-based right-bank wines, which would become revered in the second half of the twentieth century, weren't even mentioned.

At the same time, a separate classification of Sauternes confirmed Château d'Yquem's unchallenged position as the king of sweet white wines. A large part of Yquem's reputation had to do with its extremely low yield: seventy gallons to an acre, compared with more than four hundred for a leading red wine. Put another way, a single vine can produce an entire bottle of dry red wine; it produces just one glass of Yquem. The wines of Sauternes relied on the phenomenon of "noble rot," or botrytis, a fungal infection that, under precisely the right weather conditions, withered the Semillon grape to create an unctuous wine of unparalleled richness. The glory of Yquem was affirmed four years later when Russian Grand Duke Constantine, the czar's brother, placed an order for four barrels of the 1847 vintage of Yquem, paying 20,000 gold francs, four times the going rate. The purchase spread Yquem's fame and sent its market value soaring.

For Bordeaux, 1858 to 1878 was a belle epoque, blessed with favorable weather and a succession of excellent vintages. The advent of railways and steamships opened virgin markets. Gold rushes minted new millionaires. The 1860 trade treaty between Britain and France negotiated by Chancellor of the Exchequer William Gladstone, himself a claret man, reduced the tax on Bordeaux wine by 95 percent and led, over the next fifteen years, to an eightfold growth in British claret imports. Bordeaux's own wine production, over the same period, grew two and a half times, from 50 to more than 132 million gallons. The boom, which came to an end only with the arrival of phylloxera, funded the building of scores of grand châteaux, adding to the region's mercantile luster.

And so in the eighteenth century had begun a long migration, an annual diaspora of Bordeaux's most precious wines to the scattered cellars of claret lovers. Most of the wine sold fast and was drunk just as quickly. In 1788, wine from the 1784 vintage was already a rarity; Haut-Brion had only four hogsheads remaining, and demand for the vintage had pushed the price up to three livres per bottle. As early as 1829, a writer skeptical of advertisements for bottles from the famous 1811 "comet vintage" noted that, given its high quality and a relatively small crop, "it admits of a doubt whether even in the cellars of the richest individuals, any quantity to speak of now remains of the wine."

Nonetheless, vintages that were scouringly tannic when young could take decades to become drinkable, and wealthy claret drinkers held on to unusually abundant and ageable vintages. Subterranean deposits of fine Bordeaux began to accrete, like some patchy geological formation, into a far-flung stratum of old wine.

Some was kept by the châteaux. Starting in 1798, Lafite began compiling a *vinothèque,* or wine library, with examples of each of the château's vintages. A few bottles of 1797, the first contribution to the vinothèque, remain at Lafite, and are the oldest bottles in its cobwebbed cellar. The oldest bottle in Margaux's vinothèque, by contrast, is an 1848. Some of the wine went to the cellars of the premier restaurants in France. And much of the wine was exported.

Throughout the nineteenth century, the largest markets for claret were in flux. During the 1850s, the United States was the best customer. From 1860 to 1890, Argentina, flush with beef and wheat money, claimed that role. But most of the wine going to the Americas was lesser stuff, not the expensive first growths that merited cellaring for decades. Those remained the province of the British. Over the century following the 1855 Classification, untold tons of the top growths found their way across the Channel into the cellars of private houses, wine merchants, and ancient colleges at Oxford and Cambridge. Very often it was Lafite.

It was not uncommon for deposits to these cellars to outpace withdrawals. Original purchasers died, leaving stocks of wine that their children or grandchildren might have less interest in. By the middle of the twentieth century, England and Scotland had come to be riddled with underground repositories of precious old vintages. They were just waiting for someone to come along and notice.

MICHAEL BROADBENT WAS born into a Yorkshire mill-owning family, and was twenty-two before he tasted a top wine. On a summer evening in 1950, a doctor who was a friend of the family served him 1937 Yquem with nectarines. At the time, Broadbent was an indifferent architecture student at the University of London. Two years later he was drifting when his mother spotted a newspaper ad for a "wine trainee" with a merchant named Tommy Layton.

His first year in that sadly paid job, Broadbent pawned his stamp collection to make ends meet. That autumn, at Layton's suggestion, he began taking notes on every wine he tasted. He never stopped.

Over the next fourteen years he rose to national sales manager of Harvey's of Bristol, a prominent merchant. Then, in 1966, Broadbent heard that Christie's was going to start selling wine. Sending off an energetic letter to the auction house—he announced the salary he would require—he persuaded them to let him found the new department.

Broadbent did not invent the secondary market for old wine, but he did reinvent it. Wine had been sold starting with Christie's first auction in 1766, and first growths had been a staple of its auctions from 1787 on. Over the centuries, Christie's had auctioned off the cellars of kings, prime ministers, and other grandees, among them the Duke of York, Edward VII, and Benjamin Disraeli (whose homeopath, in treating the prime minister's asthma and gout, prescribed Lafite). But Christie's was bombed to the ground in the Second World War. After it was rebuilt, the sale of art, antiques, and jewelry resumed, but not wine. The market had been dormant for a quarter of a century when Broadbent arrived.

Rosebery was a harbinger. That first season, Broadbent's department held thirty-two sales, which fetched around $600,000. By 1978 the numbers would be up to forty-four sales and a turnover of nearly $5 million. Broadbent was like the man who arrived at a gold rush before it was a rush. He was first to the dig site, and over the next fifteen years he engaged in a frenzy of tomb-raiding. His most spectacular discoveries were nearly all in England and Scotland. Beneath the Earl of Strathmore's Glamis Castle, he found forty-two magnums of 1870 Château Lafite, and at the Gladstone family's Fasque estate, he found a similarly impressive trove in a damp cellar with a freakishly constant temperature of 49 degrees Fahrenheit.

Where Christie's had been a full-service auction house from its founding, Sotheby's, which was twenty-two years older, had begun as a bookseller, and had only diversified in the early 1900s. Before Christie's Rosebery sale, Sotheby's had handled an art-and-furniture sale for the Rosebery clan, and the poaching of this client awoke

Christie's rival to the fact that, though the sums of money involved were relatively small, a wine department gave an auction house an edge in attracting new business and fully servicing existing clients. The Glamis sale, in 1970, stirred Sotheby's to action. Glamis Castle was owned by the Bowes-Lyon family, one of whom sat on Sotheby's board. That year, Sotheby's launched its own wine department.

Michael Broadbent's life was awash in wine, but it wasn't all raised-pinky soirées. Auctioneering can be at once among the most patrician occupations and among the least glamorous. Even eminent gavel-bangers may double as glorified stockboys, cataloging and packing up the contents of moldy, spider-ridden basements and attics. And Broadbent's wife, Daphne, and their two children were often by his side. Easter holidays meant trips to the wine country. Weekends might be spent on hands and knees in damp, grubby, medieval cellars in France, Hungary, and elsewhere, dodging white salamanders that had never seen the sun, while assembling cardboard boxes and filling them with bottles as soon as Broadbent had cataloged them.

He was a man of habits, most of which involved drinking or work related to it. Every Sunday morning Broadbent could be found in bed, writing his monthly column for *Decanter,* an English wine magazine. Mealtime conversation was wine talk. Starting at age seven, the children were served wine with dinner (only on special occasions were they allowed the option of drinking orange juice or Coke instead). Emma found it a bore, and, after giving the wine business a short try, became a lawyer and later a judge. Bartholomew cottoned to it more; at fifteen, at Château Latour, he drank an 1865 that was a revelation. Michael Broadbent was a staunch observer of that archaic British midmorning pick-me-up known as elevenses; every day he could be found, before noon, enjoying a glass of dry Madeira, German white wine, or Champagne. At 2:45 p.m., he would take a twenty-minute nap. Toward evening he would have a glass of Champagne or Tio Pepe sherry, several glasses of claret, and perhaps a vintage Port. If the regimen sounded like that of a lush, the truth was that Broadbent practiced moderation. He drank often, but he sipped, and he was an evangelist of wine's preservative properties. His frenetic cycling didn't hurt, either.

As a result of his meticulous record-keeping, he could tell you that he had tasted more than 40,000 wines as of the mid-1980s. That was more wines than most people had ever consumed, and more old wines than anyone alive. He could tell you the best wine he ever drank (an 1870 Lafite in magnum), the wine he would want if he were marooned on a desert island (a Terrantez 1862 Madeira by HM Borges), the oldest wine he'd ever drunk (a 1653 German hock), and his favorite producer (Lafite). It wasn't just Lafite's wines that put Broadbent in mind of the fairer sex; he felt that the vineyard site itself had "almost an erotic shape."

First-growth claret, from vineyards on Bordeaux's left bank, was at the center of Broadbent's auctions, but since the 1855 Classification the stodgy Bordeaux aristocracy had grudgingly acknowledged the parity, in reputation and price if not official status, of a handful of other wines. Cheval Blanc, made in the medieval town of St. Emilion, across the Dordogne River from Bordeaux, and unusual for being produced mainly from the cabernet franc grape, ascended to the first tier via two legendary vintages, 1921 and 1947. Also on the right bank, Pétrus, a merlot-based wine from Pomerol traditionally favored by the Belgians, won the attention of the powerful English market with its 1947 vintage. And Mouton-Rothschild gained actual premier status in 1973 when, by dint of assiduous lobbying, Baron Philippe de Rothschild persuaded the French government to take the unprecedented step of elevating the estate from second to first growth.

As Broadbent's auctions gained in popularity, the price of old wines bounded upward. In the first five years of the new auctions, Latour 1949 and Mouton-Rothschild 1945 more than quadrupled in price. Lesser wines jumped 200 and 300 percent. Rising values led more people to wonder whether granddad's old bottles, which had been gathering dust in the cellar for years, might be worth something, and perhaps this Christie's chap might like to come and take a look. It *was* usually the Christie's chap. Sotheby's wine department, having launched four years after Christie's, had been playing catch-up ever since.

Broadbent was a natural at auction-house hyperbole, and seemed to wring a new record out of every sale. There was always a particular wine or vintage or combination of wines and vintages that, defined in just the right way, had achieved a never-before-seen price or volume record. There was, for instance, the Christie's sale featuring one hundred dozen bottles of the 1967 vintage of Yquem, "certainly the largest quantity of any one vintage of any fine mature white wine ever to appear at auction." It was all in how narrowly you sliced the numbers, and Broadbent was a master with the knife. The only thing that attracted more press coverage than price records was especially old and rare wines, and Broadbent excelled at producing these, too.

He had made London into the center of the international auction market for fine wine, and his dominance was undisputed. As befitted a top auctioneer, he effortlessly melded the hustle of a barrow boy and the self-deprecating charm of a courtier. He delighted in rummaging through the Christie's archives and reading aloud from leather-bound catalogs of its earliest auctions, like the sale on March 18, 1771, which featured "upwards of 100 loads of Good Hay, 6 stacks of Beans . . . a quantity of Dung . . . Four Heffers, two cows, a Ram, Swan, Poultry," and, in the wine department, "a Cask of Elderwine" and "a Firkin with some old Verjuice." In his own writing, he rendered the dross of wine description into something wicked, marshaling one randy image after another to describe the fermented grape juice he was selling: "a sexy *demi-mondaine* of uncertain age but opulent charm" . . . "a light, easy, charming middle-aged lady with her slip showing" . . . and, of course, those "schoolgirls' uniforms." Normally his wife typed up his tasting notes, but when he had written an especially salacious one, he would give the job to his secretary instead.

Broadbent was intensely competitive, and he could be defensive and catty on the topic of the rival auction house. The old saw held that Christie's was made up of gentlemen trying to be auctioneers, and Sotheby's of auctioneers trying to be gentlemen, yet there was nothing particularly genteel about Broadbent's approach to competition. "Despite the strenuous efforts of our competitors," Broadbent crowed to Christie's clients in 1979, "we continue to dominate the international fine wine market." Another time, he denounced Sotheby's "extravagant claims and misleading statements" as "pure propaganda."

The largely one-sided feud became strident in 1984, when Sotheby's wine department introduced a 10-percent buyer's commission. Broadbent was instantly scornful. "It is not a very healthy step," he told *Decanter*. "We have always strenuously opposed any buyer's premium on wine." His counterpart at Sotheby's, Patrick Grubb, retorted that Sotheby's catalogs were "of infinitely better quality than those of our rivals!" Broadbent came back with, "Maybe his buyers are happy for part of their extra 10 percent to be devoted to the glamorization of what is essentially a piece of ephemera? The Bible has a phrase for this: 'a whited sepulchre'!" Two years later, Broadbent had to eat crow as Christie's followed Sotheby's lead, adopting a buyer's premium and revamping its catalogs. Grubb then published a mocking poem, which included the lines "Sepulchral hollow laughter is heard in King Street now / Despite all protestations they've killed a sacred cow."

A few years after that, Broadbent said of Sotheby's wine department, "The lack of enthusiasm shows." Sotheby's wine department, for its part, claimed that while Christie's did a volume business, Sotheby's was the quality auctioneer. Sotheby's competed nearly as avidly in the record-chasing arena, touting, during one season in the early 1980s, its sale of "the largest quantity [of cases of Port] ever sold in any season of wine auctions this century."

BROADBENT WAS GETTING wine from his fellow countrymen, but he was selling it to Americans. By the mid-seventies, the spike in prices for first growths seen between 1966 and 1971 had become more dramatic, and the really old bottles had been priced out of reach of many connoisseurs. A magnum of 1864 Lafite that had sold for $225 at the Rosebery sale in 1967 went for $10,000 in 1981. American demand was the chief reason. The strength of the auction market had come to depend on the strength of the dollar.

American colonists had preferred fortified wines from Spain and Portugal, such as Madeira and Port, and it was Thomas Jefferson who introduced a number of his peers to the less alcoholic pleasures of table wine. Before leaving France in 1789, Jefferson shipped Sauternes, Burgundy, and still Champagne to New York for the cellars of newly elected President George Washington. As secretary of state, Jefferson placed another large order for Washington and himself. He subsequently advised three other presidents—Adams, Madison, and Monroe—on what wines to serve at state dinners. When Monroe was elected, Jefferson's congratulatory letter spent three sentences on the election and the remainder on what wines the White House cellar should stock.

Jefferson was steadfast in promoting his favorite beverage. He lobbied for lower tariffs on wine not only for selfish reasons, but ostensibly because he believed in its healthful and even moderating qualities. "No nation is drunken where wine is cheap," he wrote once, alluding to the rampant abuse of whiskey he saw around him, "and none sober, where the dearness of wine substitutes ardent spirits as the common beverage." He made little headway in this campaign with Secretary of the Treasury Alexander Hamilton, who regarded Jefferson as a fop and wine as a luxury.

Still bent on cultivating wine grapes, Jefferson tried growing them at Monticello after he returned from Europe. Again he didn't succeed, but he corresponded with John Adlum, father of American viticulture, and remained optimistic that America could rival France as a winemaking country. "We could, in the United States," Jefferson wrote, "make as great a variety of wines as are made in Europe, not exactly of the same kinds, but doubtless as good."

Jefferson claimed, patriotically if not altogether convincingly, that he had tasted wine made in Maryland that rivaled the very best Burgundy. He felt North Carolina had come the furthest in developing as a wine producer, and that its Scuppernong grape had yielded America's first "exquisite wine, produced in quantity."

He was also a proselytizer at the table, and seems to have flirted with the wine enthusiast's avocational hazard of overestimating others' interest in the topic. "There was, as usual, the dissertation upon wines, not very edifying," John Quincy Adams yawned to his diary after one White House dinner hosted by Jefferson. Through his entertaining at Monticello, Jefferson seemed to want to convert Americans, one palate at a time, to wine (as well as to a more broadly defined good life). He drank three to four and a half glasses of wine a day, and he designed a pair of dumbwaiters, flanking the fireplace, that brought bottles directly up from the wine cellar to the dining room. His sizable library included volumes treating of the most up-to-date science on winemaking. Because of trade disruptions during the War of 1812, he suffered from the depletion of his cellar, writing that "wine from long habit has become an indispensable for my health, which is now suffering by its disuse."

After Jefferson, another prominent American champion of wine would not appear for a long time. By the turn of the twentieth century, Gilded Age families like the Du Ponts and the Morgans owned substantial quantities of wine, and some of the new apartment buildings then going up in Manhattan were constructed with private cellars in the basement for each tenant. But in general,

Americans didn't drink wine. The temperance movement, together with distractions like Prohibition, didn't help.

In the late 1930s and the 1940s, despite Repeal, Americans were slow to rediscover a taste for wine. Postwar prosperity, and cheap air fares to Europe, began to change this, pushing American consumption of wine to twice what it had been before the war. It was the 1959 vintage in Bordeaux, however, that tipped the balance of power in the wine-buying market from England to America. Dubbed the "vintage of the century" by the French, the 1959s received widespread press coverage—including in *Time, Newsweek,* and an influential article by Art Buchwald—and American interest. By the time Broadbent founded the Christie's wine department in 1966, the choosiest American collectors had pent-up demand, which they unleashed both in Christie's sale rooms in London and at an annual auction Broadbent soon launched in the United States, under the aegis of the Heublein drinks conglomerate.

The debut Heublein auction, which occasioned Broadbent's first trip across the Atlantic, took place at the Continental Plaza Hotel in Chicago in May of 1969. Broadbent's over-the-top Englishness played well in America, and he hammed it up, wearing a tailcoat with a red carnation in the lapel. When opening sample bottles for the slack-jawed North American rubes, he stagily took his time with the mechanics of wine service: skimming the capsule, drawing the cork, and decanting the liquid contents. The knockdown totals (the sum of an auction's winning bids) climbed quickly, from $56,000 the first year to $106,000 the second to $231,000 the third. These were huge sums for a single auction, compared with London results. The power and scale of the American market was obvious.

Peter Morrell, a twenty-six-year-old wine retailer in New York who felt that he needed experience with pre-phylloxera Bordeaux, made news around the world in 1970 when he bid £220 (at the time about $500) for a double magnum of 1865 Lafite originally from the Rosebery cellar. When he was interviewed for television, the reporter was incredulous at how much he had paid, and quipped to viewers that even if it was vinegar, Morrell would have "the world's most expensive salad dressing." A record wine bid was newsworthy. Five hundred dollars for a bottle was still shocking.

The whole thing was a flack's dream—for Heublein, for Christie's, and for those shrewd retailers and restaurateurs who had discerned a media loophole: making a record bid for a bottle of wine guaranteed press coverage, and it was much cheaper and more impressive than a quarter-page ad. The trend really took off at the third Heublein auction, when Broadbent sold an 1846 Lafite for $5,000, a new record by a long shot. Soon the numbers went much higher, way beyond the records Christie's was setting in London. A Memphis restaurant owner paid $31,000 for an 1822 Lafite. A Dallas wine merchant topped that with a $38,000 bid for a Jéroboam of 1870 Mouton.

Broadbent sewed up the American market. In addition to the Christie's sales in London, which drew lots of American bidders, and Heublein, which was the dominant U.S. auction and which Broadbent ran through 1982, he also was brought in to run the annual Napa Valley charity auction, which began in 1981. The first year, the temperature reached 110 degrees Fahrenheit, and up on the dais, Broadbent cooled his feet, unseen by the auctiongoers, in a bucket of ice water. In 1981, in Chicago, Christie's started running its own auctions in the United States.

The wine-collecting boom was limited to a tiny slice of Americans, but there was already a palpable unease, manifest as snobbery, among British wine veterans who could see their primacy being usurped. "As a group," Decanter noted in 1986, "American doctors seem to have the world's greatest interest in great Bordeaux." The record-chasing was offered up as further evidence of American puerility. And while the California wine industry was nudging American awareness of its product forward, as of 1980 a national poll found that 23 percent of wine drunk in the United States was on the rocks.

The high end of the market, however, was coming to be dominated by Americans, and the high end of the high end had given itself a name: "the Group." They owned huge collections of wine. Marvin Overton III, a Texas neurosurgeon who sometimes wore a bolo tie combined with a fur coat, had 10,000 bottles in his cellar. Lloyd Flatt, an eye-patch-wearing Tennessean of shadowy occupation, owned two townhomes in New Orleans; one housed him, the other his 30,000-bottle wine collection. Tawfiq Khoury, a San Diego shopping-mall developer, owned 65,000 bottles, thought to be the largest private collection of wine in America at the time. As wine became detached from its traditional role as a table beverage—as it became a fetish or a trophy or an investment—it became more common to find private collections of wine that far exceeded their owners' abilities to drink them.

"Wine became the soloist," Broadbent said later.

The Group pioneered a new type of event known as a mega-tasting, which could take either of two forms: horizontal (many wines from one vintage) and vertical (many vintages of one wine). Broadbent dated the very first horizontal tasting to 1968, when a Dutch physician named John Taams brought together several wines of the 1961 vintage, but it was in the late 1970s, in the hands of these new American supercollectors, that the format gained traction. Overton hosted a forty-seven-vintage vertical tasting of Latour in Fort Worth in 1976, and followed that up three years later with a thirty-six-vintage vertical of Lafite going back to 1799. Broadbent presided, alongside Baron Elie de Rothschild.

"If it hadn't been for my time in the U.S., I wouldn't be so involved in this hobby," Wolfgang Grünewald, a German-born businessman whose 32,000-bottle collection is among the world's largest, and who before retiring to Switzerland owned a Los Angeles steel company and was a partner in the Melrose Avenue restaurant Patina, said later. "Americans have a curiosity, for special and rare things, that I haven't met elsewhere."

Not everyone in the wine world was thrilled by these events. The most common criticism was that great wines that, in isolation, would be once-in-a-lifetime experiences, were lost amid the hyper-critical, side-by-side comparisons of a mega-tasting (what one commentator termed "the crushing proximity of the giants"). What should have been pleasurable was reduced to an arid and world-weary intellectual exercise. At big tastings, great wines were spat out rather than drunk, and when served without food, they were stripped of their natural context.

The events favored "big" wines—those with lots of fruit and concentration. In such a clinical setting, these were the wines that tended to show best. And after twenty or thirty or forty wines, palate fatigue set in for most tasters, and only the biggest wines would make a taster sit up and notice. There could be dental side effects as well: an Australian study of wine judges' teeth found instances of severe damage and recommended not brushing one's teeth on the morning of a tasting, in order to leave protective plaque in place.

A low-grade dishonesty often permeated the Group's events, diplomatic euphemism taking the place of candor when a bottle brought by a fellow guest wasn't quite up to snuff. Outside of the Group, events weren't cheap; most of the mega-tastings cost thousands of dollars to attend. Some participants couldn't help feeling a bit queasy over the sheer decadence and extravagance. "I feel a genuine sadness about vertical tastings that has always left me feeling as if I needed a soul-cleansing afterwards," wrote the Los Angeles wine journalist Dan Berger.

THE MEGA-TASTINGS ALSO, of course, depleted the rarities unearthed and sold by Broadbent. Edmund Penning-Rowsell, a whiskery socialist and claret scholar who covered wine auctions for the *Financial Times*, observed that as early as 1973 there had been a lull in the discovery of English cellars. But in 1976 there was a resurgence of finds, most in Paris and Bordeaux and a few in the United Kingdom, such as Woodperry House in Oxfordshire. The next year, Penning-Rowsell was able to write of an "extraordinary recrudescence" of rare bottles in the auction room.

With the familiar sources drying up, some of this new torrent seemed quite fantastical in origin, but then, exotic discoveries were a staple of wine history. In 1925, the old-line Piccadilly wine merchants Berry Brothers had unearthed a cache of early-nineteenth-century Tokaji vintages that had been walled up by the Princely House of Bretzenheim in anticipation of the revolution of 1848. Now, in the late 1970s and early 1980s, similar hidden troves came to light. Ten Broeck Mansion, the home of a Revolutionary war general in Albany, New York, yielded a forgotten stash of nineteenth-century bottles that were auctioned at Heublein starting in 1978. Some bottles at the 1980 Heublein auction, including an 1836 Sercial Madeira, had been salvaged by divers from a ship that sank off the coast of Savannah in 1840.

By 1985, even as occasional odd finds continued to trickle in, it was clear that the heyday of claret archaeology was over. Since old cellars were a Christie's franchise, their virtual disappearance enabled Sotheby's wine department to begin to close the competitive gap. The watershed 1982 Bordeaux vintage had sent prices, along with American interest in wine, to new heights. Then, in February of 1985, the dollar hit a historical peak. The Reagan boom was cresting, and the American appetite for old wine was insatiable. For Christie's, there was money to be made, and competition to face down. Broadbent was more aggressive than ever. He wasn't about to let anyone else bring his winning streak to an end.

CHAPTER 4

MONSIEUR YQUEM

*I*N APRIL OF 1985, HARDY RODENSTOCK, WHO HAD recently moved into the lakeside home of a Munich construction heiress, told some German wine friends he'd just received a phone call about an astonishing discovery in Paris. He took the next plane, he wrote later, "and took a look at the cellar, bottles and everything." A hidden cellar had been breached when a house built in the mid–eighteenth century was being torn down. It contained about a hundred bottles. Two dozen were engraved with the initials "Th. J." They included bottles of Lafite, Margaux, Yquem, and Branne-Mouton, as Mouton-Rothschild had been called in Jefferson's day, from the 1784 and 1787 vintages. Rodenstock said he paid 20,000 French francs for the lot, which at the time worked out to $2,227. The discovery was serendipitous for a number of reasons: While in 1985 Mouton was one of the most coveted wines in the world, in Jefferson's day it was middle-of-the-pack and neither sought after nor collected; and Rodenstock had found the bottles just two years before the bicentennial of Jefferson's visit to

Bordeaux. When his friends pressed him for more details, Rodenstock clammed up.

The circle of collectors that had formed around Rodenstock by
the time of the Jefferson bottles' discovery was drawn together by
wine, and they learned little about each other that did not pertain
to it. To the world, Hardy Rodenstock presented a stolid moon of a
face, barely interrupted by small, opaque eyes and the faintest suggestion of a mouth. He was physically unprepossessing. What you
remembered about him were not the stippled-in details but the
big-brush outlines. He wore his brown hair in a boyish shag that
downplayed his forty-four years. He dressed flashily, favoring shiny
double-breasted suits with big lapels, starched colored shirts with
contrasting white collars and cuffs, sharply creased slacks, and
modishly tinted plastic eyeglasses. Despite "dressing like a banker,"
as an auctioneer recalled, he never seemed to have any money. He
had a worldly mien, a quiet self-assurance that could come across as
humility or aloofness. As he shook your hand, he would click his
heels together.

How Rodenstock became interested in wine was a story that
changed depending on who was asking him and when. There were
three stories. The one he told least often, and which was given the
least credence, was that he had started drinking wine as a child,
with his grandfather. The one he told most often involved a Dama-
scene conversion. After the funeral of a friend's father in 1976, the
son of the deceased served four of the most legendary wines in history out of the family cellar: 1961 Château Palmer, 1945 Mouton-
Rothschild, 1947 Cheval Blanc, and 1921 Château d'Yquem. Palmer,
a wine that was officially a third growth and unofficially considered
to be just below the first growths in quality, was regarded, in the
1961 vintage, as sublime. Rodenstock said that tasting the four
wines was a life-altering experience, and that he became instantly
obsessed.

The third story—and the one that those in the German wine

scene who had known Rodenstock longest believed to be the truth—was neither as simple as the first nor as mythic as the second. Rodenstock made his living managing *Schlager* acts—a style of easy-listening German pop music—and according to this version, he had booked some of his clients for a festival in Wiesbaden and gotten stiffed. The promoter had no money, and offered to pay him in cases of wine, his only currency. Rodenstock protested angrily that he drank beer and schnapps, but ended up driving a van to collect the wine. He forgot about it for a while, then during the winter he retrieved some of the bottles from his basement. They were white Burgundies, and he liked them. He bought more wine and soon did, indeed, become obsessed.

At first Rodenstock would invite music-business friends to drink with him, but as his interests turned increasingly toward the old and rare, he found their nuances were lost on those people. Many wine neophytes have a mentor who guides them through the intricacies of wine when they are just starting out. Self-taught, Rodenstock had no desire for a tutor, but he was eager to find like-minded appreciators with whom to share his experiences. He read *Essen und Trinken,* the first modern gastronomy magazine in Germany, and signed up for its tours of wine regions. Through these he met the wine journalist Heinz-Gert Woschek, and other readers, and was directly exposed to the châteaux for the first time. He found he had a particular interest in Bordeaux, and he arranged other visits privately.

When Woschek launched Germany's first wine magazine, *Woscheks Wein Report* (soon renamed *Alles über Wein*), in 1981, Rodenstock began writing long articles that gave him further entrée to the châteaux and their owners. He became a regular buyer at wine auctions at Christie's and Sotheby's in London, and at Cave Nicolas, a merchant in Paris. He was a hobbyist who bought wine, but whose commerce with it was otherwise limited to the occasional one- or two-bottle trade with a fellow collector. Though he wasn't wealthy, old wine was still relatively cheap. He lived with one of his clients, a moderately successful singer named Tina York, who was the younger sister of a well-known *Schlager* singer named Mary Roos, and her two Yorkies, in a remote area east of the Rhine called the Westerwald. It was a normal house, except that the cellar overflowed with bottles.

One of the places Rodenstock sought out wine fellowship in those early years was Fuente, a twenty-seven-seat restaurant in the town of Mulheim, near Düsseldorf. Well situated to serve the moneyed trenchermen who ran the big industrial companies headquartered in the region, it occupied an old house with a sign showing a horse being watered. Fuente was a star of the new German gastronomy, and served French nouvelle cuisine. Its lamb filet in pastry and its crayfish salad had drawn praise, and a star, from Michelin's inspectors. The restaurant had opened in 1976, just when Rodenstock was developing a taste for wine in nearby Essen, and by 1978 he was a regular customer. Rolf-Dieter (Otto) Jung, the young owner with a Dundreary mustache and a cigarette always smoldering in a long holder, had built its wine list into one of the best in the country, with 350 labels and an inventory worth some $150,000. Rodenstock was looking for someone to talk to about wine, and would come in alone with a bottle or two to share with Jung.

GERMANY, LIKE AMERICA, had only a modest tradition of enthusiasm for fine Bordeaux. At the end of the nineteenth century, one Hamburg restaurant had made a point of keeping at least one bottle of each of the sixty-two classed growths in its cellar. But the country remained essentially a beer-and-schnapps kind of place until the early 1970s, when its Western half began to experience a gastronomic awakening. As the decade progressed, wine lovers in a few centers like Hamburg and Wiesbaden started to find each other. Some were restaurant owners; some were journalists; some were private collectors. They organized tastings and traded invitations, sometimes with members of the American Group. The transatlantic alliance quickly fell apart because "the Americans were unsophisticated and not generous," said one participant. "They served some horrible bottles, and didn't reciprocate in kind." A German collector who was a half-Jewish Holocaust survivor was also put off when a member of the Group, at the Los Angeles restaurant Scandia, described fellow member Tawfiq Khoury, a Palestinian, as a "sand nigger."

The most zealous of the Germans were distinguished by an obsession with a particular kind of wine, and they nicknamed each other accordingly. Uwe Könecke, who owned a small-truck dealership, became "Magnum Uwe" because of his preference for large-format bottles. A Swiss German named Walter Eigensatz, who with his wife owned several spas, was known as "Mr. Cheval Blanc." A Munich businessman by the name of Hans-Peter Frericks was dubbed "Herr Pétrus." Hardy Rodenstock was "Monsieur Yquem."

There was something defiantly timeless about Yquem. Its syrupy concentration derived not only from noble rot but also from a meticulous, and expensive, production process. It went beyond the dramatically low yield. Each harvest, the château would send pickers through the vineyard an average of five times, and up to eleven, selecting only those grapes ready to be picked. The château hewed to rigorously high standards and, some years, released no wine at all. The result was a Sauternes that fetched astronomical prices and inspired cultish fervor, in no one so much as Rodenstock.

The wine scene in which Rodenstock began to move consisted largely of people who had amassed impressive collections, not just of young vintages but of old ones as well. They started to host tastings focused around rarities, which at first weren't so hard to find. Old Bordeaux came up fairly often at auction, and they weren't outrageously expensive. It was easy to find 1928s and 1929s of Latour and Mouton. You almost didn't need to collect; the stuff was available at the store. One shop in Hamburg carried Burgundy from the 1930s and 1940s for eight dollars a bottle.

There was a romantic aspect to it all. Rodenstock and his new friends were "drinking history," as they liked to say, and would commonly wax historical about what Goethe, Schiller, or Napoleon was doing in the year of the vintage they happened to be opening just then. There was a visual allure to the parade of old bottles, which could be delightfully heterogeneous. Because of the historic inconsistency of bottling (sometimes by customers' butlers, sometimes by merchants, sometimes by châteaux), you could see three Lafites from the same year that all looked different. This was truer of wines older than the 1920s, when Baron Philippe de Rothschild first château-bottled his entire production, the first growths following suit soon thereafter.

In many ways, the rarities game was *Star Trek* for grown-ups. No women were invited to tastings, and the male collectors' explanations for this tended to be halfhearted: There was only one bottle of each wine, not enough for spouses; it was wrong to forbid women to wear perfume, yet that would be necessary at a wine tasting. The reality was that the gender mix, or lack thereof, mirrored the wine world in general.

The boys' club fostered a competitive atmosphere, and the connoisseurs prided themselves on deciding that an authority such as Broadbent was wrong in his assessment of a particular wine. Nothing pleased them more than to discover a "shadow vintage," a year that was a great value because its proximity to a more famous vintage had caused it to be overlooked; come up with a brilliant new food-and-wine pairing; or have an inside line on esoterica such as Yquem's little-known red wine, produced in small quantities for the consumption of its pickers at harvest time. The collectors one-upped each other with individual bottles—if one had a magnum, another had a double magnum—and with the lavishness of their tastings. In 1983, Walter Eigensatz, Mr. Cheval Blanc, hosted a vertical of his favorite wine in Wiesbaden and arranged for two white horses to lead a pre-tasting parade through the streets of the city.

The collectors would also try to psych each other out. A "Parker 100" tasting in Hamburg, which featured wines that had received a perfect score from the increasingly influential American wine critic Robert Parker, included what the Germans called a "pirate," a mystery bottle—in this case, a mystery double magnum. Everyone stood around sniffing at their glasses and making guesses. Rodenstock went up to a well-fed, stubble-haired journalist named Mario Scheuermann and said he thought it was an old Pétrus. "Definitely not," Scheuermann said. "It's a '61 La Chappelle." It could not be, Rodenstock said; the 1961 La Chappelle, a red from the Rhône Valley, did not exist in big bottles. Scheuermann insisted it was, until Rodenstock conceded, "Little boy, maybe you are right." And Scheuermann was. Mischievously, the host had decanted four regular bottles into the larger bottle. Scheuermann was able to guess this because the '61 La Chappelle was his favorite wine. He had drunk it fifty times.

Egos and posturing aside, there was a genuine intellectual thrust to the tastings. The point, at least for the more serious collectors, was to learn more about Bordeaux; it was easier to begin to understand the character of a wine by comparing and analyzing different versions of the same thing than by studying things that were entirely different. "You know wine if you are able to drink good wine. In this way you get a matrix in the brain for tasting wine," Fuente owner Otto Jung explained years later. "I laugh when someone says, 'That's a typical '82,' when he has only drunk three." To really know a château, you had to have tasted its wine over a century of vintages.

To be a great taster also depended on one's palate sensitivity and palate memory. Some members of the Rodenstock clique had an almost synesthetic reaction to wines; they didn't merely smell and taste them, they saw them, each with its own shape and structure and character. Wines, for these super-tasters—as a Yale researcher has designated the small percentage of people with an especially high density of taste buds—were as starkly distinct and instantly recognizable as faces. Rodenstock was a good taster. Maybe he wasn't the virtuoso some friends described (one claimed that given a room of unmarked 1985 Bordeaux, Rodenstock could pick out each château), but he was exceptional.

Even the best palates could be humbled in a blind tasting, in which labels were concealed. Sometimes you caught a wine immediately; sometimes you could sit in front of it for five hours and still not get it. The conventional wisdom held that beginners often performed better at this, because they didn't know all the exceptions to the exceptions. Harry Waugh, the English wine merchant and writer, was once asked how often he confused Bordeaux with Burgundy. "Not since lunch," he replied.

Some tasters frowned on blind tasting. It was one thing to know the names of the wines on a table, and simply not know which glass contained which. That was interesting. But purely blind tasting was, they argued, a trivializing parlor game that wowed outsiders but wasn't a learning exercise.

The art of drinking the very oldest rarities required an extra degree of connoisseurship—almost a kind of necrophilia. The normal sequence when evaluating a wine might be look-smell-taste, but when opening an old wine, Broadbent thought that one should smell first. The color wasn't going to change, whereas with an old wine, the smell very likely would. An old wine exposed to oxygen normally evolved much more rapidly than a younger wine. The initial bouquet would tell you a lot more than the color, yet it might last only thirty seconds. Then again, an old wine could surprise you. That 1893 Margaux might first merely taste drinkable, merely be *recognizable* as wine, yet two hours later have opened up into something rich with red-berry fruit, with what some connoisseurs poetically called "the sweetness of death." This was one of the unpredictabilities of old wine that fascinated people like Rodenstock. Opening one of these bottles could be like waking something up gradually, or igniting something that burned brightly before quickly petering out. You never knew which it would be.

EVEN AMONG HIS clique of obsessives, Rodenstock stood out as a monomaniac. He segued from managing bands to collecting music-publishing royalties, and increasingly devoted his time to looking for bottles, networking, and attending auctions. He became engaged to Patricia Woschek, daughter of Heinz-Gert, who owned *Alles über Wein*. It was impossible to talk to him about anything other than wine, and nearly everyone with whom he associated was somehow involved with it. In 1980 he hosted the first of what would become annual tastings.

He chose the restaurant Fuente as the setting. At the time, tastings in Germany tended to be monastic affairs, with bland slices of bread, a few grams of cheese, and wine. Tastings in conjunction with meals were a novelty. Rodenstock supplied the wine, and Otto Jung, who was looking to boost his restaurant's profile, provided the food and service. The first year, Rodenstock's guests were a small group—"fifteen freaks," in Jung's words. A few were friends from the music business, some were wine people, and some were celebrities—mainly politicians and soccer stars—whom Rodenstock somehow knew. The tasting made the newspapers when Walter Scheel, the former president of West Germany, showed up at the tiny restaurant in a motorcade, sirens screaming.

The annual tastings quickly grew into endurance tests. Even Broadbent, who began attending the event in 1984, wasn't prepared for how grueling the black-tie affair would be. That year the group sat down to eat at noon, and didn't get up until midnight. Halfway through, Broadbent had a headache, and back at his hotel he threw up. He blamed it on the food, and the next year he made sure to have more bread and water and less rich French cuisine.

Each year, Jung and Rodenstock thought they wouldn't be able to top themselves the next, but then they would. There would be more people and better food; there would be more wines, and the wines would be older and rarer. There was an imperial quality to Rodenstock's life. It was a baroque succession of epic meals and wines, and he paid for all the wines at his tastings, which made the lucky few who were invited exceedingly grateful. As Kaiser, however, Rodenstock would get angry if someone was five minutes late. And he brooked no dissent, dropping anyone who dared disagree with him about anything.

Through his largesse, and the specter of its withdrawal, he also controlled journalists. "If someone had written negatively about the tastings," Woschek explained, "they would never have been invited again." *Alles über Wein* published nothing about Rodenstock's background or personality. Acolytes would exalt a mildly irreverent aside by Rodenstock into high comedy, laughingly recalling the time when, after buying a case of half-bottles of 1958 Latour, he announced that it wasn't great wine but it "goes well with roulade," a homely German dish featuring some filling swaddled in a roll of beef. By the early 1980s it was clear to people like Woschek and Mario Scheuermann that his knowledge had surpassed theirs.

IT WAS NOT just the tastings that gave Rodenstock his growing cachet. He was also becoming known for the bottles—often in a large format—he unfailingly served at those events. There were old Constantia wines, famous wines from the Western Cape of South Africa that had been popular in the nineteenth century; a pre-Napoleonic royal Tokaji, dating to 1649, from the Royal House of Saxony; and another from the Royal Cellar in Bavaria. Even Rodenstock's jaded friends were awed by some of his discoveries.

It was Rodenstock who years later would produce a tappit hen of 1811 Lafite at a tasting in Hamburg. A tappit hen was an extinct, extremely rare, bulbous style of bottle, and 1811 was considered the best Bordeaux vintage of the first half of the nineteenth century; it was known to connoisseurs as "the comet year," for the nine months in which the giant streak of 'light that transfixed Pierre in *War and Peace* was visible from the earth. A team of sommeliers brought the tappit hen into the restaurant's dining room in a wooden box, and the men crowded around like children about to unwrap Christmas presents. "If this bottle falls down, that's a hundred thousand marks," someone said. "No one clap your hands." Twenty people had contributed 5,000 marks each (roughly $3,000) to finance the purchase of the tappit hen, and Rodenstock donated a 1900 Margaux and an 1864 Lafite for the event.

His friends were increasingly curious where he got his bottles. From the start, Rodenstock had been unvaryingly private. As the years passed, he rarely invited anyone to his home or revealed anything about his personal life or finances. Friends knew that he had several different cellars, including one in Switzerland, but most never saw any of them. Though his tastings, with their celebrity and journalist guests, seemed geared for maximum publicity, Rodenstock was actually quite shy. He never got up and spoke, asking people like Woschek, Scheuermann, and the Austrian crystal magnate Georg Riedel to do so instead. He was similarly ambivalent about being photographed. He disliked smiling on command, and he insisted that Woschek grant him approval of which shots would be published in *Alles über Wein,* often vetoing the editor's selections. Jung, after five years of co-hosting tastings, was still using the formal "you" with Rodenstock, something Jung did with no one else he had known for so long.

It was as if you were allowed to know Rodenstock only so well. There was always a distance. At the first year's tasting, near Rodenstock's hometown of Essen, the guests were all business acquaintances; no family members or childhood friends were present. After a tasting of eighty wines, even people who spat were inevitably looser and more outgoing; Rodenstock, seemingly unaffected by the alcohol, would be as closed-up as ever. No one knew anything about his family. Woschek, who considered himself a good friend of Rodenstock's and who was poised to become his father-in-law, wasn't even sure whether Rodenstock had siblings. People gossiped about his name. The Rodenstocks were a prominent optics family in Germany, and Hardy, without ever claiming to be a member, did little to correct the assumption that he was.

In those early days it seemed to his friends that Rodenstock's main sources for old wines were the auction houses of London and Zurich, as well as the cellars of Paris merchant Nicolas. As his tastings made news, though, *Alles über Wein* began to receive letters from people, especially in Germany, saying they had private cellars and wondering how they could get in touch with Rodenstock. He was also a ferocious networker, sending letters to hundreds of wine dealers and châteaux and merchants. The history of wine was full of examples of bottles surfacing in unusual places, and Rodenstock was competing on, or beneath, the same fields as Christie's and Sotheby's. It made sense that he, too, would come upon rare finds.

THE JEFFERSON BOTTLES outshone any of his previous discoveries. Rodenstock was an insatiable consumer of wine-related media, and Jefferson's connections to wine were not a secret. In the 1980 inaugural edition of his big book, Michael Broadbent had quoted Jefferson to describe the 1784 vintage of both red Bordeaux and Yquem. In 1984, *Decanter* had published an article on the subject titled "America's first wine expert." In its first issue of 1985, *Alles über Wein* referred to Jefferson's 1787 list of the leading Bordeaux châteaux. Rodenstock himself had written a long article about Yquem two years earlier, in which he talked about Jefferson's orders of Yquem. At the time of the discovery of the bottles in 1985, he told Heinz-Gert Woschek that they had belonged to Jefferson. Nonetheless, in a letter the following year Rodenstock would state that "the identity of the initials Th. J. had no meaning to me at first." Still later, he would repeatedly say that it was Comte Alexandre de Lur Saluces, whose family had owned Château d'Yquem since before Jefferson visited Bordeaux, who first suggested that Th. J. might stand for Thomas Jefferson.

That May 3, Lur Saluces hosted a group at the Château. The Commanderie des Grands Boutilliers de France was a small fraternity of wine enthusiasts, including Rodenstock, and on this occasion, without any advance notice, he declared that he had brought with him a bottle of 1787 Yquem. Rodenstock then proceeded to open it, first breaking through the outer layer of protective wax that he had added after finding the bottles, then through the original sealing wax. And then, ever so carefully, he drew the cork.

"This suite of events sufficed in itself to fill me with joy," Lur Saluces wrote later that year, in a letter to Richard Olney, the expatriate American painter and cookbook author. "But the astonishing thing is that the wine was excellent . . . not only liquorous and still alcoholic, but very harmonious. I was stupefied to discover something so vibrant and so alive, so characteristic of a great Yquem vintage."

In his own notes, Rodenstock recorded that the wine was "excellent," "dark in color," and "sweet with a tremendous long finish." To Rodenstock this was a "historic event," not least because it proved that, contrary to received wisdom, noble rot existed before 1847. Before leaving the château, the group agreed to taste a 1784 Yquem that fall.

On June 14, Rodenstock himself wrote to R. de Treville Lawrence III, who edited a newsletter for the Vinifera Wine Growers Association, a group of Virginia winemakers. Rodenstock described his Paris find ("These wine bottles are from Thomas Jefferson's wine collection") and stated, "I have sealed all the bottles." The letter was accompanied by a photo, which showed a 1784 Yquem capped with a fresh knob of wax and labeled with a slip of paper, signed by Rodenstock, announcing that the bottle had been sealed on the sixteenth of April that year.

News of the bottles first broke in America through a press release issued on October 11 by the VWGA, and a note appended to the simultaneously published report by the *VWGA Journal*'s Lawrence gave the first inkling that the discovery might be controversial. "Questions will no doubt arise regarding the finding of these rare wines enjoyed by Jefferson 200 years ago: 1. Where was the wine found in Paris? How was it preserved? 2. The numbers on the etching on the bottle appear in a more modern style. The copy of his initials appear [*sic*] accurate and could have been put on the bottle after he received them in Paris. 3. In checking with the present American Consul General William S. Shepard, Bordeaux, and The Thomas Jefferson Memorial Foundation, Monticello, neither are aware of extant bottles of Jefferson's wines."

Three days later the second Jefferson bottle was opened. For the first time Rodenstock had decided not to hold his annual tasting at Fuente, instead choosing Die Ente vom Lehel, a Wiesbaden restaurant that was among the best in Germany. It was larger than Fuente and able to accommodate more guests. It also employed a young sommelier to whom Rodenstock had become close, and its wine list was without parallel in the country. Beautifully illustrated, the list contained a paean to Yquem written by none other than Rodenstock, who said that in a bottle of Yquem "the entire act of making love occurs . . . lust for life and depravity . . . melancholy and lightheartedness . . . poison and antidote."

The tasting took place on October 14. Lur Saluces was again present. So was Broadbent, who wrote about the 1784 Yquem in his notebook: "In the decanter the wine had a deep, luminous old gold colour but in the glass was a paler perfect amber, bright and lively.

The nose was perfect: gentle, scented vanilla, no oxidation, not a trace of acetification, no faults. After 20 minutes the remains in the glass had an indescribable fragrance. On the palate the wine was still sweet with perfect body and balance, flavour of ripe peaches and cream, excellent acidity and dry finish."

Later that day, Broadbent and Rodenstock were sitting at a table when Broadbent made a suggestion. Why not let Christie's auction off one of the Jefferson bottles? Christie's had never sold a claret this old, certainly not one that was certifiably from a specific château and a specific vintage. And the Jefferson engraving made it unprecedented. Even the rarest wines were commodities—a now-uncommon bottle might have begun as one of one hundred thousand—but the etched initials placed these bottles in the realm of singular, if drinkable, art. Broadbent was determined that Christie's should have a chance to auction one off, and Rodenstock agreed to consign a bottle for sale. Soon after, Broadbent flew to Munich, where Rodenstock met him at the airport and handed him a silver metal briefcase.

CHAPTER 5

PROVENANCE

*I*T LOOKED VAGUELY LIKE A WINE BOTTLE, BUT NOT one resembling anything for sale in a liquor store. Broadbent was back in London after collecting the bottle in Munich, and now, for the first time, he could study it at leisure. The glass had a green-amber tint. The bottle's shape was feminine. At the waist, it bellied gently. Shoulders eased languorously into neck. A rough wax cap offered a first line of defense against air penetrating the cork. Besides the archaic features, the bottle had an obvious patina of age. Calcified cellar dirt was caked halfway around it. Elsewhere, the glass was spackled with a spidery, dun-colored dust. On a section of the bottle's trunk where the glass still showed, the engraved numerals *1787* were visible. Below, in a looping script, was etched the antique spelling "Lafitte." Still closer to the bottle's base was the cryptic abbreviation "Th. J."

A 198-year-old bottle of Lafite was beyond rare; one that had once belonged to America's third president, Thomas Jefferson, was stunning. Broadbent knew that a bottle this unusual required a higher level of scrutiny than any he had previously auctioned.

Provenance—the chain of custody from a wine's creation through its consignment to the auction house—was always a concern. Mainly this was because with mature wines, condition was the number-one determinant of whether a bidder was acquiring a transcendent sensory experience or a bottle of ghastly swill. As a result, condition dramatically affected how much money a bottle fetched at auction. Two bottles of the same thing, one with wine into the neck, the other with wine only to mid-shoulder, could go for surprisingly different prices. Sound provenance was also critical to an auction house's reputation. Sell too many wines that disappointed, and you could lose the trust of customers. Broadbent had a strong incentive to be vigilant.

In compiling years of Christie's catalogs, he had helped to codify a vocabulary of wine condition that was now commonly used in the business. How pristine a label looked and whether or not the wine was "OWC" (in its original wooden case) were both clues to how it had been stored. But the primary indicator of condition was ullage, or fill level, the amount of headspace between the base of the cork and the surface of the wine. This gap could vary significantly, and to standardize the differences, Broadbent used eight descriptors, from "high fill" to "mid-shoulder" to "below low-shoulder," with matching illustrations.

Ullage meant wine had evaporated. After a few decades of aging, a certain amount was to be expected with even the most carefully stored bottles. But too much headspace suggested a faulty seal, a point of ingress for a stream of oxygen that might have wrought bacterial havoc. Past a certain point, ullage itself could be destructive. As the ratio of air to liquid in a bottle increased, the likelihood of accelerated aging, and possible spoiling, went up. This was why wine was bottled with a high fill, and why the best châteaux extended customers the courtesy of periodically topping up bottles with the same wine, to keep headspace to a minimum.

The wine in the 1787 Lafite bottle was well into the neck, a remarkable level for wine so old.

A second provenance concern, less often problematic, was authenticity. The problems that existed in Jefferson's day hadn't gone away, and the recent history of wine had in some ways been an arms race between cheats, on the one hand, and consumers and honest winemakers on the other. France had passed appellation-control laws in order to combat adulteration by unscrupulous winemakers, and winemakers had taken to château-bottling in order to guard against shady middlemen. Bottles made it harder to fake wine, but not impossible, especially when it was an inside job. When *Reichsmarschall* Hermann Göring, during World War II, placed an order for some cases of Mouton, workers at the château glued Mouton labels on bottles of ordinary wine. As a handful of leading brands emerged, outright fabrication of wines and vintages took place: fake Mouton 1894 appeared on the Bordeaux market in 1904, and in 1914, "Latour 1900" showed up in the French grocery chain Félix Potin selling at one-third the going price.

With wine, the distinction between real and fake could be elastic to the point of philosophical. Where the authenticity of, say, paintings was straightforward—a Monet either was by Monet or was not—there were degrees and kinds of vinous imposture. Maybe a bottle of Mouton contained Mouton, but in a vintage inferior to the one named on the label; maybe it contained a blend of the ostensible vintage and a lesser vintage; maybe it contained another, cheaper wine; maybe it contained something altogether different from wine.

Starting in the early 1980s, counterfeiting at the high end of the wine market became more common. In 1982 an enterprising twenty-nine-year-old California man by the name of Louis A. Feliciano was arrested after he commissioned a printer to make wallpaper with the repeating image of the Andy Warhol–designed label from the 1975 Mouton-Rothschild. Feliciano cut it up into labels and applied them to bottles of bulk California wine and of the much less valuable 1974 Mouton. Eventually, after New York wine merchant Michael Aaron helped the Bureau of Alcohol, Tobacco and Firearms conduct a sting operation that included phone taps, Feliciano was arrested at LaGuardia Airport.

Later, a price bubble caused by frenzied demand for the 1982 vintage itself, together with the rise of so-called trophy wines, proved irresistible to would-be forgers. Though some of the frauds were detected, wine bottles without labels were largely interchangeable to the eye, their contents uncheckable without opening. The wine business operated on trust to a far greater extent than many of its members liked to admit publicly.

At Christie's, Broadbent had handled enough old bottles to know that this one was legitimately old. It was mouth-blown in a shape typical for the period and characteristically uneven in thickness, the glass chunky in some places, thin as eggshell in others. If there "was any jiggery-pokery," Broadbent thought it would be in the engraving, so the first thing he did was show the bottle to Hugo Morley-Fletcher, Christie's porcelain and glass expert.

Broadbent said nothing and sat back and waited for Morley-Fletcher's appraisal. The expert agreed that there was no doubt that the bottle was the real thing, and confirmed that the letters had been wheel-engraved, the standard technique in the late eighteenth century. A friend with whom Broadbent played music at his weekend house near Bath, and who happened to be an expert on engraving, added that it would be impossible to drill on glass so old. Next, Broadbent had a handwriting expert from the British Library assess the style of lettering; he confirmed that it was characteristic of the period. The cork, Broadbent himself opined, "appears to be original," and he took added comfort from a scientific examination of the 1787 Yquem that Rodenstock had commissioned, reporting that "[t]he cork was found to be the original and the wine had an excellent constitution."

As for the Jefferson connection, Broadbent consulted *Jefferson and Wine,* an anthology of articles assembled by the editor of the *VWGA Journal* that detailed various aspects of Jefferson's interest in wine as well as some of the orders he had placed for first-growth Bordeaux. From these, Broadbent drew his unequivocal conclusion, in the auction catalog, that "Th. J. are the initials of Thomas Jefferson."

Whether the wine would be drinkable or not, and, if it was, what it would taste like, was a whole other matter. The 1784 and 1787 vintages of Yquem opened by Rodenstock earlier in the year had drawn rave reviews. But that most concentrated of the Sauternes dessert wines, with high alcohol and residual sugar, was better constituted than red table wine to withstand the vinegarizing ravages of bacteria.

Red wine was different. No merchant or wine writer was going to say, of the 1982 vintage: "Drink now through 2182." The finest Bordeaux might peak after twenty years, stay on that plateau for another fifteen, and then begin to decline. Yet old-wine drinkers routinely opened bottles that were more than a hundred years old and spoke of them as if they were still in their prime. How was this possible?

It was true that some of the wines Broadbent had turned up in pristine castle cellars had been untouched for more than a century and still dazzled tasters. But such wines were outliers, and the oldest was only 130 years or so. Even the best were appreciated more by the mind than the tongue or nose. They garnered faint praise, like "still very much alive." The best Baron Elie de Rothschild had been able to say of the 1799 Lafite opened at Marvin Overton's seminal vertical tasting in Dallas in 1979 was, "It's wine."

It was also true that some bottles from the cellars of great French restaurants and of the châteaux themselves had proved drinkable, and even pleasurable, after 150 years or more. In 1969, Steven Spurrier, an English merchant who would soon open a popular wine store in Paris called Caves de la Madeleine, attended a dinner at Restaurant

Darroze, a three-star in Villeneuve, at which an 1806 Lafite was poured. It was, he recalled more than three decades later, "still red, definitely a bouquet of wine, almost reminiscent of Lafite." At Overton's Lafite vertical, Broadbent tasted the same 1799 faintly praised by Elie de Rothschild and noted that it was "very much alive: fabulous colour, warm palish *tuilé* (the colour of a sun-faded old tile in Provence); a gently fragrant bouquet, with a touch of decay when first opened which cleared, held and even developed in the glass; light though still a meaty little wine, faded but fascinating, the finish a little dried up and tart." But wines this ancient had invariably been recorked at least once, their lives extended by topping up, often with younger wines, and by the replacement of their old corks with new ones.

Of course, many old wines disappointed. You never knew, until you opened it, how a bottle would be. When Broadbent tried an 1875 Margaux, he rhapsodized about its "extraordinary nose like crystallized violets and clean bandages!" At another event, however, he glumly lamented the state of an 1858 Mouton, wincing at its "incredibly awful creosote, tarry smell" before jotting in his notebook the ultimate condemnation: "Not tasted." One of his favorite stories involved a bottle of 1898 Lafite and the legendary Napa Valley consultant André Tchelistcheff. At one of the Heublein auctions run by Broadbent, the four-foot-eleven Tchelistcheff had sampled the old wine and told the room, in his émigré's Russian accent, "Tasting old wine is like making love to an old lady." After a dramatic pause, he had continued, "It is possible." After another pause: "It can even be enjoyable." Then, following one last sip: "But it requires a leetle bit of imagination."

To an extent, the very unpredictability of old wine was part of its allure. Even wines with platinum provenance, and which had been unmoved and lain side by side for decades, could vary dramatically. That element of surprise was thrilling, and fascinating, to some collectors. But it was disappointing, even crushing, to spend thousands of dollars on a bottle of wine that turned out to be long gone. If you couldn't afford to take that risk, you wouldn't be very happy collecting old wine.

From a salesman's standpoint, a never-breached bottle of 1787 had an aura of authenticity that a topped-up bottle did not. But a never-topped-up bottle stood less chance of being drinkable. Broadbent's challenge was to resolve this conflict, at least in bidders' minds, emphasizing the authentic oldness while, at the same time, making the best possible case for drinkability.

Given what Rodenstock had told him about the conditions in which he found the Jefferson cache—a perfectly sealed cellar with ideal temperature and humidity—as well as the visibly high fill level in the Lafite, Broadbent dared imagine that this might be a rare wine that met the challenge of the authenticity-drinkability paradox.

AT THE END of October, only a few days after Christie's announced that it would sell the bottle at its December 5 sale, an article appeared in the *New York Times* titled "Oldest Bordeaux? Yes; Jefferson's? Maybe." The doubts were those of a researcher at Monticello who, in addition to expressing the general belief among Jefferson scholars that no bottles of his wine had survived, questioned the way Jefferson's initials were punctuated on the bottle and the idea that Jefferson had even had any bottles engraved. The researcher also noted that the particular combination of châteaux and vintages Rodenstock said he had found did not tally with the detailed and thorough record of Jefferson's wine purchases.

In November, in response to an inquiry by Broadbent about Jefferson's wine-related writings, the researcher informed him that Jefferson had never specifically mentioned the 1787 vintage. Broadbent dug further into the Jefferson literature and, in an insert that accompanied the catalog, laid out a more elaborate case for attributing the bottles to Jefferson. "There is an immense amount of circumstantial evidence supporting the ordering of this wine and its identification," Broadbent wrote, "but, of course, no proof. The arguments supporting this fabulous find are related below."

Broadbent's arguments zeroed in on a handful of ambiguous references that punctuated the otherwise compulsive precision of Jefferson's ample correspondence. To account for the presence in the cache of Branne-Mouton, a wine Jefferson had never mentioned ordering or even drinking, Broadbent pointed to an occasion when the American consul in Bordeaux had told Jefferson he would send "some wine of our own chusing [sic]," without specifying which. Broadbent noted other occasions when Jefferson had asked château owners to send the "best." He pointed to the shipment of 1784 Haut-Brion that had been misrouted and had never reached Jefferson, and suggested that other such misroutings could explain the presence of the Rodenstock bottles in Paris. Broadbent quoted letters from Jefferson requesting that wine shipments be marked with his initials, and he argued that it was unlikely an engraver would ape Jefferson's eccentric mode of punctuating. Monticello's argument to the contrary was, "of course, ridiculous."

Broadbent concluded by noting, irrelevantly if tantalizingly, that 1787 had been "the year that the United States Constitution was signed . . . John Wesley wrote his *Sermons,* Mozart composed *Don Giovanni,* the 'Prague' symphony and *Eine kleine Nachtmusik.* . . . Whatever the theories, impossible to substantiate either way, we are confident that we have in this sale more than a little bit of history."

Nowhere in the auction catalog or this accompanying insert did Broadbent mention a dark rumor circulating about the bottles' origin, the whispered intimation that they were part of a smuggled Nazi hoard. The National Socialists had been as rapacious in their looting of fine wine as of everything else. Göring, in particular, was passionate about Bordeaux, filling his cellar with more than 10,000 plundered bottles. Albert Speer, architect and munitions boss for the Third Reich, later wrote that the only time he felt intimate with the 275-pound Göring was on the evening when Göring shared a Lafite with him. As for Adolf Hitler, a supposed teetotaler who didn't care about wine as a drink, he did recognize its potential to confer social status. In May of 1945, when Allied forces liberated the Eagle's Nest, Hitler's mountaintop redoubt in the Bavarian Alps, they found half a million bottles of wine, including Lafite, Mouton-Rothschild, and Yquem.

So the Nazis had their secret stocks of wine. The French did, too. Justifiably worried that the Germans would steal their wine in the early days of the Second World War, people throughout France concealed bottles by walling off sections of their cellars. In 1940, with the Germans closing in on Paris, the venerable restaurant La Tour d'Argent, which had one of the world's finest lists, culled the 20,000 best bottles from its 100,000-bottle cellar and stashed them in a secret passageway. The Germans took the 80,000 that remained in plain sight, but the hidden stock survived.

Maybe the rumor about Rodenstock's bottles was unfair—born of anti-German sentiment and nurtured by Rodenstock's cryptic remarks—but it had surprising longevity. Broadbent, for one, seemed entertained by the Nazi theory. Although it was never clear whether he subscribed to it, he would still be bringing it up in conversation two decades later.

CHAPTER 6

~

"We Did What
You Told Us"

uck them. FROM HIS SEAT IN THE BACK ROW OF THE West Room at Christie's, in London, on December 5, 1985, Marvin Shanken was watching the auction of the 1787 Lafite with growing resentment. He had flown all the way to England for this. His life revolved around wine, and for him this bottle had great meaning; he had planned to share it, to use it as an occasion to celebrate wine. The Forbeses weren't even in the business. It was just another bauble to them, yet here they were, throwing their weight and money around. Now the bidding was up to £50,000, and Michael Broadbent was about to bring down his auctioneer's hammer. If Shanken was going to stop Forbes, he would need to act quickly.

THOMAS JEFFERSON FOUNDED the University of Virginia. Marvin Shanken graduated last in his class from the University of Miami. Bearlike and charmingly disheveled, with a shrewd glint in his eye, he was a pleasure-seeker. Forbidden by his wife to smoke cigars in their Manhattan apartment, he bought the adjacent flat, turning it into a smoking lounge. As the owner of *Wine Spectator,* he had a more than social interest in wine, and having worked on John F. Kennedy's 1960 campaign, he also had a passion for American presidential history. When Shanken learned from Broadbent about the Jefferson bottle coming up for auction, he knew he had to have it. He would display it at his annual Wine Experience event so that, he later said, "people could see a piece of history."

Shanken first became interested in the wine business as an investment banker putting together West Coast vineyard real-estate deals. His cellar was stocked mainly with California cabernets. He didn't have much auction experience, and he had never been to the wine-auction mecca, the Great Rooms at Christie's in London. This wasn't necessarily the best year for him to be making his debut there, either. *Wine Spectator* was struggling, and Shanken lived from week to week. He didn't have cash to blow, much less the kind of money he knew it would take to land this bottle.

Shanken had watched as wine prices soared over the last decade, and he had no illusions: this bottle was comparable to the first edition of an old book; it was an esoteric object that would likely draw a free-spending fanatic or two out of the woodwork. The Brits wouldn't touch it, but a few Americans might have placed advance bids. The bottle could go for as much as ten grand, fifteen even. Exactly where he would get the money, Shanken had no idea, but he was determined to buy the bottle with the great pedigree. Hell, he was prepared to spend up to $30,000, which was just shy of the highest price ever paid for a bottle of wine.

Shanken was so confident he'd be returning to New York on the afternoon of December 5 with the bottle in hand that, rather than using an agent to bid for him, he flew to London so that he could savor the victory right there in the auction room. Arriving around 2:00 p.m., Shanken took a seat in the middle of the room and waited patiently to complete the formality of obtaining the bottle.

A few minutes before the afternoon session was to begin, he saw a familiar face. Len Yablon belonged to Beach Point, a country club in Mamaroneck, New York, where Shanken was sometimes a guest. Yablon was a finance guy; he had no connection to the wine business and was not, as far as Shanken knew, a collector.

When Shanken greeted Yablon and asked what he was doing there, Yablon replied, "We came to pick up the bottle." He introduced the young man next to him as Kip Forbes, son of publisher Malcolm, for whom Yablon worked. Malcolm had asked them to buy the bottle, Yablon explained, and they needed to rush it back to the Forbes Building in Manhattan in time for a cocktail party for advertisers that evening. The party would launch an exhibit in the ground-floor gallery, consisting of original letters written by Thomas Jefferson, a Jefferson table borrowed from another museum, and the bottle, for which a space had already been set aside. "The plane is waiting," Yablon said.

The plane? Shanken knew that Yablon must mean the Forbeses' private jet. The man spoke with infuriating assurance, as if their acquisition was a foregone conclusion. Forbes was a major publisher, Shanken an upstart. He knew he couldn't compete with that kind of money. Dejected, he walked to the rear of the room, taking a seat in a chair against the back wall. Five minutes earlier he had pictured himself as the bottle's owner. Now he wouldn't even be bidding; he would only be watching. *The plane!* Shanken could grimly look forward to returning to New York, empty-handed, in coach.

DECEMBER 5 WAS Kip Forbes's birthday, but he was spending it with Len Yablon running a routine errand. London was the last stop on a weeklong European tour, a whirlwind annual inventory of the Forbeses' residences on that side of the Atlantic. Courtesy of the corporate 727, they had checked up first on the Palais de Mendoub in Morocco, then on Château Balleroy in France, and that morning, after arriving at Heathrow, on Old Battersea House, their seventeenth-century, Christopher Wren–designed mansion on the Thames. Normally the routine would include a quick visit to Harrods department store to shop for gifts, then dinner at a restaurant before flying back to the States. But this year Malcolm had put in a special order for a bottle of wine.

At home, when their children were growing up, Malcolm Forbes and his wife drank wine with dinner most nights. After Charles de Gaulle spouted the separatist slogan "Vive le Québec libre!" while visiting Montreal in 1967, Forbes protested by boycotting French wine. A Portuguese rosé, Lancer's, became a familiar bottle on the dinner table.

Although the astute and self-aggrandizing Forbes made few expenditures unsuited for either a press release or a tax write-off, he had genuine enthusiasm for wine. He enjoyed drinking it. He liked its mystique. He made no bones about being an "appreciator" rather than a serious collector. Though he bought blue chips, it was for short-term drinking, not long-term investment. The family was advised in its wine buying by a sommelier from the Four Seasons restaurant in Manhattan, and whenever the man suggested that a particular wine might be suitable for laying down for future generations, Malcolm would get annoyed. He didn't intend to wait for his grandchildren. He just wanted to know when it would start to peak.

Malcolm favored Bordeaux. He owned ten bottles of 1890 Lafite, and he especially liked Margaux and, because the château was owned by his New Jersey neighbors the Dillons, Haut-Brion. He bought hundreds of bottles of the 1965 vintage, which was considered particularly horrible, at a cost of five dollars each. For years the Forbes family served that and the 1963, another poor year; most people, ignorant of vintages, were impressed merely by the label. To be fair, even bad vintages of a great wine were worthy of drinking, and such vintages could actually be harder to come by than good ones, because nobody held on to them for very long.

In the mid-eighties, on the occasion of the centennial of France's gift of the Statue of Liberty to the United States, Danielle Mitterand visited New York Harbor. In the afternoon, after a celebration, the Forbes yacht *Highlander* picked her up and motored out to sea. There wasn't a lot of chitchat—Malcolm spoke no French whatsoever, Madame Mitterand only limited English—but when they reached the cramped, glass-doored wine cellar belowdecks by the staterooms, Malcolm said: "Ah, you'll be happy to see all the wines from Bordeaux." Madame Mitterand replied, not entirely warmly, "I am from Burgundy."

Malcolm loved giving people, for their fiftieth anniversary or seventy-fifth birthday, a bottle from their marriage or birth year, always with the injunction, "If you open it, don't tell us." Once, knowing that Richard Nixon loved wine, Malcolm invited the former president to the corporate cellar on lower Fifth Avenue, where a T-shirt hanging on the wall reads, "Life is too short to drink cheap wine." Malcolm and his sons enjoyed dinner with Nixon right there in the cellar's crisp, 60-degree air. Malcolm wasn't precious about his wine, and if he had to work late, he thoroughly enjoyed popping open a Margaux to drink with a Big Mac and fries.

All the Forbes children had taken up collecting: Steve was into historic documents, Bob went for toy boats, Tim bought Americana, and Moira amassed comic books. But Kip embraced the mania most fully. It was Kip who became curator of the family's collections, and it was to Kip that Forbes senior would later dedicate *More Than I Dreamed,* his memoir of collecting. Kip wrote his senior thesis at Princeton on Victorian art, and had an abiding passion for English paintings of the late nineteenth century. As a young man he seemed to pine for a bygone world of aristocrats. At age twenty-three he married the thirty-eight-year-old German baroness Astrid Mathilde Cornelia von Heyl zu Herrnsheim, and, for a time, took to wearing

Edwardian three-piece suits with a pocket watch and chain. In 1976, Kip encouraged his father to buy the *Social Register*. By the time of the 1985 auction, Kip's Victorian painting collection had grown to some five hundred paintings, most of which he kept at Old Battersea House.

The Forbeses also collected presidential memorabilia. They owned one of Abraham Lincoln's stovepipe hats—and the opera glasses Lincoln was holding when he was shot—and they owned three letters from Jefferson on the subject of wine. One was to the chief of the Seneca Indians and said how bad alcohol was for them. Another was to a lady friend, with a gift of six bottles of wine to improve her stomach. In the third, Jefferson invoked presidential privilege to bring wine into the country duty-free.

In 1985, Malcolm had the ground floor of the Forbes Building renovated to accommodate a suite of galleries. Kip was good friends with the president of the Maryland Historical Society, and with a loaned Jefferson table that arrived just six days before the London auction, a special Jefferson display was to open that very evening in New York to inaugurate the Forbes Galleries. When Malcolm read in his Christie's catalog about the bottle coming up for sale in London, he saw it as a perfect tie-in. He told Kip to go to the auction and get it.

KIP HAD BEEN to plenty of auctions before, often on behalf of his father, but never a wine auction. Like his father, he enjoyed wine. His wife's family owned vineyards. He could be awed, like many people, by famous labels. He had a small cellar in his home, and he had even tasted some exceedingly old vintages, including an 1870s Mouton-Rothschild from the Forbes cellar, which was leaking so badly that his father decided they might as well pull the cork. The wine was "convincingly alive, at least for the first fifteen minutes," Kip later said. But that was as far as his oenological inclinations went. He had never visited Bordeaux, much less Château Lafite. And he didn't consider the 1787 Lafite a bottle of wine so much as a historical artifact. He and Yablon would bid £5,000, maybe, a huge sum. But victory was assured. They would claim their prize and drive straight to the airport.

Most of the Christie's headquarters, on King Street near St. James Square, had been razed by bombing in 1941 and rebuilt after the war, but the Renaissance façade, a four-story sheet of Portland stone, was the original. Kip and Yablon arrived at the auction house dressed for their transatlantic journey. Years before the term "brand representative" would enter the marketing lexicon, the Forbeses had been practicing the concept, and Kip wore a tie bearing the epithet CAPITALIST TOOL, and carried a FORBES CAPITALIST TOOLBAG tote. He and Yablon took their time wandering through the Christie's galleries, and then entered the West Room, where Yablon introduced Kip to Marvin Shanken.

Although it was reasonable for Forbes and Yablon to assume that £5,000 would accomplish their goal, they were also conscious of their delicate position. Malcolm had said to buy the bottle; he had not set price parameters. The relationship between Malcolm and exorbitant bids went back a long way, and he knew his own predilection for losing self-control. Once, when buying a piece of Fabergé, he had said he would bid up to $25,000; after that, Yablon should take over the bidding, and Malcolm would tell him when to stop.

Known within the Forbes family as "Dr. No," Yablon was a loyal retainer who had grown up in the Bronx thinking tennis was "a sissy sport." He had risen from lowly accountant to something akin to Forbes's minister of finance. He was the one person close to the patriarch with the power to restrain his extravagant spending. Anything concerning money, Malcolm referred to Yablon. In spite of the "Dr. No" moniker, Yablon made a point of never saying that word to Forbes. Instead, he would say he needed to think it over, which he did; then, the next day, he would have a reasoned discussion with Malcolm, for or against the expenditure. Yablon was hardly draconian. What others might view as Forbes's spendthrift ostentation, he recognized as being the mind of a savvy brand publicist at work.

Bidding for his father, Kip Forbes felt he was damned whatever he did. When his brother, Steve, bought the original survey establishing the Mason-Dixon line, he set a world price record for an American document. Malcolm had slammed his hand down on the table, called Steve irresponsible, and remained angry for nearly a year. When Malcolm instructed Kip, in 1982, to go to London to bid on the declaration of war that Mussolini had read from his balcony, Kip wasn't about to make the same kind of mistake his brother had made. The Mussolini document was estimated at a mere $8,500–$10,000, and when the bidding hit $100,000, Kip dropped out. "I thought, 'Oh no, I know how this game is played,'" Kip later recalled. But Steve came to him and told him to put on sackcloth and ashes. Far from being impressed with his son's restraint, this time Malcolm was furious not to have obtained the document. There seemed to be no pleasing him.

Now, three years later, Kip was back in London with a buy order. His anxiety was assuaged by the presence of Yablon, who had agreed on a number that seemed reasonable—after which he would drop out. If Malcolm was displeased, they would share the heat. But they didn't expect that problem to arise, given the relatively low prices of even the rarest bottles of wine. Nothing about this auction seemed that unusual. Any qualms about authenticity had been allayed by Christie's. And they were under orders. "I'm from the Bronx," as Yablon said later. "The boss said to buy it." As far as he and Kip were concerned, they were going home with the bottle in time for the Jefferson exhibit.

At first, when the bidding was low, Forbes and Yablon alternated raising an index finger or their paddle, number 231, then hung back while others made bids. This was in line with the bidding strategy favored by Malcolm—show only desultory interest at first. The bidding rapidly escalated, and Kip stayed in the game until he had left everyone else behind with a bid of £50,000.

"Any more?" Michael Broadbent asked. "Any more?"

WITH KIP FORBES seconds away from winning the bottle for the equivalent of $75,000, Marvin Shanken, in the back row, was thinking *Fuck them.* His disappointment fully transformed into anger, Shanken grabbed his catalog and stabbed the air.

"Fifty-two thousand pounds," Broadbent called out. Without breaking stride, he looked back toward Kip Forbes to see whether he'd raise Shanken to 54,000. Kip did, and a classic duel began.

No matter how many people wave paddles, an experienced auctioneer homes in on two at a time and bids them up against each other. In this case, everyone else had stopped trying. Shanken and Forbes were the only bidders left, and each was determined to possess the object at the front of the room. At £68,000, there was another pause in the bidding. Then it leapt upward, bouncing back and forth between Forbes and Shanken.

Forbes bid 78,000.

Shanken bid 80,000.

Forbes bid 82,000.

By now, he and Yablon were nudging each other, but they resisted the temptation to turn around and see whom they were bidding against. Neither had a clue it was Shanken. Yablon knew Shanken was interested in wine collecting, but he also knew that Shanken had recently been through a divorce and likely had no money.

The room was silent save for Broadbent's relentlessly upward-counting voice. When Shanken bid £100,000, Broadbent turned again to Kip. One hundred thousand was the drop-out number Kip and Yablon had agreed on. Kip knew, even before this number was reached, that he would probably go at least one bid past it, but theory was easier than practice. He paused.

Marvin Shanken felt what seemed to him a series of electrical shocks—not because he might lose the bottle, but because he might win it. An improbably long time seemed to have elapsed since he had bid, and as the pause stretched on, the jangling reality seized Shanken: he could actually be on the hook for £100,000. That was nearly $150,000. He had contracted textbook auction fever. Stunned by his own recklessness, Shanken suddenly felt very afraid. He'd be paying this bottle off for the rest of his life. Or else he would be forced to declare bankruptcy. Either way, he'd be ruined.

"A hundred and five."

Michael Broadbent was speaking.

"One hundred and five thousand pounds, in the middle."

Shanken saw that Kip Forbes had raised his finger.

Kip Forbes had raised his finger!

Broadbent looked searchingly at Shanken.

"At one hundred and five thousand pounds," Broadbent repeated. "Going at one hundred and five. Any more?"

No frigging way, Shanken thought. He kept his hand down.

"One hundred and five thousand," Broadbent said once more, and hammered the lot down.

The room roared with applause.

The whole thing had lasted one minute and thirty-nine seconds.

Kip Forbes was handed the bottle, which he laid gingerly in his green Forbes Capitalist Toolbag. Then he and Yablon, somewhat stunned, left the room while bidding on other lots continued. They had spent the equivalent of $156,000. It wasn't as if the Forbeses hadn't bought things at auction for much greater amounts of money, but for a bottle of wine this was unheard of. Kip would allow that he had suffered from "a controlled contagion." Only after exiting did he and Yablon discover whom they'd been bidding against.

"Why didn't you tell me you wanted to bid?" Yablon asked Shanken. "We could have talked."

Some people had followed them out of the room, curious to learn just who these men were, and a crowd gathered. Journalists' questions focused on the importance of this bottle, which had been earmarked for the author of the Declaration of Independence. Suddenly, Kip was in the position of having to explain and find meaning in a purchase that had begun as a quotidian chore. "It's more than a bottle of wine," he answered, when a reporter suggested his bid had been exorbitant. "It's a piece of history." He said the Forbes family had no intention of opening the bottle. He planned to celebrate by drinking a rather younger Lafite.

With the news about to go out on the wires, Kip figured he had better call his father. "Well, Pop," he told Malcolm, upon reaching him in New Jersey, "I did what you told me." When Kip said what he'd spent, his father's reaction was of the Mason-Dixon variety. Malcolm dropped the phone. When he recovered himself, he was furious. Kip held the receiver away from his ear, but Malcolm was still audible. He demanded to speak to Yablon: The guy who was supposed to take care of the money had allowed this insanity? Gladly, Kip handed the phone to Dr. No, who dutifully took his turn in the telephonic woodshed.

The idea was to fly the bottle straight to New York in time for the gallery opening that evening, but now Christie's was confronted with something it had never faced before—a bottle of wine that had sold for so much it would require an export license. A museum was also needed to certify that the bottle wasn't a national treasure, and discussion ensued as to which museum could most quickly provide this service. Broadbent's right-hand man set about making the arrangements, while Broadbent called Rodenstock to tell him the news. Like Broadbent and Forbes, the German was taken aback by the amount. While waiting for the paperwork to come through, Kip chatted with Yablon and Broadbent. Ever the salesman, Broadbent wondered if they mightn't be interested in other bottles from the cache.

By the time the Victoria and Albert Museum provided the certification, it was nighttime, and there was no way Kip and Yablon were going to make it to the party in New York in time. Export license in hand, they were driven to the *Capitalist Tool,* idling on the tarmac at Heathrow. With an eight-hour flight ahead, they put the bottle to bed in the plane's stateroom—swathed in velvet, nestled inside the carry bag, surrounded by pillows, and bound loosely to the mattress with sheets. Then they settled in for the flight, talking about how angry Malcolm was.

At Newark Airport, the head of Forbes security helped them through customs. They braced for Malcolm, but by the time they saw him, the following day, his attitude had shifted. While worrying that he would look like a horse's ass—a fear that had seldom vexed his free-spending life—he had gone on the TV program *Adam Smith's Money World,* ostensibly to talk about the economy. Inevitably asked about the purchase that was making news around the world, Forbes had grumbled, "The Forbes family would be far better off if Mr. Jefferson had drunk the damn thing."

Now he was thankful. Reporters were calling in droves, and it was dawning on Malcolm that the Forbeses had inadvertently staged, as Yablon would later put it, a "masterstroke . . . the publicity coup of the century." Marvin Shanken, in his London hotel room, received a call telling him that news reports of the Forbeses' record purchase mentioned that the underbidder was the publisher of *Wine Spectator.* The PR was nice, but mainly Shanken was relieved to have escaped without the bottle. Kip Forbes had a hard time believing this. "I think at the end [Shanken] regretted it," Forbes asserted later, "because it was a slow news moment, and it did get huge amounts of publicity."

At the Forbes Galleries, curator Margaret Kelly took over. She had learned of the price paid for the acquisition from the radio. The Jefferson table already stood against an angled wood-paneled wall in the narrow Carrère gallery on the ground floor. Recessed in the wall above the table was a diorama containing a miniature replica of Jefferson's bedroom and study at Monticello. On the table, Kelly had draped a tacky wood crate with salmon-colored velvet, and she now positioned the bottle at an angle, nestled in the fabric, with the engraving showing. Next to it, under glass, were the three Jefferson letters.

Upstairs, in the company offices, there were a lot of raised eyebrows. Malcolm was known to do crazy things, but this set a new bar. Kip's siblings, however, understood. Their father had wanted something. There really hadn't been any choice.

Years later, Len Yablon, who had a wine cellar at home but was partial to a good cocktail, would recall that at the time he thought it was "meshuggah"—*this was a bottle of wine, not a Rolls Royce!*—"but it ended up genius." Still, he acknowledged, a public company could never have gotten away with such an expenditure. That was the joy of working at Forbes—business and fun were never far apart, whether it was owning a motorcycle distributorship or a bottle of wine that had belonged to Thomas Jefferson. Yablon never knew what was next: A party in Morocco? A balloon trip across the ocean? But of his forty-one years at the company, the purchase of the bottle still ranked, two decades later, as his most unusual experience working for a very unusual man. It reminded him of a great naval battle that lasts only an hour but goes down in history.

ON THE NIGHT of the auction, in the northern German city of Hamburg, a telephone rang in a house east of Lake Alster. It was answered by Hanns Janssen, a Monte Carlo Rally driver turned wine writer who had been present when Michael Broadbent persuaded Hardy Rodenstock to let him auction the bottle. Rodenstock was calling now. What, he wanted to know, did Janssen think the bottle had sold for?

JANSSEN: Twenty thousand marks.

RODENSTOCK: No.

JANSSEN: Twenty thousand francs.

RODENSTOCK: Don't talk in francs or marks. Guess in dollars.

JANSSEN: Okay, ten thousand.

RODENSTOCK: No, more.

JANSSEN: Fifty thousand.

RODENSTOCK: More.

JANSSEN: You're crazy.

RODENSTOCK: More.

JANSSEN: One hundred thousand.

RODENSTOCK: More.

JANSSEN: One hundred fifty thousand.

RODENSTOCK: One hundred fifty-six thousand.

JANSSEN: Now, what do you think of that bottle that we drank? Was it worth one hundred fifty-six thousand?

CHAPTER 7

IMAGINARY VALUE

Immediately after the Forbes purchase, Lucia Goodwin appeared on TV for the first time in her life, driving from Charlottesville, Virginia, to the National Agricultural Library in Maryland to tape an interview. Goodwin was, in 1985, the closest thing to a full-time generalist scholar at Monticello. A research associate whom everyone called Cinder, she had a wry and studious nature. She had been at Monticello off and on since 1968, shortly after she graduated from Harvard with a degree in American history and literature. For the last five years she had been consumed with editing the Memorandum Books, Jefferson's financial diary, a project begun by her coeditor thirty years earlier. She and the coeditor had finally finished the manuscript the year before. Now she had time on her hands.

When news of Rodenstock's discovery had broken two months earlier, the staff at Monticello was instinctively skeptical. Some poor widow or other attic-rummaging type was always showing up there bearing an "original" copy of the Declaration of Independence, found in a shoebox in a closet, that turned out to be a 1944 reproduction. The percentage that proved legitimate was infinitesimal. It seemed strange, too, that Christie's had not heeded Monticello's input before deeming the bottles authentic.

As media calls began coming in, Monticello's curator decided that the seat of all things Jefferson should have an informed position on the bottles. The task of formulating it fell to Cinder Goodwin, who began her research even before the auction took place. Her interest in wine extended as far as most people's: She liked to drink it. Her obsession was Jefferson. As it happened, Monticello had compiled a comprehensive list of all the Jefferson relics known to exist. And Goodwin was very confident that she could prove, or disprove, Michael Broadbent's attribution of the Jefferson bottles.

THE PRIVATE NONPROFIT foundation set up in 1923 to administer Monticello was itself in the collecting business. In the course of his life, Jefferson assembled a substantial amount of art, furniture, and other valuables. He sold some furniture during his lifetime, when his term as secretary of state was ending and he was getting ready to move from Philadelphia to Monticello. In 1815 he sold his personal library to the Library of Congress, which had lost its collection to fire in the War of 1812. Early American artifacts were in demand even during his lifetime, and he gave a draft of the Declaration of Independence to the Philosophical Society in Philadelphia; another society in Philadelphia, dedicated to celebrating William Penn's arrival, owned one chair sat in by Penn and two made from the elm tree beneath which Penn first signed a treaty with the Indians.

Jefferson anticipated the historic value of his possessions when he gave his granddaughter's new husband the custom-made "writing box," or lap-desk, on which he had written the Declaration. "If these things acquire a superstitious value, because of their connection with particular persons," Jefferson wrote to the granddaughter in late 1825, "surely a connection with the greater Charter of our

Independence may give a value to what has been associated with that. . . . Its imaginary value will increase with years, and if he lives to my age, or another half-century, he may see it carried in the procession of our nation's birthday, as the relics of the Saints are in those of the Church." Recognizing that the object's value hinged on the certainty of its connection to the Declaration, Jefferson scratched out an affidavit attesting to its origin.

When Jefferson died, in July of 1826, his will specified the disposition of only a handful of items. He bequeathed his walking stick to James Madison and watches to each of his grandchildren. At least ten clippings of his hair were taken posthumously. His farm and account books, as well as his collection of 40,000 letters—every one that he received, plus a duplicate of every letter he sent—went to his grandson and executor, Thomas Jefferson Randolph. Most of the silver went to his daughter Martha. A number of valuables were distributed among family members.

At a five-day executor's sale at Monticello the following January, the remainder of Jefferson's personal property was auctioned. This included paintings, sculptures, Jefferson's copying machine, "130 valuable negroes," and "various other articles curious and useful to men of business and private families." Jefferson's grandchildren bought a lot of the furniture. Other items were bought by friends, neighbors, and strangers. Monticello was overrun by ghoulish tourists who walked away with whatever they fancied, including fig bushes and grapevines; Jefferson's family resorted to placing a notice in the local newspaper beseeching memento seekers to "desist from such trespasses."

Certain categories of items were handled separately. Most of Jefferson's books (he had reassembled a large library) were sold, in 1829, to a bookseller in Washington, D.C. His art collection was shipped to Boston for auction. On the journey, the paintings were severely damaged by seawater; when they went on the block in July 1828, only one sold.

In short, Jefferson's worldly possessions scattered, often without a trace. Over the years, they would briefly surface. On July 4, 1876, at a Boston celebration of the country's Centennial, the lap-desk Jefferson had given to his grandson-in-law was displayed. Robert Winthrop, a former senator who had become head of the Massachusetts Historical Society, scoffed at Jefferson's self-deprecating affidavit.

"Superstitions! Imaginary value! Not for an instant can we admit such ideas," Winthrop said. "The modesty of the writer has betrayed even 'the masterly pen.' There is no imaginary value to this relic, and no superstition is required to render it as precious and priceless a piece of wood as the secular cabinets of the world have ever possessed, or ever claimed to possess. . . . Even the table at Runnymede on which the Magna Carta was sealed," Winthrop went on, getting a bit carried away, "could hardly exceed, could hardly equal, in interest and value, this little mahogany desk. What momentous issues for our country, and for mankind, were locked up in this narrow drawer, as night after night the rough notes of preparation for the Great Paper were laid aside for the revision of the morning!" Ultimately, the desk went to the Smithsonian.

Sometimes Jefferson relics turned up in the collectibles market or came to light in an academic context. In 1904 a newspaper reported that a brass coal scuttle "said to have been at one time the property of Thomas Jefferson" was stolen from a Manhattan antique store by "a negro." Around the same time, William Jennings Bryan purchased a marble punch bowl, with original oak pestle, that had belonged to Jefferson. In 1930, Jefferson descendants consigned several items for auction in New York, including a 1776 letter relating Revolutionary news and an 1819 schematic for the buildings of the University of Virginia. In the 1940s a New York antiques dealer named Israel Sack tried selling a Jefferson clock, which had been purchased at the 1827 sale, to the White House and the Jefferson Foundation. In 1947 a scholar combing the libraries and museums of Paris on behalf of Princeton University's epic project to publish all of Jefferson's letters happened upon the original wooden models of a new and better plow Jefferson had invented.

Over the years, Monticello enjoyed considerable success in recovering Jefferson relics, or at least locating them. The provenances were often straightforward. The Jefferson table lent by the Maryland Historical Society for the Forbes exhibit had passed down through five generations of Jefferson's descendants before being purchased by a woman who willed it to the society. Many of the pieces that descended through Jefferson's heirs found their way back to Monticello either as gifts or purchases. By 1958, more than fifteen pieces of the original silver owned by Jefferson had been reclaimed; when Monticello could not get the original, it sometimes had reproductions made.

There remained a number of relics that Monticello had located but had not been able to obtain, and many more that Monticello knew about but couldn't locate. Monticello had never been able to find, for instance, a slew of paintings from Jefferson's art collection that had been referenced in Jefferson's documents. Every so often one would turn up, usually in as serendipitous a fashion as Rodenstock's wine bottles. In 1912 a Jefferson-owned portrait of Thomas Paine turned up in a box of objects at a Massachusetts auction; the owner had no idea of its venerable history, which wouldn't be recognized until the 1950s.

When it came to Jefferson's wine, no bottles had ever been found. America's early presidents had no entertaining budget, and Jefferson, in his first year of office, spent $2,800 of his $25,000 salary on wine. This kind of extravagance increased his already sizable debts, and he could no longer afford to keep deep stocks of wine. When Jefferson died, the 586 bottles left in his cellar held only wines from southern France and some Scuppernong.

In the 1960s, Monticello set about re-creating the wine cellar as it must have looked originally. It had been empty since Jefferson's death. In February 1966 the curator of Monticello traveled to London seeking empty eighteenth-century bottles. He was able to find about twenty, and sailed back to New York with the plan of making molds to produce additional facsimiles. The closest Monticello came to laying hands on an actual artifact of Jefferson's wine drinking was the discovery, in the course of archaeological digs begun at Monticello in the late 1970s, of most of a Madeira decanter and a shard of glass bearing the seal of Lafite.

IN 1985, CINDER Goodwin had her work cut out for her. Wine cherishes celebrities, and there are celebrities, certainly, who cherish wine. Nonetheless, celebrities loom much larger in the history of wine than wine does in their personal histories. While Thomas Jefferson was the foremost connoisseur of the eighteenth century, the fact received almost no mention in his biographies. The Monticello library's file on Jefferson and wine was only an inch and a half thick.

But having spent much of the past five years doing the footnotes for the Memorandum Books, Goodwin had read countless Jefferson letters and was by now an old hand with Jefferson documents. Starting as a young man, Jefferson had kept several different diaries (one about his garden, one about his farm, one about his travels), every letter he received, a copy of each of the 16,000-odd letters he wrote in his lifetime, a correspondence log noting each letter sent and received, and the Memorandum Books. These last contained a daily record of every expenditure and every receipt of Jefferson's from the age of twenty-four. There were bills for the oats for Jefferson's horse in Paris. He also kept reams of miscellaneous accounts, which included customs records that accompanied the wine shipments he received in Paris. Jefferson larded his correspondence, to a tedious degree, with the minutiae of his wine orders, from shifting exchange rates to intricate freight-forwarding logistics. At his death, several tens of thousands of pages in his handwriting were in circulation.

"He didn't have a wastebasket," Goodwin said later.

It was more than this thoroughness that made her confident. Jefferson's wine orders showed up in four different parts of the Jefferson record: the Memorandum Books, the miscellaneous accounts, the letters, and the letter log. Not in one or the other of them; most orders could be found in *all* four. Jefferson not only wrote everything down; he wrote it down several times in several places. Of course, Jefferson was human, and maybe a particular letter had been misplaced, or an entry hadn't been made; but some trace of the entry or letter would invariably show up elsewhere. "He was a hero of meticulousness," in Goodwin's words. Jefferson himself stated that he would swear on his deathbed to the reliability of the Memorandum Books, which he said had excluded only a single transaction in fifteen years.

This thorough, meticulous, and multiply redundant record had survived nearly intact. If the bottles found in Paris had indeed belonged to Jefferson, there was every reason to expect that supporting documentary evidence could be found. Goodwin called the Princeton letters project and spoke with Monticello's curators, who confirmed that none of the wine bottles exhumed by archaeologists at Monticello had been engraved. Then she began scouring the written record.

Goodwin found that for the 1784 vintage, Jefferson had recorded the purchase of only two of the four wines found by Rodenstock: the Margaux and Yquem, which he had received in 1787 and 1788, respectively. In his 1788 letter to the owner of Lafite, Jefferson had ordered the 1784 vintage, but he was informed that none was available. As for 1787, the vintage of the Lafite that the Forbes family had just bought, there was no evidence that Jefferson had ever ordered, or even wanted to order, a 1787 Lafite or, for that matter, a 1787 anything. Nor was there any indication that he had received them without ordering them. In 1790, after his return to America, he did place one order for Yquem in which he didn't specify vintage (he asked to be sent whichever was drinking best), but he had it shipped directly from Bordeaux to America, and he recorded that he received the shipment. And there was no record of his having ever ordered Branne-Mouton in any vintage.

On December 12, 1985, a week after the record-setting auction, Goodwin issued her report. She couldn't just come out and say she thought Broadbent and Rodenstock didn't know what they were talking about, so she began by flattering them: "When we learned that [Hardy Rodenstock and Michael Broadbent] were men of unquestioned knowledge and integrity, we began to reassess the possibilities of authenticity." Then she methodically proceeded to establish that they didn't know what they were talking about.

While Goodwin's report focused on the record-setting 1787 Lafite, she made the point that the bottles must fall or stand as a group. They had been found together and engraved similarly, which must have happened after they left their respective châteaux. Given that Jefferson, from 1787 on, ordered his wine directly from châteaux, deliberately bypassing merchants, this meant either that one of his intermediaries in Bordeaux had done the engraving, or that they had been engraved after reaching Jefferson in Paris.

"He seems to have made the connection between the bottles and Jefferson by a study of the records," Goodwin wrote of Rodenstock, "but it is precisely those records which make such a connection less and less likely."

Broadbent, in his Christie's-catalog provenance for the 1787 Lafite, had pointed to Jefferson's 1790 order, which included a request that the bottles be *etiquettés,* or labeled, as support for the engraving. Goodwin pointed out that to engrave the entire shipment (1,020 bottles) would have been costly and would certainly have merited mention in Jefferson's Memorandum Books, yet no such expense appeared there. Goodwin also homed in on the particular style of initials used. Jefferson had requested that the wine be marked "T.I." In other circumstances he had used a cursive "TJ" to identify certain possessions, and "Th:J," with a colon, to sign some correspondence. The form of the initials on the Rodenstock bottles was "Th.J.," which Jefferson had never used or specified.

Goodwin further noted that Jefferson had requested that the marking take place at the vineyard, which didn't explain how wines from four different vineyards seemed to have been engraved by the same hand. And she cited some letters that seemed to indicate that, by *etiquetté,* Jefferson had meant that the cases, not the bottles, be labeled. Most damningly, it seemed, the 1790 order had consisted only of Yquem and a lesser-known Bordeaux named Rausan. Not only had the shipment for Jefferson arrived successfully in America; even if the unspecified Yquem was 1787, the shipment had not included Lafite, Margaux, or Branne-Mouton.

Trying to anticipate some of the objections that might be raised, Goodwin dealt with the possibility that Jefferson had received some bottles as a gift or as part of a trade. In order for a verbal, undocumented transaction of this sort to have taken place, it would need to have been before his departure from Paris in September 1789, which was, in those days of three or four years between harvest and shipping, early for the 1787 vintage.

Goodwin also allowed that there was a slim possibility that evidence of further orders would turn up (in 1985, Jefferson's letters had only been published through 1791, and access to the unpublished letters was limited), but given the redundancy of Jefferson's recordkeeping, and her access to both his letter log and his Memorandum Books, she thought it highly unlikely. She also acknowledged that a lack of documentary evidence did not definitively prove that the bottles weren't Jefferson's. Monticello had numerous relics it had deemed authentic without having a paper trail to back them up; in those cases, however, provenance had been supported by the objects' uninterrupted passage through several generations of Jefferson's descendants.

How the particular combination of châteaux and vintages announced by Rodenstock—some of which Jefferson had ordered and received in Paris, some of which he had ordered and expressly not received in Paris, some of which he had ordered and received in America, and some of which he seemed never to have ordered, but which, if he had ordered, would in any case have been after his return to America—had all ended up in Paris, and been engraved by the same hand, was beyond Goodwin, but in her report she hazarded a guess.

"Were there not Thomases, Theodores, or Theophiles, and Jacksons, Joneses, and Juliens who also had a taste for fine Bordeaux wine, and who would have been resident in Paris in 1790 or after, when the 1787 vintage would have been in bottles? I think it is a question of someone other than Jefferson, and perhaps there is an equally fascinating story there." After making another perfunctory reference to the "honorable characters of Mr. Rodenstock and Mr. Broadbent," she concluded that she could not "make the same leap of faith they have."

WHEN GOODWIN'S REPORT came out, Broadbent and Rodenstock reacted not with gratitude that this servant of accuracy and historical truth had demolished their case for a Jefferson link, but with rage. Even the most detail-oriented person couldn't be expected to "note every vintage and source of every bottle he ever purchased or received," as one Broadbent/Rodenstock partisan wrote, especially someone as busy as Jefferson after his return to the United States.

Goodwin had made a convincing case, but Broadbent seized on three weaknesses in it. First, there was, as it turned out, a record of Jefferson having requested engraving of bottles. Shortly before leaving Paris in September of 1789, he had written to John Jay, America's foreign secretary in New York, describing a shipment of wine to him and George Washington with diamond-engraved initials on each bottle. Second, Goodwin's insistence about the form of the initials was a flimsy argument; there was no reason to assume that someone engraving the bottles for Jefferson would follow his exact and idiosyncratic mode of punctuation. Third, Goodwin had said that the only wine in the cache that Jefferson had recorded ordering was 1784 Yquem; she failed to connect Jefferson's order of 1784 Margaux with the Rodenstock find. (She hadn't caught this only because the early U.S. media reports about the cache hadn't indicated that it included 1784 Margaux.)

These points made only glancing dents in Cinder Goodwin's case, but they sufficed to give Rodenstock and Broadbent a basis to attack the entire report. "Cindy Goodwin," as Broadbent called her, had been "led astray and raised doubts almost solely because of the initials on the bottle," as had the *New York Times*'s Howard Goldberg, whose probing questions Broadbent found distasteful. Goldberg was guilty, Broadbent wrote, of "the sort of investigative journalism we are all only too used to: like a terrier shaking a rabbit." Rodenstock also supplied the *VWGA Journal* with a copy of what appeared to be a facsimile of an eighteenth-century page of Château d'Yquem's ledger showing an explicit order by Jefferson for the 1787 vintage.

In a December 28 letter to Dan Jordan, Monticello's new director, Rodenstock complained angrily that his integrity had been impugned by Goodwin. "[O]ne should courteously keep back one's dubious and unfounded remarks," Rodenstock wrote, "and one shouldn't make oneself important in front of the press." The controversy played out on the letters pages of *Decanter*. An elderly, impish Sussex winemaker named Arthur Woods, who frequently wrote letters to the editor dogging Broadbent, posed the rhetorical question, "Is it possible that Mr. Christopher Forbes, who bought the bottle, has not so much purchased a wine almost certainly undrinkable, or a genuine bottle of the period, worth perhaps £100, as a set of initials whose authenticity is likely to be vigorously challenged by those of a heretical bent?" He concluded by asking, "Did I hear somebody murmur 'Piltdown Man'? Perish the thought."

In Bordeaux, owners of the first-growth châteaux rallied behind Broadbent. Baron Eric de Rothschild, from Lafite, told *Wine Specta-tor,* "I don't question its authenticity." Comte Alexandre de Lur Saluces came next, attesting in *Decanter* to the authenticity of the Yquems that Rodenstock had found. Lur Saluces mentioned the let-ter in which Jefferson asked for bottles to be "labelled," the original of which was in Yquem's voluminous archives, and mentioned the 1784 order and "an order corresponding to 1787 as well" (Jeffer-son's 1790 order in which he didn't specify a vintage). It was the same evidence already weighed by Goodwin, but Lur Saluces put a different spin on it.

"I see no reason to doubt the authenticity of these bottles," Lur Saluces continued. "Indeed, as far as the 1787 is concerned, we have been astonished at Yquem to discover an aroma that is familiar. After the tasting, the cellar master himself confirmed to me, that simply on the nose he had been able to recognize Yquem." Lur Saluces called Rodenstock "my friend." Broadbent himself wrote a letter to the edi-tor that appeared in the July 1986 issue, in which he made the point: "I cannot imagine anyone in the late eighteenth century going to the trouble of engraving 'Th.J,' the name of the wine and the vintage, in the extraordinarily faint hope that in two hundred years' time some susceptible collector would acquire it and some muggins of an American would pay an exorbitant price for it. . . . All I can repeat is that the bottle and its contents are amazingly right."

Since neither side could prove anything, the dispute boiled down to where the burden of persuasion lay. Goodwin, a historian, made the case that it was very unlikely that the bottles were Jeffer-son's. Surely it was statistically implausible that the only Jefferson bottles ever found intact would be the exact ones excluded from his extraordinarily thorough records (even if those records weren't perfect, as evidenced by the unaccounted-for glass Lafite seal found in the dirt at Monticello). She contended that it was up to Broadbent and Rodenstock to convince the world otherwise. Meanwhile, Broadbent insisted that too many coincidences were involved for the bottles *not* to be Jefferson's. His argument rested on several assumptions, not least of which was that no one had deliberately set out to fake the bottles.

FORTUNATELY FOR BROADBENT—and for Christie's—Monticello didn't come out with its report until a week after the auction had taken place. By then, the record price had vaulted the bottle high into the mediasphere, chronicled from Stockholm to Omaha to Melbourne. CBS News called it "the most famous bottle of wine in the world." Most reports—whether in *Newsweek*, the AP, or the *Times* of London—stated unequivocally that it was Jefferson's wine.

Journalists loved tallying the prorated cost of the wine: $19,500 a glass, $4,000 a sip, $795 "for each year of the life" of the wine. Citroën ran an ad making fun of the bottle's price compared with the mere £4,165 cost of its "Van Rouge." In a cartoon that ran in a British newspaper, a paunchy, red-nosed airplane passenger passed a bottle around to his friends while turning to a seat neighbor who appeared to be having a heart attack: "I've just opened your duty-free, mate—I'll get you another bottle when she comes round!" Some muggins of an American, reveling in all the publicity, had the best of these framed and added to the gallery of press clippings that winds around the hallways of the *Forbes* magazine executive offices on lower Fifth Avenue.

There was a fair amount of moralizing about the purchase. Hand-wringing pundits spoke of Jefferson "[turning] over in his grave" because of the extravagance, or because of the Forbeses' stated intention of putting the bottle in a museum. Wine experts proffered sniffy opinions on whether the Lafite would be drinkable. Bordeaux château owners eagerly hoped the price would have a trickle-down effect on the market for their own wines. Broadbent was soon calling it "[u]ndoubtedly the major event of the wine season, of any season, anywhere."

Coming at the height of a decade increasingly viewed as one of materialistic excess, the bid would eventually take on symbolic heft. As "the most expensive wine" (by a factor of more than four), the bottle entered *The Guinness Book of World Records*. By the end of the decade, *Life* magazine, in its rundown of the 1980s, would include the purchase in a handful of year-defining events of 1985, alongside the resurrection of Coke Classic and the fad for Transformers, the Japanese toy.

In all the hubbub, any serious scholarly doubts about the bottle were forgotten, and two questions went unanswered. Years later, in interviews, Rodenstock would claim that Christie's had known about the cache and he had simply beaten them to it. But Steven Spurrier, the well-connected Englishman who owned a wine shop in Paris and served as Christie's agent in that city, had not heard so much as a whisper about the bottles' discovery. It seemed odd that whoever first found the bottles wouldn't have shopped them to the highest bidder, rather than automatically selling them to Rodenstock. Stranger still was the question of where, exactly, the bottles could have been found. In his last four years in France, Jefferson had lived at an address not in the Marais but on the Champs-Élysées, and the house had long ago been razed, replaced by a high-rise. Perhaps the bottles were a gift intended for Jefferson—a mixed case from an aristocratic Parisian friend that was never delivered because of the French Revolution. But even a week after Forbes had made news around the world, no one had stepped forward to claim he'd been the Parisian driver of the backhoe that had broken through to the hidden cache that turned out to hold the most expensive bottle of wine in history.

CHAPTER 8

THE SWEETNESS
OF DEATH

TOWARD THE END OF APRIL 1986, THE JEFFERSON table had to be returned to the Maryland Historical Society, and the Forbes Galleries staff rearranged the exhibit. They moved the 1787 Lafite to a case in the adjacent gallery. Soon after, wine merchant Bill Sokolin, who owned a shop at the corner of Madison Avenue and 34th Street, came to see the bottle. He was struck immediately by how it was stored.

The bottle basked under a spotlight.

Its environment was approximately the opposite of ideal cellar conditions.

Sokolin went over to a security guard and asked him to inform the Forbeses that they really needed to store the wine differently.

Not long after that, a member of the curatorial staff was removing the bottle from its case for a photo shoot when she noticed that something wasn't quite right. The bottle was a dark green, but despite its murkiness, she could see something floating in the wine. She looked more closely.

It was the cork.

The light had baked it, causing it to shrivel and slip.

Horrified, curator Margaret Kelly called Michael Broadbent for advice; he was, she recalled later, "surprisingly unhelpful." Since the bottle wasn't for drinking, he advised her simply to put a new stopper in it.

The Forbes family was concerned, but once they determined that there was nothing more to be done, that was that. From the beginning they had felt that what they had in their hands was not a bottle of wine but a piece of Jeffersoniana, a historical curiosity. There was never any intention of drinking it, notwithstanding the suggestion by their friend Ernest Gallo that they sample the wine by sliding a hypodermic needle through the cork. Even if there was a slim chance that the wine was potable, they had no illusions that its taste could stand up to the price tag. Better to leave it undisturbed in its glass tomb, cork bobbing in the liquid. The wax seal remained intact. And so, even after the cork fell in, the place for the bottle remained not their wine cellar but the presidential memorabilia display in the galleries.

The incident became a source of much merriment and derision among those observers to whom the purchase had been an extravagant folly, as well as among those rarefied wine devotees who had felt the wine was wasted on a vulgar, nouveau-riche American. It played right into Anglo-condescension, and the well-publicized event was unlikely to help the bottle's resale value. Still, the likelihood that there was a meaningful distinction to be made between the taste of the wine pre- and post-spotlight was slim.

In truth, very little was known about exactly what might take place in a bottle of wine sealed for two hundred years. The kinds of authenticated samples needed for studying older wine were costly, and few commercial interests—potential sources of research funding—were at stake in the question of bottle age. Scientists' knowledge of what happened in a bottle stopped at about fifty years. Wines older than that were uncharted territory, leaving unsolved the puzzle of how something could become more valuable by rotting.

Crudely, the molecular changes known to unfold in a sealed wine bottle that has been laid down for years involve the gradual interaction of oxygen and wine. Simple chemical compounds break down and recombine into more and more complex forms called polymeric phenols. Acidity and alcohol soften. The largest compounds—the harsh, astringent tannins—drift down into a carpet of sediment, taking with them the saturated, inky pigments. They leave behind a mellowed, unfathomably subtle flavor and a brick-red hue. Everything knits together, resolving into an ever finer complexity expressed fragrantly in the wine's bouquet.

At least that's how it is supposed to work. Just as oxygen yellows newspapers and browns sliced apples, it spoils wine, but the process is more complex. There is also a beneficial oxidation that helps a wine mature. Paradoxically, wine is improving even as it is being destroyed; time will kill a wine, but is also necessary to make it great. This dual process is visible after a bottle has been opened. Aeration of wine—whether by decanting a bottle, swirling one's glass, or sloshing a mouthful around—is a form of controlled oxidation. The aim is to improve the wine by helping it open up after its long confinement in bottle. Leave an uncorked bottle or glass out too long, though, and it will be ruined.

The trick that the greatest old bottles of wine pull off is keeping long enough to blossom. The tiny amount of air in a bottle of wine, the porous cork that allows a slow exchange of oxygen over decades, the coolness of a cellar that decelerates chemical reactions in the wine, the humidity of a cellar and horizontal storage that ensure a cork stays moist and maintains a seal—all these practices are aimed at fostering beneficial changes while deterring destructive ones. A wine is considered mature when it has maximized its flavor possibilities but has not yet begun to deteriorate.

There are certain truisms about how wine ages. Big bottles are believed to age more slowly than small ones, because the ratio of oxygen to liquid is lower. Wine in cooler cellars ages more slowly than wine in warmer ones. More-tannic wines take longer to come around than more-supple ones. High-alcohol, high-sugar, and high-acid wines—fortified wines such as Port and Sherry, sweet wines like Sauternes and Tokay, the deliberately heated Madeira, acidic wines including certain Rieslings—all live longer than table wines because their strength inhibits the development of bacteria.

The genius of Madeira, a sea turtle of a wine with an almost infinite lifespan, is that oxidation is the goal. "You take a wine and oxidize the crap out of it," in the words of Andrew Waterhouse, a chemist at the University of California, Davis. Madeira, like many kinds of wine, was discovered by accident, when ships' captains noticed that barrels of wine from the eponymous Portuguese island that had gone around the world in their holds, with lots of heat and sloshing around, tasted pretty good. Soon this was done deliberately, and it became common for advertisements for barrels of Madeira to boast of the miles they'd traveled, the distant ports seen. Later, and more cost-effectively, white wine would be deliberately cooked for between three months and a year, either naturally in tin sheds under the tropical sun, by pumping hot water through steel pipes in tanks containing Madeira, or by putting Madeira-filled casks in heated rooms. It was impossible to ruin something that had, essentially, perfected the taste of ruin. Further oxidation is simply making a Madeira more like itself. (Apparently inspired by Madeira's example, in the nineteenth century the manager of Château Lafite, a Monsieur Goudal, sent fifty bottles of the 1846 Lafite on a sea voyage around the world in an effort to accelerate their aging.)

With still wines, you cannot stop the undesirable process of oxidation, you can only delay it. Therefore the young bottles of wine with the greatest chance of achieving an exalted state are those with both preservatives (tannins) and potential (phenols). The red wines of Bordeaux's left bank are among the most ageable because their predominant grape, cabernet sauvignon, contains extremely high levels of phenols and tannins. The bottles that have proven, over long history, to be considered the greats—1870 Latour, say— were undrinkable in their youth.

Because the tannins serve as an antioxidant, once they start clumping together and falling out of the wine, this line of defense against further oxidation begins to give way. At this point a wine's fruity character begins to disappear, and the wine is said to "lose its fruit." Eventually, a wine becomes so leached of its original vitality that it is called faded at best, but more likely "maderized" or something worse. The Forbes bottle, two hundred years old and recently exposed to light, heat, and possibly oxygen, was almost certainly something worse.

THE FORBESES HAD not planned to taste the wine. Now, clearly, no one would. The question of how a red wine from the Jefferson-bottle cache might taste would have to wait for another of the bottles to provide an answer. But for Rodenstock and Broadbent, the stakes had heightened, and Broadbent was worried. In the six months since the Forbes sale, questions about the bottle had multiplied. Answers to at least some of them were promised by a tasting on June 3, 1986, when a 1787 Branne-Mouton from the cache was opened at Château Mouton-Rothschild.

In 1985, few wines were as highly priced in the market as Mouton-Rothschild, but in 1787, when it was known as Branne-Mouton, the vineyard had been mentioned only in passing in Jefferson's diaries, and then as a *third*-tier property. In the 1855 Classification, it was named a second growth. The French branch of the Rothschild family bought the vineyard in the middle of the nineteenth century, but it was the magnetic and multitalented Philippe de Rothschild (champion race-car driver, film producer, translator of Elizabethan drama into French), who took it to new heights of excellence and fame. He led Bordeaux in being the first to château-bottle his entire production (in 1923), brought a marketing touch unique in the fusty Médoc when he began using a famous artist—Braque, Picasso, Warhol—to design each year's label, and won the only significant change ever made to the 1855 Classification when he persuaded the French government to elevate Mouton to first growth in 1973. He also kept up the long-standing rivalry between Mouton and his cousins' Lafite, famously serving curry with the rival wine at a luncheon, a tactic certain to obliterate any subtleties of Lafite's taste. Rothschild's insistence on setting the opening price for Mouton's new vintages higher than Lafite's had been a primary cause of the early-1970s price spiral in Bordeaux.

Mouton had been one of the so-called "wines of the vintage" in 1982, a bumper year that brought unprecedented speculation into the Bordeaux market. Rodenstock had visited the château in 1984 and written a long article about Mouton for *Alles über Wein*. The presence of Mouton among the Jefferson bottles was an extraordinary stroke of fortune.

The idea for the event at Château Mouton-Rothschild was Rodenstock's. As with the Yquem opened at Yquem the year before, he liked the notion of bringing this Mouton home to taste in its birthplace with the great baron himself. The bottle had been brought to the château by hand, six weeks earlier, and left standing upright, to allow enough time for the sediment to settle to the bottom. It had been locked away in the baron's personal cellar, to avoid a cellar staff person's reflexive laying of the bottle on its side. Just to make sure, a sign was placed next to it enjoining anyone from moving it. The château had the best collection in the region of nineteenth-century Bordeaux, but the oldest bottle of its own wine was an 1853 (the year the Rothschilds bought the property), and it had been acquired just a few years earlier, at Christie's.

Among the nineteen tasters who attended were several of

Hardy Rodenstock's German cronies, including Mr. Cheval Blanc, Herr Pétrus, and Magnum Uwe. Michael Broadbent arrived just as the tasting was beginning, wearing gray flannel slacks, a blue blazer, and, shrewdly, a Mouton necktie. He promptly began retelling the story of the Forbes cork fiasco.

The group crossed the gravel walkway to the cellar slowly and solemnly, as at a funeral. Leading the way in blue overalls and Adidas sneakers, a candle in his hand, was the aged cellarmaster Raoul Blondin, lower lip petrified in a shrugging Gallic *pffftttt*. Blondin said that the wine would be "passé. Zéro."

The bottle was in the shape of a flask, with shoulders in a Burgundy-style slope. Etched in the glass were "Branne Mouton 1787" and "Th. J." A wax bulb sealed the top. There was significant ullage, the wine's surface nearly three inches below the bottom of the cork. Everyone looked intently at the bottle. Broadbent opened his notebook and began recording his impressions. "Level?" he said aloud. "Ah, mid-shoulder. Very interesting."

Rodenstock had brought with him Ralf Frenzel, the young sommelier of Die Ente in Wiesbaden, who was a kind of personal wine steward and surrogate son to him. Frenzel carried the bottle upstairs and out onto a gravel path near the original patch of vineyard called La Motte. He placed it in a bowl on the ground, crouched in front of it, and gently began tapping at the wax seal with an antique sommelier's hammer given him by Rodenstock. Though only in his twenties, Frenzel knew what he was doing. The soft percussion of his tool dislodged the cork, which plopped into the wine.

Then came the sound of glass cracking. A lateral hairline fissure opened, a few inches from the bottle's base. Wine seeped out into the bowl.

"*Schnell! Schnell!*" the Germans cried.

En masse, the group hurried back down into the cellar to get a decanter Rodenstock had brought, a hollow glass bust of George

Washington with a cork in the crown of his head. It was vital that the wine be removed from contact with the cork and the wax that had collapsed inward with it, before either could corrupt the wine. And the crack threatened to expand. Frenzel carefully but quickly decanted the rest of the wine, then the group relocated again to the tasting room.

Now that the wine was safely transferred, the Médocain sun filtered dimly through its murk, and it was possible to assess the color. It was in no sense red. The body of the wine was molasses brown, the rim amber. All to be expected in a wine so old. But the concentration of color was improbably youthful.

"*Extraordinaire!*" several of the French murmured.

The hue reminded Broadbent of a 1900-vintage Bordeaux. It had a sheen that an oxidized wine would not.

Frenzel wasted no time, pouring it out into glasses. Baron Philippe was sick and bedridden, the guests were told, and his grandson Philippe now lifted his glass and asked if it would be all right to take it to his grandfather upstairs. He then departed to share the precious gift with the baron, who in truth was not there because he refused to meet with the Germans; his first wife had died in the concentration camp at Ravensbrück.

The smell of the wine was restrained at first—even the hypersensitive Broadbent found it scentless. There was none of the acrid tang of vinegar or the deep mustiness of oxidation. There was nothing. Broadbent was surprised. In spite of his touting of the Forbes bottle, and his earlier suggestions that it might have survived the centuries in drinkable form, he knew it was nearly impossible for a red claret to do so.

This one had a relatively low fill level, had been untouched for two hundred years, and had been stored who knew where. "But at this age," as Broadbent put it later, "no news is good news." And, after four minutes, the wine had a discernible fragrance. It blossomed, filling the room with a kind of sweetness. Was it the proverbial sweetness of death? As the tasters plunged their noses into the depths of their glasses, they found that the bouquet kept changing. After ten minutes it had what Broadbent described as "a rich, warm, wholemeal, gingery smell."

"Dunked gingernuts," he remarked.

"Lovely coffee," Rodenstock intoned.

Jancis Robinson, an English journalist who was the only woman present, was taken aback. Over forty-five minutes, the wine kept getting more delicious, a feat "even for a young wine," as she later put it. "This relic of pre-revolutionary days" was "richly juicy and fighting fit" and "the most exciting liquid I ever expect to drink." An hour after the pour, Broadbent found cabernet flavors in the nose. On the palate, he experienced "a beautifully sweet rich wine, with good body, extract and absolutely perfect acidity and balance. The flavour had hints of coffee and caramel, the effects of a long but sublime form of oxidation in the bottle, and it was delicious to drink."

"I've never tasted anything like it," Raoul Blondin said, over and over. The last drops of wine in the decanter were trapped at the tip of George Washington's nose, so Blondin tipped the cracked bottle upside down, emptying its viscous dregs into a giant glass and tasting it. "It's delicious," Blondin said. "No bitterness. They wouldn't have done any egg-white fining in those days, you see." Such fining, more common in modern times, was a technique in which egg whites were stirred into wine, before bottling, to help precipitate out coarse solids. The result was clearer, more stable wine, and a sediment that could have an unpleasant astringency.

Blondin was in his mid-seventies, and had tasted many of the oldest vintages of the wine to which he had devoted his life, but none was as old, or noteworthy, as this one. He reveled in the symmetry of the bottle's being opened right next to the vineyard whence it had sprung, the plain known as the Carruades, which had originally constituted the whole of the property. He passed the glass around. When it got to Robinson, the dominant smell note was a blend of sundry colognes and tonics transferred from the hands and faces of all the Germans who'd already handled it. It made it hard for her to absorb the wine's essence, but she was still impressed by its high quality.

Young Philippe Sereys de Rothschild returned and reported that his grandfather, who had shared his *maître de chai*'s skepticism that this wine could possibly be drinkable, was amazed and delighted. (The baron would die a week later.) Rodenstock was clearly pleased with himself, nodding his head and smiling inscrutably as he said, "The Paris cellar was so effectively blocked up, it was almost hermetically sealed, you see." Broadbent, whose jaded palate made him cool and detached about most wines, was almost manic, probably as much because the wine vindicated his and Christie's imprimatur for the Forbes bottle as because the wine was inherently exciting. "I thought it would be a bit acidic, a bit decayed, but there wasn't a trace. If there was any doubt, forget it. This wine is genuine. No doubt about that."

After tasting such an antique, it was time for something younger: an 1858 Mouton. "It tasted so light, so *modern* after its predecessor," Robinson later recalled. Then Rodenstock showed off a bottle he had in the trunk of his car: a Jéroboam of 1945 Pétrus.

It was time for lunch, which was served next door at Philippine de Rothschild's *petit château*, decorated in the Louis XVI style. An 1865 Margaux would be among the wines to be drunk. Rodenstock mentioned that he had a complete vertical of Mouton from 1945 to 1982. He suggested opening the '45 Pétrus Jéroboam, but this idea was scuttled by grandson Philippe, who suggested it would be a waste to drink it without having decanted it sufficiently ahead of time. An equally likely reason was that powerful right-bank Pétrus might well show up the elegant left-bank wines.

Broadbent, who had a dinner to attend in London that evening, flew out on a 2:25 p.m. flight. He felt reassured by the day's events. The cork's collapse, as suggested by the Forbes bottle's fate, was a reliable feature of old wines. The Mouton bottle's cracking suggested there was no way that an engraving could have occurred recently. Even Blondin's comment about the lack of fining in the eighteenth century was a reminder that wine, in Jefferson's day, was for early drinking; the 1787 vintage would have been bottled in 1788 and ready for consumption in 1791. "[M]ost of the party anticipated a funeral. It turned out to be a resurrection," Broadbent crowed in a *Decanter* article headlined "No More Doubts."

CHAPTER 9

SALAD DRESSING

*B*EFORE THE FORBES AUCTION, BROADBENT HAD SAID the 1787 Lafite was probably the only bottle "of its kind" that would ever come up for sale. Arthur Woods, Broadbent's *Decanter* letters-page tormentor, was having none of it. "One now supposes that after a discreet interval another bottle will appear for auction," he wrote in June 1986; "next December or early in 1987 perhaps?"

As it happened, in December, one year to the day after the Forbes sale, Michael Broadbent auctioned off another of Rodenstock's Jefferson bottles. This time he was selling a 1784 Yquem, the same wine that had piqued his interest when Rodenstock opened one at the October 1985 tasting in Wiesbaden. In the catalog, Broadbent called it "the last but one bottle of 1784, and the only occasion this vintage is ever likely to come on the market."

In spite of Monticello's doubts, and the unfortunate incident with the Forbes cork, the Mouton tasting six months earlier had benefited Broadbent and Rodenstock in two ways: it had authenticated the wine while adding to its value by finding it drinkable; and this new bottle was an Yquem—a Sauternes with a greater chance of surviving than a red wine—and of a vintage that had already been opened successfully. It had a track record, which Broadbent distilled as "perfect in every sense: colour, bouquet, and taste."

Broadbent also happily reported that a German laboratory had analyzed the bottle opened earlier. "[T]he wax, the cork, and the wine have been rigorously examined by Professor Eschenauer whose methods are said to be the most acceptable, reliable and accurate," Broadbent wrote in the catalog for the December 1986 sale. With the bicentennial of Jefferson's visit to Bordeaux just months away, the moment seemed too perfect not to put another Jefferson bottle on the market.

As with the Forbes/Shanken match-up one year earlier, the contest on Thursday, December 4, 1986, rapidly narrowed to two serious bidders. After bidding £35,000, the owner of a wine shop in Syracuse, New York, was sure the bottle was hers, but then a buyer in the front row, an olive-skinned man with glossy ringlets of black hair and a small mustache, topped her and won the bottle for £39,600, or $56,628.

The buyer gave his name as Iyad Shiblaq, and identified himself to reporters as a Jordanian Muslim. He took pains to say that the bottle was not for himself, as his religion required him to be a teetotaler. He said he was buying the wine for "a friend of mine in New York" who had given him £50,000 to bid. Shiblaq wouldn't name the friend, saying he had "no idea what he is going to do with" the bottle and that the friend simply wanted it "because of the label." Shiblaq then rushed away without answering further questions.

This Jefferson bottle, too, set a record: it was the most expensive *white* wine ever sold. Like the Forbes purchase, it made news around the world. A transatlantic guessing game commenced as to the identity of the mystery buyer. On December 5, the *New York Post*'s Page Six floated several names, including Malcolm Forbes,

William Zeckendorf Jr., and Daniel Rose (both of the latter were Manhattan real-estate developers), investment banker Ed Marks, and Dodi Al-Fayed, son of Harrods owner Mohammed Al-Fayed, who years later would die in a car crash with Princess Diana. All denied it, and the *Post* concluded that none was the buyer.

"WHOOPS!" Page Six corrected itself the following day. The buyer was Al-Fayed, after all. "Wine is meant for drinking," a Christie's specialist named John Boodle had opined after the auction. "It is not a thing of beauty. You can't hang it on the wall." Now, Al-Fayed's spokesman told Page Six, "He's just going to keep it as if it were a piece of art." Christie's said it might auction another Jefferson bottle soon.

THE SHIBLAQ/AL-FAYED purchase came at a moment of broadening American awareness of Thomas Jefferson's interest in wine. The first serious attention paid to his precocious connoisseurship had occurred in 1976, during the national Bicentennial, when the Wine Museum of San Francisco put on an exhibit called "Thomas Jefferson and Wine in Early America."

Jefferson had planted scores of grape varieties at Monticello, and in many ways had foreshadowed the kind of systematic experimentation that eventually led Robert Mondavi to revolutionize American winemaking in the 1960s and 1970s. Now it was primarily citizens of his home state who led the way in dusting off this forgotten aspect of Jefferson's life. In 1976 the Virginia Wine Growers Association, which would later break the news in the United States about the Rodenstock discovery, published its *Jefferson and Wine* anthology. The same year a winery called Barboursville opened in the shadow of the Blue Ridge Mountains, around the ruins of one of the five homes Jefferson had designed in his lifetime; it named a wine Octagon after the shape of some of the rooms. (Virginia's wine industry would soon take off, expanding from six wineries in 1979 to forty-one in 1991 to 122 in 2006.) In 1982 a former National Security Agency linguist of Virginian extraction opened a winery called Monticello in the Napa Valley, and included a Jefferson Cuvée cabernet among its bottlings.

This rediscovery of Jefferson and wine came to a head in the mid-eighties, around the time of the record Forbes purchase. Monticello itself, in 1985, copied Jefferson's planting of 1807, sowing twenty-one of the twenty-three varieties of white and red grapes (French, Italian, domestic) Jefferson had planted in the quarter-acre northeast vineyard. In 1986 a winery named Jefferson Vineyards came out with its first vintage; it was made from grapes grown on the neighboring land once worked by Filippo Mazzei, the Italian wine grower Thomas Jefferson had sponsored.

With the bicentennial of Jefferson's 1787 visit to Bordeaux approaching, the scattered group of people with a particular combined interest in both wine and Jefferson arranged a series of celebrations. Travel agencies promoted tours of French wine regions visited by Jefferson. Treville Lawrence, editor of the *VWGA Journal,* approached Monticello about the possibility of either Hardy Rodenstock's opening a bottle there or of the VWGA and Monticello jointly auctioning the bottle to benefit the VWGA. Monticello's board of directors turned down the request. "The major problem relates to a doubt in our mind about the Jefferson connection," director Dan Jordan wrote in a letter to Lawrence, "but the tradition here has also been to generate revenues in ways other than auctions."

Edward Lollis, the American consul to Bordeaux, spent more than a year researching and organizing a slate of events that roughly tracked the dates of Jefferson's visit. In a small triumph of amateur scholarship, Lollis deduced an explanation for Jefferson's epistolary mention of seeing Latour's vines, given the lack of evidence that Jefferson actually visited the estate. Latour's vines grow near the Gironde, and Jefferson, an able flatterer, could plausibly imply he had glimpsed them as he sailed north along the river away from Bordeaux.

Things kicked off on March 28, 1987, with a black-tie dinner at the Château de Clos de Vougeot, in Burgundy, keynoted by the president of the Jeffersonian Wine Grape Growers Society in Charlottesville, Virginia. On June 1, the American ambassador to France traveled from Paris to Bordeaux, where a changing-of-the-cork ceremony was scheduled to take place at Château Lafite for a 1787 Jefferson bottle still in the possession of Rodenstock. The same day, Château Haut-Brion unveiled a plaque honoring Jefferson's visit two hundred years earlier. In the afternoon, at the downtown building that had once been the Palais Royal and now housed the Chamber of Commerce, a Jefferson impersonator spoke, and the "world premiere" of an American Express tourism video, "Bordeaux at the Time of Jefferson," was screened. In the final scene, filmed using a helicopter, a group of wine bottles rose into the sky.

Three weeks later, during Vinexpo, the massive trade show which brought the wine world to Bordeaux every other summer, Lollis welcomed visitors to the American consulate for a tasting of 140 wines from seventy-one American wineries. Jefferson had dreamed of this: the wines—whites downstairs, reds upstairs— came not only from Napa, but also from Missouri and some ten Virginia wineries. Christie's, meanwhile, had announced that it would sell a third Jefferson bottle at Vinexpo.

ON THE FIFTH and final day of the trade show, two and a half hours into a four-and-a-half-hour, four-hundred-lot auction, Christie's put the Jefferson bottle on the block. This one was a 1784 Margaux (the engraving said "Margau") and was a 375-milliliter half-bottle shaped like a mallet. The fill came almost to the top of the shoulder. Michael Broadbent quoted from two Jefferson letters that referred to his buying 1784 Margaux, and a French colleague opened the bidding at $21,600.

The bids quickly added $5,000 to the asking price. One of the leading contenders, an absentee buyer who had left a commission bid authorizing Broadbent to raise the paddle on his behalf, was Marvin Shanken. Though thankful not to have spent $156,000 on the 1787 Lafite, the publisher of *Wine Spectator* was still annoyed that he had gone home empty-handed. When Broadbent called to say that another Jefferson bottle was coming up for auction, Shanken prudently decided to stay away from the saleroom but told Broadbent to bid up to $30,000 in his name.

When the price hit $26,600, a phone buyer, whom Broadbent identified to the room only as an Arab "bidding for a friend," countered with $28,300 before dropping out in response to Shanken's automatic bid of $30,000. Shanken had his bottle, and yet another record had been set. This one was for the most expensive *half*-bottle of wine ever bought.

A writer for Shanken's magazine, in an article about the auction, seemed suspicious of the mystery bidder who had dropped out only when Shanken's limit had been reached. So was Shanken. "You know what?" he said later. "In the auction business, you never know. Who knows even if there was another bidder?"

Before Shanken would take delivery of the bottle, he insisted that Broadbent have it recorked at Margaux, both to avert a repeat of the Forbes spotlight debacle and to validate the wine's authenticity. Estate director Paul Pontallier, fearful of the bottle's fragility and uncertain of its origin, wouldn't touch it. The bottle stayed in Bordeaux until Broadbent was able to return in August. Then, with the cellarmaster and Pontallier looking on, Broadbent performed the operation himself.

Broadbent first removed the capsule by chipping gently at the wax (the bottle's glass neck was thicker than that of the bottle broken at Mouton). When he removed the cork, which was black and wizened, its length surprised him. He poured a little of the wine into a glass, and he and the other two men each sampled it. "Despite its oxidation, the colour was a fairly healthy orange-rimmed red brown," Broadbent noted, "with just a whiff of what clearly might once have been a marvellously rich wine."

Except for a Rodenstock-sourced 1771 Margaux he had been served that May, this 1784 Margaux was the oldest dry red wine Broadbent had ever tasted; the Mouton he had drunk was a 1787, and the 1784 a sweet white Yquem. Without topping the bottle up, Broadbent delicately eased in a new wedge-shaped cork he had brought with him. Then he heated some wax, gently dipped the neck and cork into it to form a seal, and gave the bottle a twirl. To his relief, it didn't break. When Broadbent called Shanken to say "mission accomplished," he reported that "you could still taste the fruit." Broadbent slipped a sock over the bottle, secured it in a wooden box, and carried it by Concorde, at Shanken's expense, to New York.

Shanken's purchase made less news than had its higher-priced forerunners, but lent important new credibility to the Jefferson bottles. Forbes and Shiblaq/Al-Fayed were rich, showy, wine-world outsiders. Their bottles were bangles. Shanken was something else. As the owner, publisher, and editor of the premier wine magazine in a country increasingly obsessed with wine, his decision to buy a Jefferson bottle was meaningful. And his purchase, unlike Forbes's, came after the scholarly doubts about the Jefferson attribution had been well aired. If Shanken still believed the bottle was for real, then it was no longer just Broadbent and Rodenstock and Château d'Yquem standing behind the cache. Margaux's willingness to let Broadbent recork the bottle at the château—thereby bestowing its official imprimatur—provided still another blue-chip endorsement.

BROADBENT SOON HAD a chance to taste two more of the Jefferson bottles. At Rodenstock's annual tasting in September 1987, this one at the Arlberg Hospiz Hotel in western Austria, the German opened a 1787 Margaux. "Slight ullage," Broadbent noted, "wizened black cork, thick, gritty, puce-coloured sediment, the wine itself deeper than expected; little nose at first but exposure to air revived it quite sweetly; richly flavoured, well balanced."

The following year, Rodenstock traded a Jefferson bottle to Lloyd Flatt, a fifty-year-old member of the Group who was planning a monumental tasting. Flatt, who lived in New Orleans, was routinely described by wine writers as an "aerospace consultant," but he was widely rumored to be involved in the design or sale of weapons. ("He bragged that he sold the Argentines the missile that sank the British cruiser in the Falklands," recalled a guest who attended his tastings.) Flatt was lean and tall, with a neatly trimmed beard now going gray. His customary outfit of a tailored suit dapperly offset the triangular black patch he had worn over his right eye since a childhood accident. A little boy once walked up to him at an airport and asked if he was a pirate. "Yes," Flatt responded, in his native Tennessee drawl. "Now go away."

Flatt had begun buying wine in the late sixties, at Heublein in the United States and Christie's in London. He thought nothing of setting his alarm for 3:00 a.m. in order to arrange a phone connection to a morning auction in England, and he scoured wine shops around the world. His bottles were nearly all French, and most of those were Bordeaux classed growths. Flatt owned lots of nineteenth-century vintages, and he liked big bottles. Among his most prized wines were a Jéroboam of 1929 Mouton-Rothschild, and double magnums of 1806 Lafite and 1953 Pétrus. Flatt claimed to have tasted more vintages of Pétrus than anyone alive. Later he added Burgundy, aged Champagne, Port, and eaux-de-vie to the mix. He didn't buy just any old wine, only bottles he felt had impeccable provenance. By the 1980s, the collection at his house on Ursuline Street in the French Quarter was so big that he moved to another house nearby, air-conditioning the vacated house at 55 degrees, installing neutral lighting to facilitate accurate color appraisal, and filling the house entirely with wine.

It was not a museum cellar. Flatt liked to say that he wrote off the cost of a bottle upon purchase, so that even if it appreciated in value, he wouldn't feel inhibited about popping it open. For people like Flatt, who drank wine almost as ardently as he bought it, wine did not offer the usual psychological balm of compulsive collecting: the satisfaction of completeness, the security of ownership. Wine was different from paintings or stamps or cars. Its very purpose was to be consumed, to register sense impressions and then disappear. It was also, of course, more social. Sharing meant sharing—not, as with paintings, having visiting hours, but actually giving away some of one's possession.

But even if Flatt's cellar was meant for drinking, with a rumored 30,000 bottles it was undeniably excessive. This was one of the tacit rules of supercollecting: steadfastly declare that you buy your wine for drinking, not for collecting, despite owning far more bottles than you could ever possibly drink. Another: preach about wine as the drink of moderation while, at the same time, reeking of personal eccentricity. Flatt lived both axioms.

He had attended many of the events organized by fellow members of the Group, and these tastings, like those of their German counterparts, had become trials of one-upmanship, their scale and scope expanding every year. "You'd say to yourself, 'I haven't had that. I want that. I must have that,'" Flatt said later. "It became very competitive."

By the late eighties, Flatt had hosted sprawling verticals of Pétrus, Mouton, Cheval Blanc, and Ausone, which was the one other St. Emilion wine considered to be Cheval's equal. But the tasting of Lafite that Flatt decided to throw in October 1988 was by far his most ambitious. Of all the Bordeaux in his collection, Lafite reigned supreme. Flatt had more examples of it than of any other wine, and it was his favorite, "an entity within itself," as he put it, "truly the first of the great growths. It has great finesse, subtlety, elegance and staying power."

The tasting would take place over three days. Flatt already owned 3,000 Tiffany wineglasses, and he ordered an additional two thousand. And Flatt made sure the entertainment would live up to the rest of the event. The Storyville Stompers, a Dixieland jazz band, would parade the tasters to lunch at a restaurant. Another meal would have the theme of a plantation feast. Peter Duchin, the New York society bandleader, would perform at the 120-guest, black-tie dinner-dance at the Meridien Hotel, which would bring the weekend to a close.

As for the wine, Flatt's tasting would make Marvin Overton's pioneering 1979 "Lafite in Texas" shindig seem like small beer. Overton had assembled thirty-six vintages, at the time a huge number. But for this 1988 tasting, which had been in the planning for more than a decade, Flatt assembled no fewer than 115 vintages of the first-of-first growths.

Working in Flatt's favor, Lafite was perhaps the most collectible wine ever made, built to last and especially popular with those compulsive cellarers in England and Scotland. People kept it around for a long time, and more nineteenth-century vintages of Lafite had survived than of any other red Bordeaux. Even before ramping up for this tasting, Flatt already owned sixty vintages. All had perfect résumés, coming from Lafite itself, from other Bordeaux châteaux (they customarily traded samples with each other), or from the impeccably maintained cellars of great French restaurants.

Now, to round out his tasting, Flatt homed in on the remaining vintages he wanted to include in the vertical. He was especially interested in serving the 1806, which he had acquired at auction in 1976 and which hadn't appeared in earlier Lafite verticals. An 1803, having already been in the lineup at Overton's 1979 tasting, interested Flatt less. He watched the market intently, constantly checking in with auctioneers and merchants; whenever a Lafite surfaced that he didn't yet own, he pounced, checking another vintage off his list. The wines most difficult to acquire were not the pre-phylloxeras, which were expensive but came up for auction on a fairly reliable basis. The really hard gets were the justifiably obscure vintages: nineteenth-century wines blighted by phylloxera or the powdery fungus called oidium; certain years from the unfortunate decade of the 1930s (Broadbent: "It opened with three atrocious vintages"); and even a few more recent "off" vintages, such as 1951 and 1965.

Flatt faxed updates to friends, and they joined in the bottle hunt. Peter Meltzer, a journalist who had been writing about Flatt for years, was able to contribute a rare 1956. Broadbent considered the vintage so poor that drinking it was "a penance," but Meltzer happened to own some because 1956 was the year of his wife's birth. David Milligan, a New York importer of Lafite, got the château to contribute a 1905, a 1931, and a 1941. As the tasting approached, Flatt was still trying to add to the list. When an 1822 came up for auction at Christie's in September, Flatt bid on it, but as the bidding soared, he dropped out. It would have made a nice inclusion, but even he had his limits. The bottle ended up selling for $20,900.

The rarest Lafite of all was provided by Rodenstock, who bartered with Flatt for a 1784 from the Jefferson cache. Whatever its longer-term provenance, the bottle's recent history was shaky. Rodenstock had personally delivered the bottle to Malibu, where Flatt kept another home, and Flatt had then carried the bottle by private plane to Washington, D.C., and then to New Orleans. The flight was turbulent. The bottle began to leak. Flatt dipped his finger in the wine and thought it tasted "good."

On a weekend in October, Flatt's guests converged in New Orleans for an event billed as "200 Years of Lafite-Rothschild." There were fourteen of them, the number of people who could comfortably fit at Flatt's table and reasonably divide a single bottle for tasting purposes. They included Overton, thrower of the 1979 Lafite vertical that was about to be left in the dust, as well as Rodenstock and Michael Broadbent, who had wangled an invite for his son by volunteering Bartholomew's services as a pourer. Before the weekend was over, Bartholomew, nicknamed Bollew, would repay the kindness by sneaking a glass of Coke into a lineup of brown, older wines his father was appraising. Michael Broadbent would say that for an old wine the color looked about right, yelling, after he smelled it, "Bollew, you little shit!"

Day One of the vertical got under way with a flight of five wines: 1950–54. It was followed by a seven-wine flight (1902–08), which was followed by a five-wine flight (1868–72). The progression was typical for a tasting of this kind, moving backward in time from younger to older, simpler to more complex, more powerful and pleasurable to subtler and more intellectual. The final stop in the day's time travel was 1784. Rodenstock's leaky Jefferson bottle.

The wine's level was into the shoulder, ominously low. The room went quiet as Ralf Frenzel set to work. Save for his youth, Frenzel looked the sommelier's part, with a black waiter's vest and a silver tastevin dangling from his neck. Having learned his lesson when the Mouton cracked two years earlier, Frenzel now eschewed his antique bottle-breaching toolkit in favor of a plastic Screwpull.

Sure enough, the cork crumbled, a piece breaking off and falling into the wine. Someone lit a candle stub in a silver stick, decanting the wine according to the traditional method. This involved carefully pouring a wine off its sediment, with a flame backlighting the stream, and stopping as soon as sediment began to flow with it. Frenzel inserted a metal funnel filter in the neck of a curvy, modern decanter to catch cork particles and poured the wine through it. Flatt brought the intact stump of cork to his nose and inhaled.

Writer Terry Robards would later point out that, notionally, this Jefferson bottle was worth "at least as much" as the Forbes bottle, since it was three years older. It might even be worth more, since 1784 was considered a superior vintage. But then Flatt's guests tasted the wine. This was the first of the Jefferson bottles to be opened and tasted in America, at an event neither run by Rodenstock nor populated exclusively with his loyalists, and the comments about the wine seemed to reflect these less controlled circumstances. Robards and Frank Prial, a writer from the *New York Times,* both deemed the wine "vinegar." Bartholomew Broadbent would later call it "one of the best balsamic vinegars I ever tasted."

"The term 'salad dressing' was on everyone's lips," Robards wrote later, adding, "Only a handful of the other old Lafites proved to be undrinkable, and each of these was basically oxidized, showing the odor of Madeira that is typical of many tired old wines. . . . What bearing this discovery had on the authenticity of the 1784 Lafite was not immediately apparent, but it was clear that something very different had happened to this particular wine."

There was that word again: *authenticity*. The best wines were such a singular experience (the spice of Mouton, for instance, or what Michael Broadbent called the "slow strip tease" of Lafite) that seasoned tasters could readily notice a deviation from it. And Robards had observed, in his considerable experience of old wines, that they all followed the same course—paling in color, thinning in aroma and taste, weakening in structure. This wine was markedly different, being very dark and vinegarishly acidic. He speculated that younger wine might have been added, triggering a secondary fermentation in the bottle.

Questions about the Jefferson attribution had been raised nearly three years earlier, and skepticism about the origin of the bottles had circulated as well, but Robards's comments, which appeared in the December 15, 1988, issue of *Wine Spectator,* were the first to suggest publicly that something might be amiss—not merely spoiled, but strange and uncharacteristic—with the wine inside of those bottles. Previous rumors of a Nazi affiliation now seemed almost quaint next to suggestions that the wine itself might not be as old as the engraving indicated.

Rodenstock and Broadbent were, of course, staunch defenders of the wine. "An ullaged bottle," Broadbent recorded in his notebook. "Alas, but unsurprisingly 'over the top,' oxidised: colour dark brown; nose like pure balsamic vinegar; despite the rich components—undrinkable." Few knew what a bottle so old should taste like, anyway. The number of people who had experienced pre-1800 wines was tiny, and of that handful, Broadbent and Rodenstock had tasted the most. This—a presumption of infallibility about old wines because he had tasted more than anyone else—was increasingly Rodenstock's fallback posture when questioned.

"I cannot believe that it is anything but genuine," Broadbent said. "I thought the bottle alone was worth 10,000 pounds."

IN THE THREE months following the Flatt tasting, Rodenstock privately sold four more Jefferson bottles. The buyer of all four was William Ingraham Koch, the scion of a Kansas oil-and-gas fortune. For the past eight years, Koch (pronounced like the soft drink) had been at the center of an epic feud with his family, including his twin brother, David. It had ignited in 1980, when Bill Koch attempted a coup by proxy fight to oust his older brother, Charles, from Wichita-based Koch Industries, then the second-largest privately held company in the country; Charles outmaneuvered him, and Bill, who worked from the Boston area, ended up jobless at age forty. Bill sued his brothers. Their mother told Bill he wasn't welcome in her house. Eventually, in 1983, Bill took a buyout of his piece of the company. He walked away with $470 million.

Before the Koch brothers cut a deal, Bill's wealth was illiquid, and he had been in a several-year funk. After receiving the windfall, Koch went on a hedonistic tear. He spent his newfound money on

·eating and drinking, and collecting houses, art, and wine. Koch had been interested in wine since the 1970s, when he noticed how much better Montrachet, the most famous white Burgundy, tasted than run-of-the-mill stuff. But it was the big payday that turned him into a collector. He started buying an average of 5,000 bottles a year, an acquisition rate he would maintain through the late 1980s.

Systematically, Koch set out to assemble deep verticals of four iconic wines; eventually he would own 95 years of Pétrus, 100 years of Latour, 120 years of Mouton, and 150 years of Lafite (as well as 33 vintages of Hennessy Cognac, back to 1851). It was while assembling these verticals that, in November of 1988, Koch bought a 1787 Branne-Mouton, a Jefferson bottle, from a Midwestern firm called the Chicago Wine Company. Koch was then approached directly by Farr Vintners, the London brokers who had obtained the bottle from Rodenstock and sold it to Chicago Wine.

Farr said they had three more, and partner Lindsay Hamilton flew to New York with the bottles—a 1784 Branne-Mouton, a 1784 Lafite, and a 1787 Lafite, all inscribed "Th.J."—in a big leather lawyer's briefcase and delivered them to Bill Koch at his Fifth Avenue apartment. For the group of three, Koch paid £116,000, or about $200,000. One month after buying the three Jefferson bottles from Farr, Koch bought another batch of (non-Jefferson) bottles from the brokers, including three eighteenth-century wines (1737 and 1771 "La Fitte," and a 1791 "La Tour") sourced from Rodenstock and priced, collectively, at £91,000 ($159,250).

Where were all these bottles coming from? 1771? *1737?* They were Koch's oldest wines. The 1737 was way beyond anything even Broadbent had encountered. When Broadbent auctioned the Forbes bottle, a mere 1787, it was the oldest authenticated vintage claret Christie's had ever handled. Even the earliest Christie's catalogs, published during the 1760s and 1770s and 1780s, made no specific mention of red wine as old as the bottles Koch had just bought. In Broadbent's *Great Vintage Wine Book,* 1771 and 1791 were among the very few eighteenth-century vintages mentioned, and not because he had tasted them, but because they had been acclaimed in their time. Their turning up now seemed a remarkable coincidence. But selling the bottles to Koch put them in the hands of an enthusiastic collector, not a scholar, and using the private market for the transaction meant that it went unobserved by most people in the wine world.

The bottles were of a piece with a curious phenomenon in the old-wine scene in the latter half of the 1980s: the appearance of ever-rarer rarities. The 1970s and early 1980s had seen the progressive depletion of the buried stocks of Europe, thanks largely to Broadbent. "They don't exist now," Broadbent told an interviewer once. "They've been explored like the Pyramids or the tombs of the Nile. They've all been desecrated by me." Yet in the years since his streak of discoveries, several more bottles from the eighteenth century had surfaced. A possible explanation was that Broadbent had done the strip-mining, and a new breed of bottle hunters was digging deeper. Then again, it seemed strange that the bottle hunter raising his shovel in triumph was invariably Hardy Rodenstock.

Koch, in the mold of Forbes and Shiblaq/Al-Fayed, was a deep-pocketed outsider whose extravagant purchase of the bottles did nothing to validate them to wine-world insiders. For Chicago Wine Company and Farr Vintners to sell the bottles, however, was to provide yet two more seals of approval for Rodenstock and his bottles. The list of respected wine-world players willing to vouch for the bottles—Michael Broadbent, Christie's, Marvin Shanken, Château Margaux, Château d'Yquem—had just gotten a little bit longer.

Farr, in particular, was a major player, an upstart which, in a very short time, had emerged as the foremost London broker of

Bordeaux futures as well as a leader in the rarities market. "We used to call them 'the weasels,'" Broadbent recalled. Now Farr was the top seller of Jefferson bottles. Four—the number Farr had sold to Koch, three directly and one through Chicago Wine—was one more than even Broadbent had sold. And Farr had sold a fifth.

~

CHAPTER 10

A PLEASANT STAIN,
BUT NOT A GREAT ONE

ILL SOKOLIN WAS MAKING HIS WAY ACROSS THE ROOM to see Rusty Staub when he had the first inkling that something had gone terribly wrong. It was Sunday, April 24, 1989, and Sokolin was at a black-tie, $250-a-head, seven-course, seventeen-wine dinner at the Four Seasons. During the week the restaurant played host to Manhattan's power elite; on Sundays it was often closed to accommodate the great and grand of the wine world at private events such as this. Sokolin, a wine-shop owner, was a controversial figure among his colleagues, known for his roster of well-heeled clients, his loopy newsletter soliloquies, and a Barnumesque promotional style (when a newspaper once termed him "an incorrigible hypemeister," Sokolin wrote to thank the editor). At this moment, the proprietor of D. Sokolin & Co. was navigating the Pool Room, a high-ceilinged, midcentury-modern space bordered with stubby palm trees and surrounding an elevated, square, white marble pool rippling with azure water.

Nearly two hundred people were here, among them every wine retailer of note in the New York area, including Michael Aaron from

Sherry-Lehmann and Don Zacharia from Zachys. Former major-league baseball player Staub, now a restaurateur, had brought Mets first baseman Keith Hernandez. But what Sokolin was most excited about, what had goaded him to bring the bottle, were the guests of honor: Châteaux Margaux owners Laura and Corinne Mentzelopou-los and Paul Pontallier, the estate's urbane director.

Sokolin happened to be in possession of a Margaux the likes of which most of these people had never seen. A 1787 Margaux. A Jefferson bottle. The most expensive bottle of wine in the world, as far as Sokolin was concerned. Guinness might bestow that honor on Malcolm Forbes, but Sokolin's bottle was insured for $212,000, $56,000 above the price of the Forbes Lafite. Tonight, Sokolin couldn't resist showing the bottle around, and as a former minor-league baseball player, he was especially eager to show it to Staub.

The realization that something was dripping on his leg was not immediate. Sokolin kept walking, but the sensation of moisture didn't go away. He looked down at his tuxedo pants and saw a dark patch.

Had someone spilled coffee on him? He hadn't noticed it. Had he had an accident? He wasn't *that* old. But then—

No.

No.

Sokolin stopped walking.

He turned around and retraced his steps, as if doing so would unwind what he dimly feared was happening.

He got back to the table where he and his wife Gloria were sitting with the heads of Campari and Chateau & Estate and Southern Wines & Spirits and an executive from American Express.

His leg was still wet. No use putting it off any longer: He opened the bag.

Wine had spilled out. Worse, there were two large holes in the side of the bottle. A pair of irregularly shaped pieces of glass lay at the bottom of the bag.

"I broke the bottle," Sokolin announced, locking eyes with the Campari executive. "I'm going home."

There were gasps. He looked around the table, in shock. The people sitting there looked at him, speechless. And Sokolin walked back across the room, aware of nothing beyond himself and the bottle he clutched upright in its soggy bag. Red drops were falling now, on the blue-and-gray carpet.

Sokolin's Margaux was already dodgy in the eyes of a number of colleagues in the room. It was one of the controversial Jefferson bottles. The level of wine seemed improbably high for something so old. The seal looked new. And in hindsight, his actions at the dinner would strike several guests as suspicious. Sokolin was, after all, a notorious self-promoter who had been touting the bottle aggressively. He had brought a fragile, extremely valuable bottle to a crowded event. He had handled it clumsily. The bottle was insured for a lot of money. And once Sokolin had fully grasped what was going on, he had fled the room.

The bottle's ill-starred journey had begun in late 1987, when Farr Vintners partner Stephen Browett flew from London to Munich. Hardy Rodenstock met him at the airport with the 1787 Margaux, and Browett flew straight to Manchester, where he handed the bottle, tucked inside a tennis bag, to Tim Littler, who had agreed to buy it for £37,000. Littler hailed from an old Cheshire wine-trade family. His grandfather had bought Whitwhams, a Manchester-area merchant, and by the 1980s it was a significant player in the rare-wine market. Browett had lunch with Littler, then boarded a train back to London.

The standard Whitwhams markup was 100 percent, and the bottle was listed in its February 1988 catalog at £75,000. No sooner had the catalog appeared than Littler thought: What's the point of selling the *second*-most expensive bottle of wine in the world? The Forbes bottle had gone for £105,000. In the next Whitwhams catalog, which came out that September, Littler upped the price of his bottle to £125,000.

In the Whitwhams cellar one day, an employee noticed that the bottle was leaking through a bubble in the heavy wax that capped it. One of the firm's directors flew the bottle to Bordeaux to have it recorked at Château Margaux. With Paul Pontallier and Corinne Mentzelopoulos looking on, the cellarmaster added a bit more than an inch of 1959 wine and inserted an unusual, wedge-shaped cork. It fit loosely. Back in Manchester, Littler saw that the bottle continued to ooze.

This time he decided to recork it himself. Recorking was a specialty of Whitwhams, which performed the service on 2,000 bottles of wine a year. Some connoisseurs objected to the practice, and had found wines recorked by Whitwhams, in particular, to be subpar. But Littler defended recorking, which provided a merchant with an opportunity to assess a bottle's contents before reselling it, as a quality-control mechanism that benefited customers.

Normally, recorking a wine was straightforward: take out the old cork, put in a new one. But you had to be careful putting a new cork into the oldest bottles, as the increased air pressure could blow out the base. A 1787 Margaux called for extra caution. Like the Forbes Lafite, this Margaux was in a hand-blown bottle, heavy at the bottom and much thinner near the top. Worried that the glass would shatter, Littler taped the neck and eased the cork out with his hands.

He couldn't let this opportunity pass. He tipped out a few drops of the wine into a glass. It was the color of iodine. Littler tasted it. Later he wouldn't recall the flavor, other than "prunes" and that it was "certainly much more than" merely "interesting" or "alive." He resealed the bottle.

The old-wine market ebbed and flowed. Littler might go half a year without selling a bottle, then move six in a week. All it took was one interested buyer. But after several months he still hadn't found a customer for the Jefferson bottle. Meanwhile, a New York retailer he knew named Bill Sokolin said he had a client who was interested but wanted to see the bottle before committing.

Sokolin had pretty much fallen into the business started by his father. After attending Tufts, where he excelled at baseball, he had played for a string of teams in the Brooklyn Dodgers farm system, then was drafted into the army. Stationed in Virginia, he was spared from combat by his assignment to the service baseball, basketball, and football teams. Sokolin completed his service and, as a stopgap, went to work for his father. At the time, his father sold mainly hard liquor; what little wine he carried was plonk.

This was in the late 1950s, just when well-off Americans were becoming more interested in wine. Bill Sokolin saw an opportunity, and he rebuilt his father's business around Bordeaux. When wine prices started to soar in the 1960s, Sokolin became an evangelist of wine as investment, ultimately writing two books on the topic. William Buckley Jr. was a longtime client; in his memoir, Buckley wrote of Sokolin's enthusiasm for wine, "It would positively have killed Bill Sokolin if he had been born, say, in Saudi Arabia. I suspect both his hands and both his feet would have been amputated by the time he was sixteen, because Bill Sokolin cannot be kept from wine tasting."

When the ballyhooed 1982 Bordeaux vintage came out, Sokolin sided with a few old-guard critics in arguing that it was overrated, taking out full-page ads in the *New York Times* in which he dismissed the gushing praise for the '82s by up-and-coming wine critic Robert Parker. Sokolin was colossally wrong about the vintage, which proved to be the best investment in wine history and made Parker's name as a critic.

Over the years, through his business, Sokolin met several U.S. presidents. Just after Ronald Reagan was first elected, he called Sokolin and said, "Where's my wine?" Reagan had ordered some from Sokolin on the advice of Bill Buckley. "In front of me," Sokolin replied. He had been unable to deliver the wine to the White House without the approval of the Secret Service. With the approval, Sokolin could get the wine to him in three or four hours. Reagan took care of it right away.

But it was a dead president who tugged at Sokolin's imagination. Having heard of Thomas Jefferson's interest in wine, "I started to read a little, and then I started to read a lot." Sokolin bought more than a hundred books about Jefferson. When Sokolin met Jimmy Carter, he took the opportunity to discuss Jefferson with a sitting president. Sokolin also used the newsletters he sent regularly to his clients as a platform to talk about Jefferson. In one essay, Sokolin argued that it was Jefferson who first introduced wine futures to America. Sokolin had a mystical streak and, in a commentary of which he was especially proud, imagined a three-way conversation among Ernest Hemingway, Jefferson, and Winston Churchill. Another time, he wrote a letter to Ambassador Jefferson as if he were still alive.

Sokolin first heard of the Jefferson bottles when he read an account of the Forbes purchase in *Wine Spectator*. Later, when he visited the Forbes Galleries to view the 1787 Lafite, he was shocked that it was displayed under a spotlight and warned the security guard. Then, when the cork slipped, Sokolin says, Kip Forbes called him and asked what to do. Sokolin told him there were two options: either throw out the wine, or let Sokolin jump on a plane and take it to Lafite for recorking. The Forbeses decided to keep the bottle as it was.

Sokolin learned that he might be able to get his own Jefferson bottle when Littler, with whom he'd done business in the past and who knew of his Jeffersonian proclivities, called and said, "Bill, I think I've got your bottle." Littler said he could arrange for Sokolin to take the bottle on consignment. The two men began to explore their options for complimentary transport. Air France offered to fly Littler and the bottle to America by Concorde, but that would require Littler to get to London. British Airways flew straight from Manchester, and volunteered two first-class tickets—one for

Littler, one for the bottle. After making sure Sokolin had obtained insurance, on Friday, October 22, 1988, Littler set out for the Manchester airport.

British Airways issued a press release about the flight and photographed Littler and the bottle checking in and taking their seats on the plane, where a clutch of publicists and flight attendants dressed up the Margaux, peeking out of the same tennis bag in which Littler had received it, with blanket, headphones, and seat belt. Landing at JFK in New York at 6:00 p.m., Littler went through customs, gave the bottle to Sokolin, turned on his heel, and boarded a return flight to England. There, a hand-scrawled fax from his friends at Farr Vintners awaited him. It accompanied one of the pictures of Littler and the bottle that had appeared in a newspaper, and said, "Don't Die of Ignorance: Always wear gloves when you've got your fingers in a punt." In the photo, Littler's thumb was in the "punt," the concavity in the base of a wine bottle.

The following day, Sokolin's interested party had a heart attack while playing golf and died, Sokolin told Littler. Therefore he no longer had a customer. Littler said he was going to be in New York a month later and would collect the bottle at that time. But then Sokolin said he had another client who was interested, and Littler's trip was pushed back a few months. The bottle stayed with Sokolin.

Sokolin displayed it in his shop and encouraged wine journalists to write about it. He also sent a fax to Malcolm Forbes with the latest D. Sokolin price list, touting the arrival of the 1787 Jefferson Margaux:

> *Dear Malcolm,*
>   *This is an event of some magnitude. And it ain't the price—250,000 for this bottle.*
>   *Th. Jefferson's spirit is in this bottle.*
>   *He and G Washington had a COMPANY—called the WINE COMPANY—chartered in 1774.*

*THE PURPOSE—to get the DEMON RUM out of the
Colonies—The equivalent of drugs today.*

And replace it with WINE . . . WINE

*It's a good story and better than the ones the candidates have
chosen.*

*This little bottle will start drugs out as requested by the SPIRIT
OF JEFFERSON . . .*

Sounds nuts—?

*I think the bottle would make nice duo at FORBES—and the
story is the point . . .*

> *All the best,*
> *Bill Sokolin*

The story *was* the point, but Forbes wasn't interested. Heeding
the salesman's adage that if at first something doesn't sell, you should
ask for more, Sokolin kept hiking the price, first to $394,000. Then,
after seeing a rickety footstool sell at auction for $290,000, which
Sokolin thought absurd, he repriced the bottle at an entirely arbi-
trary $519,750.

IT WAS DURING this lull that Sokolin attended the Four Seasons
event. The sponsors were Chateau & Estate and Château Margaux.
By the late 1980s, an annual U.S. roadshow was *de rigueur* for the
top growths of Bordeaux. While, on a mass scale, America had
come late to wine, its high-end collectors had exercised a dispro-
portionate influence on the market since the late 1960s. As of 1990,
a quarter of all Pétrus and half of the production of the Domaine de
la Romanée-Conti, the most esteemed producer in Burgundy,
would be going to the U.S. In the spring of 1989, the Margaux team
were in New York to promote the 1986 vintage, considered one
of their strongest showings since the Mentzelopoulos family had
bought the estate more than a decade earlier.

Corinne Mentzelopoulos began the evening by getting up and talking about the special vintages, 1953 and 1961, that Margaux was providing that night, and about the 1986 wine that would be tasted. Then the meal got under way. A few courses had already been served when Sokolin realized he should have brought the bottle with him. What better occasion to show off this extraordinarily rare bottle of Margaux than at a dinner to honor its makers? He said so to his wife Gloria.

"Don't be ridiculous," she said.

"Nope," he said. "I'm going to get it."

Sokolin took a taxi to the prewar building where he lived on the Upper West Side, across a darkened lawn from the Museum of Natural History. Entering his ninth-floor apartment, Sokolin passed an oversized retro poster ad for Mumm's Champagne and foyer bookcases packed with works about wine and Jefferson. He crossed the blond parquet floor and turned into the dining room, where, instead of wallpaper, the ends of wooden cases that had once contained great wines were arranged in a vinous mosaic. A shelf displayed two reproductions of Jefferson's wineglasses, a gigantic Lafite bottle opened after Gloria's mother's funeral, and an eighteenth-century Madeira decanter Sokolin had opened for the party to launch his book *Liquid Assets*. He retrieved the Jefferson bottle from a freestanding refrigerated wine closet in the corner of the room.

When he arrived back at the Four Seasons, half an hour after he had left, he brought the bottle directly to the Margaux table and said to Madame Mentzelopoulos, "I bet you never saw a bottle this old." She had, of course, seen this very bottle, during its recorking for Whitwhams. Sokolin left it with the table for thirty minutes. "He was showing it to everyone," Julian Niccolini, then the maître d', recalled later. "Everyone was suspicious of this bottle." Before dessert, Sokolin retrieved it from the Margaux table and took it to show to Rusty Staub.

Sokolin was cradling the bottle in a bag, with his left arm, when

it happened. Niccolini saw the whole thing. Just inside the Pool
Room, to the left of the door, stood a gueridon, a low, metal-topped
trolley used as a service station by waiters. When Sokolin was a few
steps into the room, headed toward Staub, he brushed past the
gueridon. Wine immediately began to spill onto the carpet.

Minutes later, Sokolin was running from the room, trailing
splotches of what looked like blood on the pale stone underfoot. He
strode down a long, white marble corridor that led to the Grill
Room, past the hostess station, and down the stairs to the lobby,
which was scattered with black Barcelona chairs. When Sokolin put
the bag and bottle down on a counter as he retrieved his coat, more
of the wine leaked out, and three people dipped their fingers in it.
One, licking his finger, said the wine was "cooked." Niccolini
thought it tasted like mud.

Now in his overcoat, Sokolin pushed out through the double
doors onto an especially charmless block of midtown Manhattan
and flagged down a taxi. Back in the Pool Room, in the spot where
he had last been standing, a crowd gathered. In the chaos of his
departure, Sokolin had left the two loose bottle shards at the restaurant. Howard Goldberg, from the *New York Times,* took one piece as a
souvenir, and Paul Kovi, the co-owner of the restaurant, took the
second. Meanwhile, Gloria Sokolin, unaware of what had happened,
was wondering where her husband was. Then she saw Goldberg.

"So, the bottle's broken," the *Times* reporter said.

Gloria did a double take. "Excuse me?" she said.

"Bill broke the bottle," Goldberg repeated.

At first Gloria had a hard time believing that her husband could
have left without her, but as she continued to look for him without
success, it began to sink in. This was a problem. She had no money. She
didn't even have the ticket to retrieve her fur coat. Somewhat embarrassed, she had to borrow five dollars from a tablemate for a taxi.

Fortunately, her husband had at least had the presence of mind, in his rushed departure, to leave her coat-check ticket with the attendant.

Gloria took a cab home, and on the way, a news report came on the radio about what had happened. She arrived home and, understandably annoyed, allowed herself an I-told-you-so. But she knew how bad it felt to break something. A few years earlier she had been removing her silver chest from its hiding place inside the wine closet when she accidentally broke an 1874 Lafite. She and Bill had literally lapped it up off the floor. He had been understanding then, saying, "Accidents happen."

Now she found her husband "bereft," as she later put it. "Bill was inconsolable." Arriving home, Sokolin had gingerly removed the bottle from its carrier. Only about five ounces of wine, or 20 percent, remained. He went into the kitchen, where the walls were covered in paper, designed by Gloria, featuring a repeating pattern of signatures of great modern French chefs. *Paul Bocuse. Jean Troisgros. Alain Chapel.* Sokolin poured a small glass for himself, then put the rest of the wine in a small plastic container, which he put in the freezer. He tasted what was in his glass. It was recognizable as wine, but by no means tasted good. He put the empty bottle on a table in the living room.

At midnight, with the arrival of April 25, he turned fifty-eight. Forty minutes into Sokolin's birthday, Howard Goldberg, the *Times* reporter who had made off with a piece of the bottle, telephoned, eager to secure his scoop. He asked if Sokolin had been drunk. Sokolin said he'd only had a single glass of Champagne and hadn't finished any of his glasses of Bordeaux.

"I did something terrible," Sokolin told Goldberg. "I'm very unhappy. I was in shock. I committed murder."

The next morning, Tim Littler was staying with friends in Geneva when his host knocked on his bedroom door and said a reporter was calling from the *New York Times*. Littler didn't think anyone knew where he was, so he wasn't sure how the reporter had tracked him down, but he took the call. Goldberg delivered the bad news. At first, Littler thought it must be an April Fool's joke, but it was already the fourth week of the month, so he quickly gave up on that idea. Several more newspapers called that day.

Littler wasn't worried about the money. His attitude was a shopkeeper's: you break it, you buy it. At first he thought, knowing Sokolin, that it might be a publicity stunt. But once he learned of the precise pattern of breakage, Littler ruled out that theory. If the bottle had fallen on the ground and shattered, that would be one thing, but no one could intentionally and cleanly puncture such an old bottle.

The next several days were a blur of media attention. Sokolin walked to a TV studio, bottle in hand, to appear on Regis Philbin's show. "Murder at Four Seasons" was the headline in *U.S. News & World Report*. *People* went with "Oops!" and dubbed Sokolin's misfortune "the world's most expensive puddle." The *New York Post* blared: "Grapes of Wrath: Clumsy Vintner Breaks a 519G Bottle of Wine." For Fleet Street tabloids, the episode served as a platonic illustration of Yank barbarism. "What a Plonker!" screamed one, while another tossed off a "Thought for Today: There's only one thing worse than an American with no taste: One who buys it, then drops it."

Cartoonists had a field day. "Okay, stand back," a man said to a crowd gathered around a puddle in one cartoon, "and let it breathe." In another, a man opined, of a splotch on the floor, "It's a pleasant stain, I think, but not a great one." Paul Kovi, at the Four Seasons, sent Sokolin a bill for the $360 it had cost the restaurant to have the rug cleaned. Sokolin ignored it. His feeling was that Kovi had gotten about "ten or twenty million dollars'" worth of free advertising out of his gaffe. (It would be dwarfed, seventeen years later, when casino developer Steve Wynn put his elbow through a $139-million Picasso.)

When the reporter from *People* came to his home, Sokolin reached for the bottle, which still stood on the table where he had set

it down, and almost knocked it over. Sokolin put his hand to his chest
as the bottle swayed, but it remained standing. Sokolin retrieved the
plastic container from the freezer and let the reporter smell it. It
"looked like chocolate-brown goo and emitted an intense aroma
not unlike that of stewed prunes," the reporter wrote.

"You think I did it on purpose, don't you?" Sokolin said to the
reporter, who concluded that it had been a true accident. Two of
the key questions muttered by suspicious colleagues after Sokolin
broke the bottle had ready answers: the level of wine was so high,
and the seal new, because of the recent recorkings by Margaux and
Whitwhams.

Sokolin by now was embracing his fifteen minutes—mugging
for the camera, bugging his eyes out, and holding the bottle forth
defiantly. He said the bottle had been "worth maybe $10 million or
maybe more." He and Gloria, a real-estate broker, found themselves
invited to social gatherings that previously would have eluded them.
It wasn't clear whether they were guests or entertainment. At one
high-powered dinner party, the host introduced Sokolin as "But-
terfingers."

The *New York Times* saw a morality tale in what had happened,
publishing an editorial that read, in part, "Everyone who has saved a
perfume for a worthy occasion and found its lilies have festered by
the time she gets around to opening the bottle knows what it is to
be a William Sokolin." A William Sokolin! He had become a cau-
tionary archetype. The lesson, the *Times* concluded, was that wine is
for drinking rather than saving.

A month after breaking the bottle, Sokolin removed the frozen
wine from his freezer and defrosted it. No decanting, no ceremony.
He just drank it from a glass. A strange thing had happened in the
last month. "It was good, but it wasn't wine," Sokolin recalled. "It
was grape juice." The freezing had removed the alcohol, and with it
the impurities. At least that was Sokolin's take.

Sokolin says he asked Hardy Rodenstock for a replacement bottle,

and Rodenstock replied that it would cost $800,000. "You're crazy,"
Sokolin told him. The insurance company Frank Crystal & Co. eventually made out a check to "Whitwhams and William Sokolin" in the
amount of $197,625 and dated June 7, 1989. The money would go to
Tim Littler, who had intended to reclaim the bottle in June, since he
had an interested buyer in Japan.

Soon after, Littler and Michael Broadbent were chatting at the
Imperial Hotel in Tokyo, when a man approached, ringing a small
bell. Littler and Broadbent were old friends, and Whitwhams handled
Christie's shipping and customs clearance in Japan. Broadbent was
doing an auction there. "Mr. Littler," the bell-ringer said, "you have
a fax." It reported that the insurance check had arrived.

"I guess we've lost the record," Broadbent said.

CHAPTER 11

THE DIVINER OF WINES

*I*N THE LATE 1980S, HARDY RODENSTOCK TOLD HIS friend Georg Riedel that he wished to create his own line of mouth-blown wineglasses. Riedel was the tenth generation in a remarkable glassmaking dynasty. It had begun in the Bohemian forest three centuries before and, after World War II, relocated to the Alpine Austrian village of Kufstein. Georg's father, Claus, had a simple, brilliant insight: the shape of a glass—the size of the bowl, its curvature, the diameter of the rim—affects how a wine smells and tastes. Claus produced a glass for each of the classic wine regions, including Bordeaux, Burgundy, and Châteauneuf-du-Pape, in the Rhône Valley. They were beautiful and functional. The *grand cru* Burgundy glass was enormous, with a flaring lip. The Museum of Modern Art in New York City acquired one for its permanent collection.

If Claus was the creative pathfinder, it was Georg who would make the glasses into a coveted commodity and transform his father's breakthrough idea into conventional wisdom. In the 1970s, with the emergence of New World regions such as California and

Australia, the wine world began to move away from speaking of wine in terms of place (a glass of Bordeaux) and toward speaking in terms of grape varietal (a glass of Cabernet Sauvignon). Georg set out to market varietal-specific glasses: Chardonnay, Pinot Noir, Cabernet Sauvignon . . . Several of the glasses were identical to those designed by his father, and had simply been relabeled, but Georg also oversaw the design of a number of increasingly special-ized glasses. The thirty-three different glasses that would eventually constitute the high-end line included one expressly for Chardon-nays from Burgundy's Montrachet appellation, one for Rheingau Rieslings, and one for white wines from the Loire Valley.

Georg Riedel was custom-tailored both in his suits and in his soul. He wore pocket squares that matched his ties, and, still in his forties, had already planned the wine to be drunk at his funeral, set-ting aside sixty bottles of a late-harvest Austrian Riesling, a 1979 Trockenbeerenauslese from Freie Weingärtner. Riedel's relation-ship with Hardy Rodenstock dated to 1982, when Riedel supplied the glassware for Rodenstock's third tasting at Fuente. In return, he was invited to the event, and since then Riedel had attended and supplied the crystal—several thousand pieces of stemware—for every Rodenstock tasting.

He and Rodenstock grew close. It was through Rodenstock that Riedel learned about old wine and tasted the vintages that he con-sidered to be his peak wine experiences. He first tasted the leg-endary 1870 Lafite at a Rodenstock tasting; he tasted the 1811 Yquem, the best wine that ever passed his lips, three or four times, all at Rodenstock tastings; and it was through Rodenstock that he tasted the "most perfect" wine he had ever enjoyed, the 1921 Mou-ton in Jéroboam. In his everyday drinking, too, Riedel favored mature wines—he wouldn't touch a Bordeaux younger than ten years—and he became a regular customer of Rodenstock's.

When Thomas Jefferson was alive, glasses were typically smaller and didn't curve in at the top. Not until the twentieth century were significant changes made to the shape of wineglasses. A line called Les Impitoyables—The Pitiless—appeared in the United States in the 1980s, and consisted of four outsized, rather severe-looking mouth-blown crystal tulips. But Les Impitoyables was sometimes faulted for its glass-half-empty approach; as their name suggested, the glasses highlighted a wine's flaws as much as its virtues. Riedel, ten years later, was the revolutionary glassware that caught on.

A tireless pitchman, Georg Riedel put himself wherever wine was being bought and drunk, at auctions and fairs and tastings and trade shows. He did this very simply. One nose at a time, he demonstrated the glasses side by side with the competition. By and large, his test subjects, people who were already very interested in wine, approached the demonstration with skepticism and came away true believers.

Riedel made a big push into the United States after the dollar started bleeding value in 1985; suddenly the demand for Riedel's luxury gift items (bowls, vases, figurines) dried up. He needed to reposition the company, and wineglasses were the way. His first breakthrough in the American market was with the Mondavis, the pioneering California wine family, in January 1990. Like everyone else, the Mondavis initially reacted as if Riedel were peddling snake oil. But after being treated to his stock show-and-tell, they were converted; they got rid of all their old glasses, placed a large order for Riedels, and, like all good converts, began to spread the word themselves. Riedel did demonstrations for important wine writers, making a special trip to Maryland to demonstrate them for Robert Parker, who lived in the small town of Monkton. Parker was blown away. "Do I have to rewrite all my notes?" he wondered aloud to Riedel. In June 1991, Parker sang the glasses' praises in his newsletter.

Riedel soon scaled up his efforts. At Marvin Shanken's 1997 Wine Experience in New York, he made a presentation to one thousand noses at once. Riedel had a set speech: the glass was a loudspeaker for the wine; it transmitted the passion sealed in a bottle. Riedel took to saying: "Mondavi made wine, Parker wrote about it, we brought the glasses."

Riedel glasses were an idea for their time. Wine connoisseurship was in a phase of accelerating precision. In the two centuries since Thomas Jefferson's imprecise language for communicating about wine, attempts to describe the evanescent sensations provoked by tasting had been fitful. The romantic era of wine appreciation, which lasted well into the twentieth century, yielded such curlicues as this 1932 description, by H. Warner Allen, of the Latour 1869: "The palate recognised a heroic wine, such a drink as might refresh the warring archangels, and the perfection of its beauty called up the noble phrase 'terrible as an army with banners.'"

In the latter half of the twentieth century, the idea of tasting notes had taken hold, and their descriptions had become increasingly sensory. The untrained nose might think it absurd to detect a grocery list of smells in a glass of wine, but it had an empirical basis—a wine could contain some of the same phenolic compounds as did said groceries—which was why different tasters often came up with the same adjectives. The apotheosis of this hyperdelineated linguistic movement came in 1990, with the invention of the "Wine Aroma Wheel" by a chemist at the University of California at Davis named Ann C. Noble. The wheel attempted to come up with a standard nomenclature. Pineapple, melon, and banana were examples of "tropical fruit" flavors, which, along with citrus, berry, tree fruit, and dried fruit, made up the "fruity" family of aromas. "Wet dog," "burnt match," and "skunk" were examples of "sulfur flavors," which, along with "pungent" and "petroleum" flavors, formed the "chemical" family. In all, the wheel delineated nearly a hundred scents.

Some of the new precision was grounded in science. Much of it just looked as if it was. Attempts to rank various wines dated back to antiquity. The Classification of 1855 had been, in its way, an effort to differentiate among the Bordeaux hordes. Modern systems ranged from Michael Broadbent's zero-to-five stars to the twenty-point systems of U.C. Davis, *Decanter,* and English critics Clive Coates and Jancis Robinson. But the reigning paradigm, starting in the early 1980s, was the 100-point scale pioneered by Robert Parker and copied by other influential tasting authorities, including *Wine Spectator.* The very fineness of the scoring system's gradations cast doubt on its validity. Critics argued that it was absurd to suggest that there was a meaningful distinction between an 86 and an 87, or between a 92 and a 93. The endless verticals and horizontals were empirical studies of a sort. Was such-and-such vintage—the 1945, the 1961—still up to snuff? Was Pétrus really the best Pomerol? Which of the two Rothschild rivals—Lafite and Mouton—would prevail in a multi-vintage showdown? Was Latour truly the longest-lived of the first growths? Did the '29 Pétrus taste different in different-size bottles? These were studies without scientific controls.

Another area of wine appreciation that had become more nuanced was the pairing of food and wine. A few rules of thumb (red wine with meat, white with fish) and a handful of traditional combinations—Sauternes and foie gras, Port with Stilton, Chablis alongside oysters—had given way to a much more complex picture. There were, after all, some fish (salmon) that went well with some reds (pinot noir). You could find people who swore by idiosyncratic combinations like "Margaux and chocolate,"[*] and denounced pairing them with anything else. Rodenstock went so far as to suggest that when one was serving Yquem, its temperature should depend on what it was accompanying (43–46 degrees Fahrenheit with foie gras, 46–50 degrees with desserts, 50–53 degrees with Roquefort or Stilton). Many of the pairings did, at any rate, taste pretty good.

Until the late 1980s, the Riedel glass suggested for Sauternes was the one designed for mature white Bordeaux. Rodenstock believed Sauternes required its own glass. He made some sketches and gave them to Riedel, who turned them into designs and gave them back to Rodenstock, who made a couple of changes. Prototypes were made. The bowl of the glass tapered almost to a point at its base, and swelled elegantly to a bulge near its top. The shape tempered the dessert wine's sweetness and emphasized its minerality, transforming intensity into finesse. The narrow mouth of the glass concentrated the wine's inimitable nose, showcasing the sweet, yeasty aroma redolent of baked raisin bread. For Rodenstock, having his own line of Riedel glasses, the HR-1 Series, was the ultimate status symbol.

RODENSTOCK'S FAME HAD spread since the auction of the Forbes bottle. The publicity from that one sale had made him known internationally in wine circles, enabling him to launch a robust career dealing wine. He had made a tidy sum just by selling off several more of the Jefferson bottles. In 1986, in partnership with an innkeeper in Austria's Wachau wine region, he had begun to organize annual commercial tastings, where he provided the wine and guests paid sums into the thousands of dollars to attend. His wine business now extended to the Far East, where he also owned a Taiwanese company that packaged condoms in hazelnut shells and marketed them as gag gifts. At the end of his tastings, Rodenstock would give the nuts away.

His knack for unearthing sensational wine rarities had not ended with the Jefferson bottles. The publicity from the Forbes sale, he said, had led to his being approached about old bottles found in Russia. The czars in St. Petersburg had been well-documented procurers of Yquem, and Rodenstock soon acquired four bottles purportedly dating to between 1740 and 1760. At his 1986 tasting, he had produced an Yquem he said he had obtained in Leningrad. Bulky and adorned with enamel flowers, the bottle was undated but bore the name Sauvage, the family that owned Yquem before it became a Lur Saluces property. "The rarest of all these rarities," Jancis Robinson later described the bottle, extolling "these glasses of unctuous history."

Rodenstock spoke of a confederate, in the employ of Lufthansa, who smuggled Yquems out of Russia for him. He told friends that he had found another trove, for which he had paid a million dollars cash, in Caracas, Venezuela. "[F]or ancient wines," Edmund Penning-Rowsell wrote in 1989, "[Rodenstock] appears to have similar powers of discovery to water diviners, in their more pedestrian calling."

Rodenstock had become wealthier, his tastings more lavish every year. They were now located in the chic ski resort of Arlberg, in western Austria, lasted an entire weekend, and included nearly seventy guests, many of them European celebrities. Rodenstock, who had never ended up marrying Heinz-Gert Woschek's daughter Patricia, had traded up to richer, more socially prominent girlfriends. In addition to wine, he now collected porcelain and watches, and always wore something unusual on his wrist. He was also a tax exile, officially a resident in Somerset Maugham's "sunny place for shady people"—the haven of Monte Carlo—and kept additional homes in Munich and at Lacanau, a seaside resort outside of Bordeaux. (A few years later, he would add homes in the Spanish beach town of Marbella and in the Austrian ski village of Kitzbühel.) Though the few people who saw the homes noted that none was very large, the addresses helped him to gain entrée to a circle of people who were flashy, well-heeled, and generally dismissive of outsiders—or at least to look as though he had.

Up to now, Rodenstock had shied away from publicity focused personally on him, but with his business growing, he decided to grant a handful of carefully chosen journalists the kind of access necessary to write big features that would spread his name among prospective customers. In December 1988, *Wine Spectator* put him on its cover, a glass of Yquem in one hand, a No. 2 Davidoff cigar in the other, with the words "Money Doesn't Matter: The World's Most Extravagant Wine Collector."

The picture that emerged in the articles, clearly supplied to the journalists by Rodenstock, included several previously unreported details. Among them: Rodenstock credited his organizational abilities to his father, who he said had been the regional railway director in Essen. Before working in the music business, Rodenstock had been an academic lecturer in surveying and mathematics, "the youngest such person in North-Rhine Westphalia," and had written "a series of scientific reports and books on geodesy." He had left academia, he revealed to a friendly Austrian journalist, because "he was urged to join a political party if he wanted to achieve greater academic honor. That didn't suit the independent-minded young man at all."

The articles were not exactly hard-hitting. One of them noted that Rodenstock was a Sagittarius, referred to him simply as "Hardy," and described him as "an artist of life." He said he regularly received blank checks from American collectors begging for a spot at one of his tastings, but that he turned them down because wine wasn't about money for him. Rodenstock described himself as "a battle drinker," and said that when he tasted a great wine it was like "all hell is breaking loose on my palate."

IN THE FOUR years since Rodenstock's discovery of the Jefferson bottles, mega-tasting mania had escalated. Every week, it seemed, there was another attempt by a collector to outdo everyone else. Hans-Peter Frericks, Herr Pétrus, held a thirty-two-vintage vertical of his namesake wine at the Residenz, a centuries-old palace in Munich. There were magnums and Jéroboams, and the tasting was followed by dinner at the Egyptian Art Museum. "There was a mummy on one side and 1.8 kilos of caviar on the other," Otto Jung said later. "It was totally decadent." Outside the party, protesters picketed the use of a government building for an elite affair. Lloyd Flatt arrived at Rodenstock's tasting at Arlberg in a chauffeured Range Rover, fresh from having had a liver transplant. Arne Berger, a Hamburg collector, held several "100 Point" tastings, featuring only wines that had been anointed with perfect scores by Robert Parker.

The game was starting to exceed the means of people like Mario Scheuermann, the journalist. For one "best bottle" tasting, to which everyone attending had to contribute the best bottle from his cellar, a guest seeking an invitation had to write a letter to the organizing committee and impress them with the bottle he'd bring. And he had to be able to bring two bottles of it, or one magnum, to ensure that everyone would get a decent pour. Scheuermann proposed bringing Haut-Brion '61. This was a first growth in a vintage widely considered to be one of the greatest of the century. It traded at auction for nearly $300 a bottle. Scheuermann only squeaked in. His was the cheapest, and youngest, bottle at the tasting. Everyone else had brought legends like '45 Mouton, '47 Cheval Blanc, and '28 Latour. The tastings had become "a society game," says Jung. He became uncomfortable accepting all this very expensive wine when he was no longer contributing. The 1989 Rodenstock tasting would be the last he would attend.

The tone of these events was also becoming more serious. So much money was at stake now, and so much ego, that some long-time members of the scene felt there was a hubris to it all, a hollow and cancerous competitiveness. The collectors would revel in the fact that, often, they owned or had tasted more vintages than the people who made the wine. A veteran Rhône collector in Hamburg, a law professor, surprised Gérard Jaboulet, a major Rhône producer, with a breakfast vertical (the Germans seemed to take pleasure in scheduling these events for 9:00 a.m.) of Jaboulet's flagship wine, La Chapelle, including every vintage from 1945 to 1961.

Several of these vintages Jaboulet himself hadn't tasted. "Jaboulet was shocked," Scheuermann recalled. "This was just because this poor guy had never had these vintages."

Rodenstock's own tastings had progressed steadily. Each year the wines were rarer, the selection better, the condition better, the bottles bigger. Nothing, however, was as grand as the Rodenstock tasting in 1989.

It was at this, the tenth of Rodenstock's annual tastings, that his HR-1 line of Riedel glasses debuted. Woschek's teasing description of Rodenstock as living an imperial lifestyle took on a literal quality that year. Most of the September tasting took place at the Kurhaus Stüberl, a restaurant in southeastern Bavaria, but on Saturday the twenty-third, the festivities moved to Schloss Herrenchiemsee, a palace on an island in a nearby lake, which had been built by King Ludwig II as a copy of Versailles. As with the Frericks event at the Egyptian Art Museum, the tasting caused protests. Newspaper editorials denounced the use of a government building for this decadent event for the *schikeria,* or "chic people." That Saturday evening, eighty guests ferried across the Chiemsee for the re-creation of an event that had taken place a century earlier.

In the summer of 1867—the midpoint of Bordeaux's twenty-year golden age—luminaries from across Europe had descended on Paris for the Universal Exposition, and on June 7 a historic dinner had been held. Attended by Czar Alexander II of Russia, his son and heir Alexander III, and Wilhelm I of Prussia, future first emperor of Germany (as well as by Chancellor Otto von Bismarck), it was called the Three Emperors Dinner. The meal was prepared by Adolphe Duglére of the Café Anglais in Paris, the most famous restaurant of the period.

Rodenstock's 1989 reenactment called for guests to wear period costumes, and people showed up in everything from a Cossack getup to an American admiral's uniform to Styrian folk garb. Beyond the usual German-speaking suspects, the guests included some of the most prominent American collectors, such as Lloyd Flatt and Bipin Desai, who dressed as a maharajah; internationally famous winemakers such as Italy's Angelo Gaja; the English wine-writing and -importing couple Serena Sutcliffe and David Peppercorn; and Mario Adorf, an Italian-German movie star. Rodenstock went as Napoleon, and brought as his date an actual member of the Rodenstock optics family, Inge, an internationally known collector of modern art. Hardy Rodenstock had found a way to merge, at least temporarily, with the famous family whose name he shared.

The dinner, which began at 8:00 p.m., took place in the rectangular Second Antechamber, ornate with gilt, mirrors, chandeliers, haut-relief friezes, a frescoed ceiling, and paintings of Louis XIV and his family. Two long tables were set, parallel to each other and running the length of the room. The meal, which replicated the 1867 menu, was a barrage of excess: hot quail paté, ortolan canapés, lobster *à la parisienne,* and on and on. The centerpiece of the event, and the hardest to pull off, was the collection of wines. Rodenstock had brought together each and every one of the rarities served at the original dinner: Madeira 1810; Sherry 1821; Château d'Yquem 1847; Chambertin 1846; Château Margaux 1847; Château Latour 1847; Château Lafite 1848; and Champagne Roederer Frappé.

Amid the spectacle, Walter Eigensatz nursed rising suspicions. Eigensatz, Mr. Cheval Blanc, had been a core member of Rodenstock's inner wine circle since the early 1980s, but he had only begun to doubt his friend a few months before. For his fiftieth birthday, Eigensatz organized a tasting going back one hundred years to 1889, and featuring Mouton, Margaux, and Lafite in Jéroboam. The event included a comparative tasting of the 1959 Lafite in every bottle size from regular up to Impériale, a test of the conventional wisdom that inversely correlates bottle size and rate of aging. "The Impériale was still too young," Eigensatz recalled later.

The next flight was all Impériales from 1929, and aimed at

anointing the best wine from that vintage. The contenders included a Cheval Blanc and a Pétrus, both bought at auction, a Mouton donated by Lloyd Flatt, and an Ausone that came from Rodenstock. To Eigensatz, it was obvious that the Ausone was something other than Ausone. "I was suspicious at the time but didn't say anything," Eigensatz said later.

This was on top of his nagging questions about what happened to the corks and empty bottles after Rodenstock's tastings. In the 1980s, whenever anyone would try to get a close look at a Rodenstock cork, Frenzel the sommelier would quickly put it in his pocket. After the annual event at Arlberg, Rodenstock would leave some bottles with Adi Werner, the co-host, but always took the best ones away with him. Eigensatz had never seen where they went, and when he once asked Rodenstock, the answer was vague and unsatisfying: Rodenstock said that "a crazy guy" had paid him 10,000 marks—less than $5,000—for all his empties.

Other times, Rodenstock said he was collecting bottles for "a bottle museum." In 1987, as a fortieth-birthday gift for a noted German circus director and clown named Bernhard Paul, Rodenstock had presented three rare wines—an 1847 Yquem, a 1947 Cheval Blanc, and an old port. They were drunk at the birthday party, which was organized by Hans-Peter Wodarz, at whose Die Ente restaurant in Wiesbaden Rodenstock had held his 1985 tasting. Afterward, Rodenstock said he had intended only the contents as a gift, and he wanted the bottles back. Over the next two years he wrote twenty-five letters to Wodarz demanding the bottles be returned to him. He addressed the chef alternately as "Woody" and "Woodybaby," threatened to "make hamburger" of him, and dismissed Paul as a "circus twit." Ultimately, Rodenstock claimed he'd gotten two of the bottles back and donated them to an "Oppenheim museum."

At the 1989 Rodenstock event, at a tasting at 1:30 a.m. the night after the Three Emperors Dinner, Rodenstock poured Pétrus, in Impériales, from 1921, 1924, 1926, and 1928. Walter Eigensatz was at a table with Serena Sutcliffe, David Peppercorn, and Cheval Blanc manager Jacques Hébrard. Sutcliffe looked at Eigensatz and said, "Walter, these are all the same." All the vintages tasted alike to her. They seemed to be one wine in four different packages. Sutcliffe was less skeptical of other wines served at the tasting. "Then there are grand occasion wines," she wrote later, in a roundup of the most remarkable wines she had tasted in 1989, "which impose themselves even amid an array of historic superstars. Such was Hardy Rodenstock's Château d'Yquem 1847 in magnum, brought from Leningrad for his re-creation of the 1867 Three Emperors Dinner. Liquid cocoa and coconut milk on the nose, fireworks on the palate—not just length, but breadth, remaining constant in the glass for half an hour. *Incroyable.*"

On the subject of the Pétrus, though, tablemates Hébrard and Peppercorn agreed with her: This was one wine in four different bottles. The presence of Pétrus in large formats from the 1920s was surprising on its face because the vineyard's rise to fame had begun only after World War II. Before that, it had been little more than a farmhouse, and its wine had been shipped mainly to Belgium. Christian Moueix, whose family had become one of the estate's distributors in 1945 and half-owner in 1964, had attended the Pétrus vertical hosted by Hans-Peter Frericks in Munich, and had been skeptical then of the big bottles of 1921 Pétrus supplied by Rodenstock. When Moueix had asked Ralf Frenzel to see a cork, Rodenstock's young sommelier had replied "*Nein*," putting the cork in his pocket. After the suspicious Pétrus flight at Rodenstock's 1989 tasting, Moueix told Eigensatz he doubted that any Impériales had been bottled in the 1920s. "Moueix served me a '28 Pétrus," Eigensatz recalled. "It was bad. The twenties Pétruses were *bad.*"

Eigensatz found himself reevaluating all the Rodenstock wines he had drunk in the last several years. "I served them. I bought them," Eigensatz said of the wines supposedly purchased in Caracas.

Among these wines, which Eigensatz bought in 1987 and served shortly thereafter, were a double magnum of 1893 Cheval Blanc, an Impériale of 1893 Lafite, and a double magnum of 1893 Pétrus. "Pure raspberries," Eigensatz recalled of the Cheval Blanc. "Incredible. The Lafite was excellent. The double magnum of Pétrus was very good. I know they were fakes. I'm convinced. I never had a Cheval Blanc again in this way—it's always forest berries, never raspberries."

~

CHAPTER 12

A BUILT-IN PREFERENCE
FOR THE OBVIOUS

*F*OR A LONE PRIVATE COLLECTOR WITHIN THE GERMAN-speaking segment of the wine scene to have doubts was one thing. But more far-flung and influential people, not just those at the Three Emperors Dinner, were growing skeptical of Rodenstock, too. The German's most important ally in Bordeaux had been Comte Alexandre de Lur Saluces, the proprietor of Château d'Yquem. Lur Saluces knew many serious collectors of his wine, but none so avid as Rodenstock, whom even he called "Monsieur Yquem." Rodenstock had opened the 1787 Jefferson Yquem at the château in 1985, and when Rodenstock asked whether he might hold his 1986 tasting at the château, Lur Saluces assented. Rodenstock promised a wine of equal rarity for this tasting, the flower-painted bottle, presumed to be from the mid–eighteenth century and supposedly discovered in Leningrad, inscribed with the name of the Sauvage family.

Lur Saluces wasn't entirely prepared for what he was getting himself into. Rodenstock devoted an entire day to the question of which water to serve at the event; after sampling dozens, he concluded definitively that the simplest, most tasteless H$_2$O was a particular Belgian spa water. The event, attended by forty-two guests, began at 1:00 p.m. and ended at 1:00 a.m. the next day. After one flight, a well-marinated Michael Broadbent had to remove his vest to walk in the vineyard. Jancis Robinson, who found herself drinking 1964 Lanson Champagne to wash down aspirin, left her tasting booklet at the château, to the annoyance of Lur Saluces, who felt it would be indelicate to address the matter, as it would draw attention to the fact that she might have overindulged. Later, Lur Saluces agreed to trade Rodenstock a number of older vintages of Yquem from the château cellar, including several 1921s, in exchange for another, full Jefferson bottle, a 1784.

In Bordeaux, Lur Saluces was the bluest of bluebloods, Yquem the bluest of blue chips. The count's validation was key to legitimizing Rodenstock. Some châteaux, including Pétrus and Margaux, kept their distance. Once Rodenstock asked Margaux general manager Paul Pontallier for certificates validating some of his old bottles. Pontallier refused. "He's not an unpleasant person at all," Pontallier says. "But we've never reconditioned bottles for him or participated in his tastings. Not that we had proof of anything, but we just weren't comfortable." Over the next few years, however, several other leading châteaux, including Yquem, Lafite, and Cheval Blanc, vouched for Rodenstock's bottles by recorking them, which was tantamount to guaranteeing their authenticity. The day after the tasting at Yquem, the city of Bordeaux honored Rodenstock with a commemorative plaque.

But Lur Saluces gradually became disillusioned. When they'd first met, in the early 1980s, Rodenstock had been humble, respectful, knowledgeable, and laconic to the point of awkwardness. Over time he became increasingly arrogant, pronouncing himself the authority on Yquem. A collision with Yquem's leader seemed inevitable, and in the late eighties it happened.

Near the end of the growing season in 1987, in Sauternes, it rained. A late rainfall was one of those things that could kill a vintage. If grapes were wet when picked, the entire crop could be diluted. A new technique called cryoextraction offered a solution: freeze the grapes, then mechanically separate them from the ice. The unripe grapes would freeze first (the riper grapes' higher sugar content making them more resistant to freezing), so pressing would render juice only from the ripest grapes. Though the word suggested a futuristic, high-tech procedure, Lur Saluces viewed cryoextraction as basically "a cold room next to a press."

When he explained the process to Rodenstock, however, the German wrote a letter to Lur Saluces, denouncing the innovation and insisting that he stop using it forthwith. In the traditionalist view of Rodenstock, Lur Saluces was forsaking the venerable method of individually picked berries, bringing mechanization to a bastion of handwork. Instead of limiting his criticism to a private letter, however, Rodenstock sent copies to several journalists, and a big article appeared in *Der Spiegel,* sounding the alarm about Yquem's new "horror machine." Lur Saluces took umbrage. "This was a German giving orders to a Frenchman," as journalist Heinz-Gert Woschek later put it.

Lur Saluces was shocked by the attack and seriously considered suing Rodenstock. A few years later, Rodenstock further antagonized Lur Saluces when he tried to market a vase with Yquem's insignia. Lur Saluces was at the time embroiled in a seventeen-year fight with Davidoff over its unauthorized use of Yquem's name for one of its cigars, and Rodenstock's venture seemed a clear provocation. Lur Saluces didn't sue, but Rodenstock could forget about being asked to join the Académie du Vin, a fraternal organization led by Lur Saluces. When California collector Bipin Desai hosted a big Yquem vertical in the early 1990s, he had to disinvite Rodenstock after Lur Saluces said he wouldn't attend if Rodenstock was there.

"When Hardy attacked Yquem," collector Wolfgang Grünewald said later, "the whole Bordelais community was behind Alex. That was a huge blunder by Hardy. He lost an invaluable relationship. Hardy would not be good at politics."

MORE THREATENING TO Rodenstock's thriving business dealing wine were the proliferating questions about the contents of his bottles. At the high end of the market, doubts about the authenticity of certain old wines, while sometimes privately held, were seldom publicly aired. Châteaux, auction houses, and established merchants were fearful of spooking buyers, collectors of devaluing their cellars, and wine writers of being disinvited from exclusive tastings. Ambitious middlemen balked at interrogating their gray-market suppliers. In the late eighties, however, a handful of American collectors on the West Coast became more vocal.

They were generally more private and intellectual than the big-money collectors who formed the Group. At the center of this mostly Los Angeles–based contingent was Bipin Desai, a theoretical physicist at the University of California's Riverside branch, who on the side organized commercial tastings featuring grand assemblages of old and rare wine.

Born into a wealthy Indian merchant family in Rangoon, then raised in Bombay, Desai had been a math prodigy, graduating from high school at the age of fourteen. After his family moved to the United States, he ended up getting his doctorate in physics at UC Berkeley and specialized in making predictions about the mass and behavior of subatomic specks like quarks, bosons, and leptons.

A teetotaling Hindu in his youth, he had come to enjoy an occasional glass of wine after traveling in Europe. But after he attended a horizontal of 1961 Bordeaux, Desai became an obsessed tasting organizer. (He also became a gourmand; during a three-month sabbatical at CERN, the nuclear research lab in Switzerland, he dined two dozen times at the three-star restaurant of Fredy Girardet.) His events tended to be brainier and more focused than Rodenstock's:

Each would explore a single theme; dress would be merely coat-and-tie; there were fewer celebrities; they would typically only last two days; and, of course, Desai didn't foot the bill for his tastings.

Other key members of this group included Geoffrey Troy, an oenophile who ran a company that trucked automobiles around the United States; collector Edward M. Lazarus, a lawyer of right-leaning political convictions (at a vertical tasting of the Spanish cult wine Vega Sicilia, he proposed a toast to "El Caudillo"—the dictator Francisco Franco); Dennis Foley, an auctioneer at Butterfield & Butterfield in San Francisco who advised Gordon Getty on his wine purchases; collector John Tilson, an investment banker who, with Foley, published the newsletter *Rarities;* and Albert Givton, an Israel-raised Canadian who also published a wine newsletter. They were many of the same people who for several years had held an annual tasting jointly with their German counterparts. Desai's events often included bottles sourced from Rodenstock.

These were experienced tasters, and many of them weren't that awed by Europeans like "Rodey," as Lazarus sardonically referred to the German, or even Broadbent. After a tasting run by the British auctioneer in October 1983, Givton snarled to his diary that the event had been "very poorly organized" by "His Majesty," signing off, "Bon Voyage!" The two men would soon square off on the letters page of *Decanter,* where Broadbent, disregarding the fact that Givton had grown up in Jerusalem, wrote that "the North American palate . . . has a built-in preference for the obvious." As for Rodenstock, Givton was suspicious from their first encounter, at the September 1985 German-American Rarities Group tasting in San Francisco, where Ralf Frenzel decanted many of the wines and frequently whispered into his master's ear. At a Mouton vertical during the four-day event, Rodenstock was able to guess the 1945 correctly, even though Givton found it odd-tasting and impossible to identify.

"How could he have known that this poor bottle was the 1945?"

Givton wrote in his diary. "Anyway, this German wine collector makes me nervous. I can't quite figure him out. He seems too sleek."

In 1987, Troy and Lazarus organized a vertical of Mouton, back to 1853, in Los Angeles. Among the bottles was an 1865 bought from Rodenstock, via Desai, for a substantial sum. Several tasters found the wine bizarrely young; one noted that it had a pronounced cabernet franc character, odd for a wine that made scant use of that grape. Troy was certain, after examining the cork, that the wine was a fake. The style of the branding, and the quality of the vintage lettering, made it clear that someone had drawn the cork from a young Mouton, sanded off the vintage, and inked "1865" in its place. Troy stopped short of fingering Rodenstock as the faker, allowing for the possibility that Rodenstock had himself been duped by whoever sold him the bottle. Troy asked Desai for his money back, but nothing came of it.

In Los Angeles a week later, Desai hosted a vertical of Pichon Lalande, one of the so-called Super Seconds, second-growth Bordeaux often of a quality equal to the first growths. Among the bottles in the lineup were two from Rodenstock: an 1893 double magnum and a 1900 magnum, both purportedly from his big Venezuelan find. David Molyneux-Berry, the Englishman who headed Sotheby's wine department, was a guest of honor at the Pichon tasting, and he stood up to talk about the château's wines. As he spoke, someone came up behind him, tapped him on the shoulder, and put a cork in his hand. It said "1893" and bore the château brand. But it was oddly short. After he finished speaking, Molyneux-Berry showed the cork to May-Eliane de Lencquesaing, the château's proprietress. She told him, "We just don't use corks like that."

Troy, who had spotted the fake at the Mouton tasting a week earlier, examined the cork from the magnum of 1900 Pichon Lalande and saw that it was strikingly like the Mouton cork he believed to be bogus, with a vintage obviously sanded off and replaced with an uncharacteristically faint "1900." The wine itself tasted thirty years old. "It was outrageously young," Molyneux-Berry recalled. Another Englishman, John Avery, an old old-wine hand whose family had been in the wine business in Bristol since the eighteenth century, stood up and said, simply, "These two bottles are not real." Seasoned collector Ed Lazarus was puzzled by the "vanilla-chocolate-mint aroma," later writing of the two bottles, "I had never experienced anything remotely similar in an older Bordeaux, or in fact anywhere else, except perhaps at a Baskin-Robbins ice cream shop."

A similar outcry happened that year at a commercial tasting in Beverly Hills organized by Desai, a fifty-eight-vintage vertical of Margaux that included the 1771 and 1791 vintages. The latter had been supplied by Rodenstock, gratis, when he saw Desai in Germany; Rodenstock said both were from his Venezuelan haul. Carrying them back to the States, Desai sweated through customs, fearful of being hit with a massive antiques duty. The customs agent disappeared for a while; when he returned, he said he'd called a dozen wine stores, asking how much a "typical" 1771 and 1791 Margaux were worth. They all laughed at him. He ended up charging Desai less than a dollar, basing his calculation on the amount of liquid in the bottles rather than their age.

At the tasting, Desai remarked that the older wines smelled like an old Hindu temple. "Because there are a lot of droppings from bats in those temples," Desai recalled. "That's all I meant, but it was quoted several times and was taken as if I meant it was really spiritual and mysterious." A number of tasters found the bottles surprisingly youthful.

Controversy flared up in 1989 at yet another Desai event, a vertical of Figeac, a St. Emilion property which abuts the more famous Cheval Blanc and is unusual in making a right-bank wine dominated by cabernet sauvignon and cabernet franc rather than merlot. At the tasting, which took place in Paris, a magnum of 1905 brought by Rodenstock struck many participants as atypical, being strangely youthful, full-hued, and uncharacteristic in flavor. Edmund Penning-Rowsell, the dean of English wine writers, yelled out that it was "a complete fraud." Rodenstock, put on the spot, declared that he had bought the magnum at Butterfield & Butterfield the year before, but the San Francisco auction house subsequently reported that it hadn't sold a 1905 Figeac in the last four years. At that point Rodenstock said he had made a mistake: he had actually bought it in 1987 at Christie's Chicago, and he produced a receipt from the sale. The wine had been advertised as a bottle, but Rodenstock said this was an error and it had turned out to be a magnum. Desai was convinced by the documentation, and thought, in any case, that it would have been ridiculous to fake a 1905, an off-vintage. He noted that Rodenstock had given him the bottle at no cost.

Around the same time, an assemblage of Pétrus from the best vintages of the 1920s and 1930s, all in large formats such as Jéroboams and double magnums, came on the market, at a per-bottle price in excess of $20,000. Ed Lazarus, asked by a prospective buyer to authenticate them, was immediately suspicious. Despite decades of experience with old and rare wines, he had never encountered large-format, pre–World War II Pétrus. Neither had Dennis Foley, the San Francisco auctioneer. Harry Waugh, the eightysomething *eminence grise* of wine who had been one of the first English merchants to import Pétrus, said he never even heard of such bottles existing and was skeptical that any did. Christian Moueix, the proprietor of Pétrus, echoed this opinion. And the unnamed seller, according to *Rarities,* the short-lived newsletter that served as the Group's unofficial house organ, refused to allow on-site inspection of the bottles, declaring it "out of the question!"

Whether or not Rodenstock was the seller of that particular batch, he, too, became known for his large-format Pétrus bottlings. When questioned about them, the German said he'd bought the

wine from an English cellar. This assertion was itself later challenged as improbable, since England wasn't a traditional market for
Pomerols, although *Wine Spectator* reporter James Suckling, a regular at Rodenstock's tastings, vaguely reported the existence of old
merchants' catalogs showing that Bordeaux, including Pétrus, was
being offered in large formats even in the 1920s and 1930s. Rodenstock argued that all the skeptics were motivated by jealousy, that
they lacked sufficient experience with pre-phylloxera wines to
know how they should taste, and that in the past wines were much
less uniform, coming from barrels, not bottles.

He was particularly annoyed by the argument that his old
Pétrus big bottles must be fake because Pétrus hadn't made any
large-format bottlings before the Second World War. He chalked
such "stupid assertion[s]" up to "would-be connoisseurs . . . Such
a nonsense is unfortunately also spread by the château owners
although they have no more documents in their archives. Wine has
always been filled into big bottles and every other declaration is
pure nonsense! . . . It's ridiculous that despite such pieces of evidence some idiots still pretend that wine hasn't been filled into big
bottles in former times."

Ralf Frenzel, on the subject of big bottles, struck a metaphysical
note. On the day when he had opened the 1787 Mouton at Mouton,
while everyone else was eating lunch upstairs, Frenzel went into the
cellar with Raoul Blondin, and watched as the cellarmaster poured
two bottles of Mouton 1926 into one magnum bottle, thereby creating a magnum of 1926 Mouton. "So the question is," Frenzel said
later, "what *is* a real magnum?"

Rodenstock's bottles continued to draw questions. At a December 1989 Latour vertical at the restaurants Patina and Michael's, in
Los Angeles, three pre-phylloxera vintages struck several knowledgeable collectors as suspect. Four experienced tasters thought
some older vintages were fake, while Harry Waugh was ambivalent
and the bottles were defended by Belgian collector Frans de Cock, a

major customer of Rodenstock's who was a laminate-flooring tycoon. (With the very largest collections, a loosely inverse correlation often obtains between the size of the collection and the glamour of the collector's profession.)

The tasting notes of Givton, a Canadian, are illustrative. Of the 1865, he wrote, "Round, fruity, not unlike a younger Ausone rather than an old Latour. Some tobacco. Nice finish but artificially sweet. Unusual." About the 1870 he was more blunt: "Impressive dark color. Coffee or chocolate liqueur, and fresh wine on the nose. A fake." Likewise the 1874: "Toasty, fresh Cabernet Franc nose mixed with crème de cacao liqueur. Didn't taste at all like Latour or any other claret. Described by someone as 'young Mondavi cabernet and coffee or chocolate liqueur.' Obviously a doctored wine." Another taster likened it to "a Rolex bought in Hong Kong." Alan Hare, chairman of the château, told the room: "This is fake." Geoffrey Troy, de facto cork inspector, examined the 1865 stopper and found that it, too, seemed to have received identical treatment to the earlier Pichon and Mouton corks that he deemed fake. He assumed this bottle came from the same source.

Crème de cacao . . . coffee liqueur . . . Baskin-Robbins! This was a departure from the old relabeling or revintaging or topping up of real wine. The known universe of the fake had expanded to include bottles filled with liquids not derived from grapes. While the Los Angeles collectors continued to hold private tastings among themselves, and Desai kept organizing smaller commercial tastings, the grander events came to an end. The string of incidents with suspicious bottles had demoralized them and shaken the soundness of the rare-wine market. In nearly every case the wines could be traced back to Rodenstock, though his name was rarely mentioned in published complaints about the problem. Instead, observers made defamation-proof comments such as noting that the corks in all the questionable wines were similar to one another, and different from the standard corks to be expected in each wine. "What are we to conclude from all this?" wrote Ed Lazarus in *Rarities*. "Sadly, that a person or people have been engaged in the creation and marketing of fraudulent bottles of what purports to be unadulterated rare old wine, and further, that there is big money to be made from such activity."

Lazarus went on to say that the best bet for guaranteeing an authentic old bottle was to make sure that it was either a never-recorked specimen from an English or Scottish castle, a bottle straight from the cellar of a Bordeaux château, or a bottle with some other transparent, unimpeachable provenance. Meanwhile, several leading châteaux, including Latour and the Domaine de la Romanée-Conti (DRC), enacted stricter recorking policies. The DRC stopped recorking altogether. Lafite, Margaux, Mouton, and Pétrus determined they would only recork bottles with the original corks and capsules, and in which the wine was authentic and unspoiled.

Troy, more cynically, laid out a recipe for how to fake old bottles of wine:

1. Find an empty bottle of an old vintage of Bordeaux. It should preferably be pre-Phylloxera as these vintages are worth a great deal of money and relatively few people know what they should taste like. The bottle should have an original label in good condition, if possible, because this adds greatly to the value of rare old wines.

2. Fill the bottle with a carefully made combination of young Bordeaux, Rhône, Beaujolais, Crème de Cacao, etc. Use your imagination to make a good blend!

3. Remove the cork from a bottle of young wine of the same château as the empty bottle you plan to recork. Do not use a conventional corkscrew, as that will ruin the cork, however an Ah-So cork puller that has the two prongs that slide down the side of the cork would work fine. It is very unlikely to damage the cork.

4. Carefully sand the vintage date off the cork.

5. Brand the correct "new" date on the cork to match the label of the old bottle being recorked.

6. Recork and recapsule.

"Now you have a beautiful bottle of rare old claret," Troy concluded, "and you can make your haul as soon as an unsuspecting collector can be found who will purchase your fake bottle!"

AS RODENSTOCK'S CREDIBILITY was being widely debated in the rare-wine scene, Broadbent defended the German, saying that the tasting notes Givton had adduced as evidence of fraud were consistent with his own notes on bottles that had not come from Rodenstock. In essence, Broadbent argued that since no two old bottles are the same, just about anything is possible. While he conceded the paucity of affirmative evidence of prewar large-format Pétrus bottlings—no Pétrus bottles of any size, in fact, had appeared at Christie's before 1940—the auctioneer said that he had shown the large-format labels to a British Library expert on paper and print, who had deemed them authentic. And he said that he had found some prewar large-format Pétrus he had drunk, courtesy of Rodenstock, to be believably old. He allowed that "one or two" bottles at Rodenstock's annual event tasted "too good to be true," but noted that even wines with impeccable provenance (such as the Glamis Castle 1870 Lafite) could seem so young and fresh as to induce skepticism. He likened the evidence against Rodenstock's bottles to that in favor of airplane parts believed to come from Amelia Earhart's plane; there might not be proof that they were the real thing, but there wasn't proof that they weren't, either.

"Is Rodenstock a poseur, a cheat?" Broadbent asked rhetorically in a letter to *Rarities*. "Deceitful or just ingenuous? Plausible cer-

tainly, a little worrying perhaps. But to suggest that every marvelous tasting old bottle, or strange and 'off' bottle, is the result of
his manipulation is distinctly unfair and, I believe, wide of the mark.
But I wish he would be less secretive. It merely adds to everyone's
suspicions."

A divide was opening around Rodenstock's bottles. Depending
on where you stood, it was either a substantial factual disagreement
or a philosophical schism. The L.A. contingent, for the most part,
deemed atypical bottles to be suspect, prima facie. Rodenstock and
Broadbent argued that such bottles were illustrative of the very
diversity they found thrilling in old wines. In this view, almost any
flavor, no matter how weird, could be explained away as an artifact
of some unknown circumstance in a wine's maturation (storage
conditions, say, or bottle variation—a truism about mature wines is
that there are no great wines, only great bottles).

Insiders' skepticism seeped into the wider wine world's consciousness, as the leading wine magazines began to sneak occasional
snide asides into their copy. In December 1987, *Decanter* reported a
record price paid for a Jéroboam of Pétrus 1961 ($14,000), attrib-
uting it partly to the wine's "rarity following a burglary at the
château. Christie's say they know of no other Jéroboam, so this was
probably a unique chance for a wealthy buyer (unless Mr. Hardy
Rodenstock of West Germany happens to have a cache). As far as is
known, Thomas Jefferson did not buy this wine."

Two years later the *Wine Spectator* published an April Fool's
account of a $5.7-million bid for a "red wine believed to have
belonged to Julius Caesar." The spoof went on to say that "[t]he
ancient clay amphora, which bears the initials 'J.C.,' was found in a
bombed-out cellar in Beirut, Lebanon, by well-known West German collector Hardy Rodenstock." Moreover, Michael Broadbent
had "verified the amphora as genuine" and stated that "[i]t may well
be [drinkable]. . . . Only last year I tried a 2,100-year-old red wine
from Crete. Although the color was somewhat faded and the flavors

had dried out a bit, it still retained a delicate bouquet of pine resin, ancient Roman sandals, and Minoan bull droppings." Rodenstock had been raising eyebrows for some time, but open mockery of the venerable Broadbent was something new.

The effects of the creeping cynicism on the rare-wine market were more serious, as auction houses experienced a softening of demand for old wines. At a June 28, 1990, sale at Christie's London, only a few of the dozen nineteenth-century Bordeaux on offer sold.

The doubts caused rifts in Rodenstock's inner circle, even before Walter Eigensatz became disillusioned. In 1987, Mario Scheuermann, the Hamburg journalist who had known Rodenstock since the late 1970s and had been to every one of his big tastings, attended the first Masters of Food & Wine event in Carmel, California. There, everyone asked him about rumors that Rodenstock's bottles were fakes. Upon his return to Hamburg, Scheuermann called Rodenstock and told him what people were saying. Rodenstock reacted angrily. Scheuermann responded that he was just the messenger, but Rodenstock wasn't pacified. He stopped speaking to Scheuermann. And once Eigensatz began openly expressing doubts about his bottles, Rodenstock several times threatened to sue his former friend.

Rodenstock increasingly alienated people in Bordeaux, with both his dispute with Lur Saluces and another campaign he waged against Christian Moueix, the young head of Pétrus who had publicly doubted Rodenstock's big Pétrus bottles from the 1920s. This time his target was Moueix's use of filtration, a controversial modern technique for clarifying wine before bottling. Rodenstock presented himself as a defender of tradition, and Bordeaux winemakers such as Lur Saluces and Moueix as destroyers of it.

Rodenstock's personal elusiveness was now writ larger. He moved among his many homes, communicating mainly by fax, as he continued to solicit new clients. In 1989, when Adnan Khashoggi, the Saudi arms dealer who was Dodi Al-Fayed's uncle, was briefly imprisoned in Berne, Switzerland, Rodenstock told people he had sent him a bottle of Pétrus and that, after his release, Khashoggi had placed a large order with him.

There was a sense of innocence lost among the German collectors. "In the beginning, we were all friends, interested in what each next wine would reveal, be like," Frenzel said later. "There was a wonderful sense of camaraderie. The problem was, when the newspapers wrote stories, then came jealousy and competition. The tastings became bigger, there were more journalists, who were more and more competitive with each other. There were more people who weren't into wine but were there for their image and the glamour. And then the women started coming to the tastings in 1989 or 1990, which made it worse. They brought out the worst qualities in their husbands: 'Oh, you have a big watch, mine's bigger.'" Frenzel thought it was the appearance of the big profile of Rodenstock in *Wine Spectator,* with its cover photograph of him chomping on a cigar, that turned many of his friends against him.

What had earlier been a sense of playful competition was now more acrimonious. Collectors who contributed rare bottles that showed badly resented Rodenstock's bottles, which always seemed to come out smelling like roses, and spread rumors that the bottles must be rigged. "It's the kindergarten syndrome," Scheuermann said. "The five children in the sandbox won't let the sixth in." But none of the rifts was as public and bitter, or had farther-reaching repercussions, as that with the man known as Herr Pétrus.

HANS-PETER FRERICKS lived in a southern suburb of Munich, not far from where Rodenstock had moved after leaving the tiny Westerwald town of Bad Marienberg in 1985. Frericks had gotten rich selling bicycle and car accessories, such as windshield wipers, in supermarkets. When the German government passed a law in 1988 requiring that every car contain four pairs of PVC "anti-AIDS" gloves in their glove compartments for first-aid purposes, Frericks made a killing. He had anticipated the legislation and filled a warehouse with the gloves.

Despite his vaunted enthusiasm for Pétrus, some of his fellow German collectors viewed him as more of a status drinker than a serious wine person. Bearded and shiny-domed, Frericks was wont to get loud and drunk, and he once posed for a magazine photographer in a restaurant kitchen wearing an apron with nothing underneath, buttocks exposed. By the end of the 1980s, his interest in wine was waning, and in 1989, Frericks decided to dispose of a substantial portion of his cellar. He asked Sotheby's to handle the sale. The head of the auction house's wine department, at the time, was David Molyneux-Berry, whose habitual look incorporated a bow tie, glasses, Vandyke beard, and ponytail. He had been with the department since its founding in 1970, and had recently become director. Broadbent, competitive as ever, later recalled Molyneux-Berry as "something and nothing, really . . . When I knew him when we were both at Harvey's, it was just David Berry. He became Molyneux-Berry when he went to Sotheby's."

Molyneux-Berry took Count Heinrich von Spreti, who would later become head of Sotheby's Germany, along to translate, and they drove to Frericks's villa. In the cellar they found astonishing rarities, including two Jefferson bottles, a 1784 Lafite and a 1787 Lafite. Rodenstock had sold them privately to Frericks shortly before the Forbes auction revealed how high a price the bottles might fetch, and Frericks had paid only 15,000 and 12,000 marks respectively (equivalent to around $5,100 and $4,000).

The cellar also boasted an Impériale of Mouton Rothschild 1924. That was the year Philippe de Rothschild hired the Cubist-influenced poster artist Jean Carlu to do the label, a bold move in stodgy Bordeaux. Seeing the bottle, Molyneux-Berry gulped. How on earth had this Frericks fellow gotten his hands on *that*? It surprised him that the bottle had a large label. Molyneux-Berry had sold one of these bottles himself at Sotheby's a few years before, and it had a regular-size label. Here in the Frericks cellar, there were also magnums of Mouton from exceedingly rare years, and magnums of Pétrus 1928. Nearly all were in perfect condition. The magnums felt somehow off to Molyneux-Berry; there wasn't anything specifically wrong, but they somehow weren't right, either. Then he realized: On several of the labels, the colors were incorrect. What was supposed to be red was more of a pink; what was supposed to be green was closer to turquoise. Molyneux-Berry believed he was surrounded by fakes.

Frericks had a perfectly maintained cellar book, and without looking at it, Molyneux-Berry began moving around the room, calling out the names and vintages of the bottles he thought were bogus. Behind him, von Spreti, reading from the immaculately kept cellar book, said, "Origin, Rodenstock." Over and over, "Origin, Rodenstock." Rodenstock had sold eighty bottles to Frericks, for a total of 150,000 marks, or $71,000. They included, besides the two Jefferson bottles, Lafites from 1844, 1858, 1864, and 1875; Yquems from 1852 and 1869; and Pétrus, all in double magnums, from 1921, 1924, 1926, 1928, and 1929. Every one of the bottles Molyneux-Berry thought were counterfeits turned out to have been sourced from Rodenstock.

Molyneux-Berry took another look at the '24 Mouton Impériale. Its colors were off, too, but there was something else. Not only were they wrong, they were wrong in a way that was vaguely familiar to Molyneux-Berry. Where had he seen those colors before? Suddenly, Molyneux-Berry remembered. A few years earlier, Mouton-Rothschild had published a coffee-table book, an illustrated history of its artist-commissioned labels. The book had reproduced the label colors in exactly the same wrong way. It was an artifact of the printing process.

After returning to London, Molyneux-Berry did further

research. He called Mouton, which confirmed that only three Impériales had been produced in 1924, and that it was highly unlikely any would have had a large label. Molyneux-Berry also phoned Monticello, which informed him of the scholarly doubts about the attribution of the Jefferson bottles. And following the Three Emperors dinner that fall, he heard reports of the suspect Pétrus bottles served there.

Only twice in his twenty years in the auction business had Molyneux-Berry refused a cellar. In one of the situations, "the guy was clearly involved in crime." In the second, the cellar, containing forty cases of 1982 first growths and 1982 Pétrus, belonged to a South American diplomat in Belgium; the auctioneer was convinced that drug money was being laundered. Now, Molyneux-Berry refused his third. On December 1, 1989, he sent a carefully worded letter to Frericks, politely declining the opportunity to auction his cellar and mentioning "significant doubt as to [the] origin" of some of the wine. "It was code," Molyneux-Berry said later, "for 'these bottles are fakes.'"

Soon after, Molyneux-Berry had another encounter with some Rodenstock wines. This time they were consigned to Farr Vintners, the London broker that had recently sold Bill Koch his four Jefferson bottles. The wines included an eighteenth-century Latour, which the head of the château wanted to give to a valued Japanese client. But first he asked Molyneux-Berry to assess the bottle's condition and provenance for him. Molyneux-Berry went down to the Farr offices and examined the bottle. Supposedly it came from the million-dollar cache Rodenstock claimed to have found in Venezuela. The bottle was old, but there was no provenance attached to it whatsoever. "I can't say it is," Molyneux-Berry concluded, "and I can't say it isn't."

By now, Molyneux-Berry was convinced that Rodenstock was a forger. It wasn't just the Frericks cellar or the Latour. Molyneux-Berry also recalled how several of the bottles Rodenstock had bought from Sotheby's had extremely low ullages. There had been a 1921 Trockenbeerenauslese like that, and later Molyneux-Berry had heard that Rodenstock had sold a bottle of the same wine, this one filled to the brim. Another time, Rodenstock had bought an empty Cognac bottle from the 1811 Comet vintage; later he had sold a full bottle of the same. Molyneux-Berry couldn't prove they weren't entirely different bottles, but they added to his doubts. Molyneux-Berry had come to believe that Rodenstock was "quite an evil man. If you look in his eyes, you see there's something cruel about him. They say, 'You don't know that I'm tricking you.' He's having a massive laugh at the wine world." The auctioneer went to Grey Gowrie, then Sotheby's chairman, and asked if the auction house might expose Rodenstock. The chairman, as Molyneux-Berry would recall later, replied that there was no percentage in alienating a potential client.

Early in 1991, Molyneux-Berry was flipping through an industry weekly called *Harper's Wine & Spirit Gazette* when a Christie's ad caught his eye. There, reproduced and silhouetted, were four large bottles of Pétrus and a 1924 Impériale of Mouton. He recognized them immediately as having come from the Frericks cellar. Molyneux-Berry called Broadbent. "I blew a wobbly," Molyneux-Berry said later. "It's not often that I lose my rag, but I said to Michael, 'How dare you do what you're doing? I'm certain they're fakes.'"

"What Pétrus?" Broadbent said.

What Pétrus? As if Broadbent sold 1920s Pétrus all the time? Molyneux-Berry was enraged.

"Michael, how dare you?!" Molyneux-Berry said. *"How dare you?!"*

"Well, anyway," Broadbent said, "Rodenstock has made Frericks withdraw the bottles. They're not going to be in the sale."

CHAPTER 13

RADIOACTIVE

ICHAEL BROADBENT—NOW IN HIS SIXTIES, hair gone white—stood in an administrative room on the campus of GSF-Forschungszentrum für Umwelt und Gesundheit, a government research institute in a desolate northern suburb of Munich. Before him was a long table covered with a white cloth. Hans-Peter Frericks and a couple of French journalists from Gault-Millau were to his left, a pair of German scientists to his right, all side by side in a line, all focused on one thing. Frericks had decided to have his bottle of 1787 Lafite forensically analyzed by scientists. It was July 19, 1991, and Broadbent had flown in from London for this. With a set of small hammers, he had just breached the seal. It was clearly less than ten years old. Broadbent drew the cork. It crumbled but came out quite easily, uncommon for a very old wine. Broadbent was worried.

The public doubts about his authentication of the Jefferson bottles hadn't dissipated. In 1990 a British article on counterfeit wine had quoted Monticello's Cinder Goodwin, who had married and was now Cinder Stanton, as saying, "I am not particularly impressed with Christie's research." Just this year *Wine Spectator* had run a cover story about Jefferson, "America's First Wine Connoisseur," accompanied by a sidebar about the Jefferson bottles, titled "Authentic Old Bottles, but Were They Jefferson's?" Though it took on faith the assessment by Broadbent that the bottles were legitimately old, and failed to mention that the magazine's proprietor, Marvin Shanken, owned one, the short piece rehashed the old arguments about the attribution to Jefferson. The recent furor between Rodenstock and Frericks posed the most serious challenge yet, and Broadbent was increasingly troubled by Rodenstock's refusal to reveal—even to him, even now—anything more about the bottles' provenance.

NOT LONG AFTER David Molyneux-Berry had turned down Frericks's cellar on behalf of Sotheby's, the Munich businessman had consigned it to Christie's. When Rodenstock subsequently learned about it, he insisted that he had sold bottles to Frericks on the condition that they would drink them together and with the understanding that they weren't for resale.

Alleging that he had sold Frericks the Jefferson bottles at a "friendship price" and strictly for the purpose of a Lafite vertical to which he, Rodenstock, was to have been invited, Rodenstock persuaded Broadbent to postpone the sale of the Frericks cellar. Frericks responded by obtaining a court order, issued on December 4, 1990, enjoining Rodenstock from publicly claiming that they had had such an agreement, on penalty of 500,000 marks or six months in jail. Rodenstock appealed the injunction, but later withdrew his appeal.

In the meantime, Frericks, now acutely suspicious, pulled his bottles from Christie's and began telling anyone who would listen that Rodenstock's objections to a resale must be due to the bottles being inauthentic. The two men traded accusations in Munich's tabloids. Frericks suggested that Rodenstock himself had tampered with the bottles. Frericks considered having the wine scientifically analyzed, but hesitated before doing so. If his suspicions were wrong, he would be destroying an irreplaceable historical artifact that had cost him a lot of money to buy. Ultimately, however, he resolved to have one of the two Jefferson bottles tested by GSF. Rodenstock then turned the tables by producing before-and-after photos purporting to show that the seal on the bottle when Rodenstock sold it to Frericks in November 1985 was different from the seal on it now, and that the corks and ullage had changed as well. On July 15, 1991, Frericks swore in court that "[a]t no time did I alter the bottle . . . I never had the bottles resealed or sealed." Four days later, on the outskirts of Munich, he and Broadbent came together to open it.

At GSF, Broadbent held the bottle in front of a candle: the sediment looked authentically old. Manfred Wolf, a bearded chemist in a short-sleeved shirt, poured two-thirds of the wine through a funnel into a glass container for analysis. Broadbent splashed a small amount out of the Jefferson bottle into a wineglass. Holding a sheet of white paper out as a backdrop, with Frericks looking on, Broadbent tilted the glass sideways against it, the wine becoming a wider, shallower, more translucent pool. He peered through his half-moon reading glasses. The brownish hue indicated great age. Broadbent sniffed, then sipped. The nose and palate, too, suggested an ancient wine. It tasted, Broadbent said, like the Mouton opened five years earlier at Mouton. He felt relieved. It remained only for the scientists to confirm his sensory impressions.

For much of his career, Broadbent's eminence as a taster had owed nothing to Rodenstock. In 1980 the Christie's auctioneer had published his magnum opus. *The Great Vintage Wine Book* was an encyclopedia of tastes, a compendium of notes on every wine that had passed Broadbent's lips since he first began jotting down his impressions in 1952. The oldest red Bordeaux he had tasted, and the only one from the eighteenth century, was the 1799 Lafite he had tasted one year earlier at Marvin Overton's vertical in Fort Worth. He had tasted no big-bottle Pétrus older than 1945. The oldest Yquem dated to 1867. There were no notes from Rodenstock tastings, and the German's name did not appear in the book.

By the time Broadbent updated the book in 1991, his reputation had become wholly entwined with Rodenstock's. Nearly all of the oldest and rarest bottles he had tasted, from a 1747 Yquem to a 1771 Margaux to the Jefferson bottles to a series of prewar Pétrus in large formats, were supplied by Rodenstock, whose tastings Broadbent had attended annually starting in 1984. In this edition, Broadbent said he had now tasted "one thousand wines" at Rodenstock tastings, and, with the GSF results pending, felt the need to include an appendix laying out his old case for the Jefferson bottles' authenticity, as well as retailing Rodenstock's claim that he "was not aware of the significance of the initials T. J. until the first bottle (of the 1784 vintage) was opened at Château d'Yquem."

In the six months after the opening at GSF, Broadbent would also fly twice to Bordeaux to see the printer of the labels on the large-format Pétrus bottles that had been at the center of much of the skepticism about Rodenstock. The wines dated from as far back as the 1920s, but the printer named at the bottom of the labels, Imprimerie Wetterwald Fréres, was still in business. On the first visit, Broadbent took along a double magnum of Pétrus 1945 that had come from Rodenstock, and a regular bottle of Pétrus 1945 from an unspecified "impeccable source." The bottles had different labels, but the printer explained to Broadbent that while offset lithography was used for regular-size labels, a different method was used for larger ones. Broadbent came away believing the double-magnum label to be "genuine." He next returned to Bordeaux with a double magnum of Pétrus 1921 from Rodenstock. "Wetterwald and his printers looked at it through magnifying glasses and pronounced it correct," Broadbent wrote later. If the GSF tests on

Frericks's Jefferson bottle went as well, maybe the whole controversy could finally be put to rest.

ON THE DAY of the test in Munich, Yeter Göksu, standing near Broadbent, had taken a sip of the wine and thought it tasted horrible—sweet and insipid. In her opinion, only an idiot would buy this wine for so much money. An elegant Turkish-born physicist in her forties, with black hair and green eyes, Göksu had recently been conducting experiments on whether food irradiation, the practice of zapping food with gamma rays or electron beams to extend its shelf life, had negative health effects. She had been focusing mainly on dried spices.

Half a liter of the wine in the Frericks bottle went to Wolf, the chemist, who worked in a different branch of the institute; Göksu got the dregs. She would use thermoluminescence, the same technology with which she analyzed irradiated cumin, to date the sediment. Her lab was a suite of rooms in a massive building across the road from her office. They were kept cool and lit by a dim red bulb. If the materials to be studied were exposed to light, it would contaminate the signal they yielded; it was the wine's purported history of containment in a dark bottle in a dark cellar that allowed it to be dated now by thermoluminescence.

In her lab, Göksu first poured out the five centimeters of liquid remaining in the bottle. Half she set aside for two other scientists to work with; the other half she would analyze herself. Then she turned the bottle upside down to shake out the sediment. A flat, rectangular object with a reddish, coppery hue clunked out onto the table. This was strange. What was a piece of metal doing in the bottom of a two-hundred-year-old bottle of wine? She gave it to some colleagues, Bernhard Hietel and Friedrich Schulz, who operated a linear particle accelerator elsewhere on the campus.

Their specialty was bombarding objects with a high-speed beam of protons fired down a barrel that began in one room and went through a wall into another. By measuring the wavelengths of the energy thrown off by the collision, the physicists could determine the constituent elements of the target. The piece of metal was, as they suspected from its appearance, solid lead. They next bombarded some of the wine itself to see how much lead was in it. Their test showed 11.3 milligrams of lead per liter, a toxic concentration. But this was inconclusive, as other nineteenth-century control bottles, which didn't have pieces of lead resting in their sediment, also showed a lead content five times as high as some bottles of Bordeaux from the 1980s. To the two men, the lead appeared to be a piece of the protective foil "capsule" that envelops the mouth and neck of modern wine bottles.

Göksu, meanwhile, was busy preparing to conduct her tests. The sediment from Frericks's Jefferson bottle was silty, with a few crystals mixed in. Göksu had to clean and dry it, ridding it of organic material by soaking it in alcohol, then letting the liquid evaporate. She also washed the dried sediment in an ultrasonic bath. She needed to isolate clean crystals. She ended up with enough for five samples.

Thermoluminescence relies on the recording, over the last several decades, of radiation levels around the world. Scientists know how the intensity of radiation in India differs from that in Iran, which differs from that in Canada, and they know how the intensities in each of these places have fluctuated year-to-year over the past half-century. Tell Göksu a radiation level, and she can say where and when it was recorded.

Crystalline materials such as feldspar and quartz are natural radiation detectors, trapping exactly as much energy in their structures as there is in their immediate environments. Tiny grains of these substances are ubiquitous in nature, and in the microscopic dust that invariably settles on plants. Even after plants have been processed—into, say, the spices Göksu had recently been studying, or the wine she was being asked to assess now—the crystals can be isolated. By heating them, and measuring the light emitted, Göksu could gauge the amount of radiation trapped inside. And that level, because it would exactly mirror the crystals' original environment, would reveal where, or at least when, the wine originated.

Göksu and a colleague flew to Paris and spent a day, with a Gault-Millau journalist as their guide, visiting three old cellars near the Bastille. Using a scintillator, an unwieldy device similar to a Geiger counter, they took baseline radiation measurements. She needed to factor in any natural environmental radiation that might have been present in the cellar where the bottle was said to have reposed for centuries. Paris, like Munich, was built on chalky ground, and the results were low.

Back in Munich, Göksu also measured the natural radiation in the now-empty bottle, in order to have a clear idea of whether the bottle itself had affected the radiation level of the sediment. She took several small foil containers, each holding crystals, taped them to strings, and lowered them into the bottle with the strings flowing out for later retrieval. She taped additional packets to the outside of the bottle, both along its trunk and in the punt. She wrapped the head of the bottle in white tape, secured it with a red rubber band, fastened the bottle to a tray with black tape, and left it undisturbed for the next 226 days.

In March of 1992, eight months after the opening of the bottle in Broadbent's presence, Göksu was able to measure the radiation of the sediment and compare it with her Paris and bottle baselines. How old the wine itself was would be for her colleagues to assess, but she could confidently say that the sediment was 220 years old (confidently, that is, after allowing for a plus-or-minus ninety-two-year margin of error). In other words, it was definitely between 128 and 312 years old, meaning it came from some vintage between 1680 and 1864. It might, as advertised, come from 1787.

At GSF's Institute for Hydrology, meanwhile, Manfred Wolf

was getting some surprising results. A chemist whose work normally involved assessing the nuclear contamination of, say, different depths of the Munich aquifer, Wolf's expertise was radioactive isotopes whose clockwork decay could be exploited to date organic materials. He had tasted the wine on the day the bottle was opened and found it "not so bad." After doing all the tedious prep work necessary to isolate a lab-worthy sample of the wine, he first tested it for tritium, an unstable element that had risen in atmospheric concentration starting in 1945, when the first atomic bomb was detonated, and peaked in 1963, when the Partial Test Ban Treaty brought open-air testing to an end. Tritium levels had been declining steadily ever since. If no tritium showed up in the test, it was a certainty that the wine predated 1945.

What Wolf found, however, was that the wine possessed an extraordinary amount of tritium, a level consistent only with either 1962 or 1965. He repeated the test to be sure, using a less sensitive method since there was so much tritium present, and got the same result. It was just a bottle of wine to Wolf, but he was mildly shocked. He had assumed the bottle was what it purported to be, a two-hundred-year-old relic.

Next, Wolf's assistant tested the wine for carbon-14, which had a much longer half-life and could be used to date older things. But C-14, too, had peaked in the nuclear era, and the test showed a level of the isotope that indicated either 1962 or 1976–79 as the date of origin. The result was so unexpected that, to be absolutely certain of it, Wolf sent a sample to the University of Toronto. Toronto had an expensive piece of equipment, an Accelerator Mass Spectrometer, which could do more-precise carbon dating. That test yielded the same result. Combining the two findings, Wolf concluded that in all likelihood the wine dated to 1962.

So the sediment was old, as Broadbent had correctly identified, but the wine was young, as he had not. Leaving aside whatever questions these results raised about the reliability of the auctioneer's vaunted palate, the bottle had clearly been tampered with. The questions were when, and by whom.

On June 23, a year after GSF first opened the bottle, it held a press conference to announce the results. In short order, Frericks issued a press release. He noted Monticello's continuing skepticism and averred that "the person who is responsible for the falsification of the wine, which is now scientifically proved (and it has to be believed that other old bottles are also affected), apparently has ambitions to rank among the great counterfeiters of our times." Frericks encouraged the owners of other Jefferson bottles to step forward and have their bottles tested. The next day, taking Frericks' lead, a Munich tabloid announced: "The most expensive wine in the world is watered down . . . the Konrad Kujau of the grapevine has been exposed!"

THE COMPARISON WITH Kujau, forger of the Hitler diaries, was richly apt. The diaries had come to light in 1983, two years before the Jefferson bottles. Whatever the origin of the bottles—whether real or fake—both cases involved sensational discoveries of supposedly long-lost objects at historically serendipitous moments: the Hitler diaries on the fiftieth anniversary of the Nazis' ascension to power, the Jefferson bottles on the bicentennial of Jefferson's visit to Bordeaux. In both cases, tantalizing documentary references to misplaced objects existed (a missing trunk of Hitler's possessions, a misrouted box of Jefferson's wine), specific enough to make a discovery plausible, vague enough to make it irrefutable. Like the editors of *Stern,* the German newsweekly that was misled into publishing what it thought was the scoop of the century, Rodenstock claimed that skeptics were motivated by jealousy. Like Gerd Heidemann, the *Stern* reporter who obtained the spurious diaries, Rodenstock kept changing his story as to why he couldn't reveal his supplier, sometimes claiming tax reasons, sometimes saying he'd

"promised" his supplier he wouldn't name him, and sometimes saying he wanted to write about it himself one day. Like both Kujau
and Heidemann, Rodenstock made use of the Iron Curtain to
obfuscate the origin of many of his bottles, especially his Yquems,
claiming they'd been smuggled out of Russia illicitly. With regard to
large-format bottles of Pétrus, Rodenstock cited an explanation
identical to one used by Heidemann: the lack of prewar records.
And in both cases, celebrated experts had authenticated the objects.

Reaction to the GSF results in the wine world came quickly.
James Laube, a columnist for *Wine Spectator,* publicly called on
Rodenstock to come clean about the provenance of the Jefferson
bottles. And the repercussions were felt beyond the tiny club of rich
men who owned the bottles. Auctioneers and merchants from
Germany to Switzerland to the UK reported severe disruptions in
the old-wine market. "There is almost no interest in nineteenth- or
eighteenth-century wines anymore," Stephen Browett, whose Farr
Vintners had sold more Jefferson bottles than anyone else, told
Wine Spectator in early 1993. "Since the story broke in the press last
June, collectors have treated pre-1900 bottles with skepticism."

Even Broadbent seemed fed up with it all. "I just wish Hardy
Rodenstock would say how he came by these bottles," he told a
newspaper. "It's doing a tremendous amount of damage to the old
fine and rare market."

~

CHAPTER 14

LETTERS FROM HUBSI

DARKLY SUGGESTING THAT THE FIX WAS IN, Rodenstock claimed that the Frericks bottle had been doctored in order to hurt his wine business. He also issued a statement in which he asserted that "the renowned Jefferson Institute [i.e., Monticello] has found enough evidence . . . to prove that Jefferson indeed ordered the wines." Alleging that it was the "assumption of many wine experts" that Frericks had replaced the original wine in the bottle with new wine and changed the seal, Rodenstock filed a complaint with the Munich state prosecutor charging Frericks with "making a false public oath." Under German law, the prosecutor was required to take the complaint at face value, and he launched an investigation into Frericks.

Rodenstock sought to cast suspicion on GSF as well. He pointed to the facts that GSF had not charged Frericks for the test and had failed to examine the cork and sealing wax scientifically. GSF responded that Broadbent had said that the cork and wax were no more than ten years old (to which Broadbent said he had only been referring to the wax seal). The lead in the wine was reported to be modern lead foil (thus evidence of tampering), though how that exculpated Rodenstock and implicated Frericks was unclear. The state prosecutor ordered a police raid on GSF, and the cork, bottle, and seal were confiscated.

In the ensuing proceedings, Frericks presented several pieces of evidence, including a letter to his wife, Marianne, calling Frericks "a sick, bald-headed fool," accusing him of an extramarital affair, and signed "Uschi Berthold." A handwriting expert testified that the letter had almost certainly been penned by Rodenstock. Frericks wanted his money returned. "A reliable dealer would do that voluntarily," he said.

Frericks said that Rodenstock's before-and-after photographs must be "a photo montage" or "an optical trick" or, if real, that there was no way to certify when exactly they had been taken. Rodenstock responded to this by bringing forward a Bad Marienberg photo studio he said could confirm that the photos had been taken in 1985, before Rodenstock sold Frericks his Jefferson bottles. Frericks's lawyer retorted that he had plenty of eyewitnesses who could attest that the seal on the bottle as presented to GSF was identical to the seal at the time when Frericks first purchased it. Rodenstock responded, "[Clearly] Mr. Frericks didn't expect me to have the bottle photographed in its original condition in 1985. . . . I sold the bottle to Mr. Frericks in the same condition I bought it—in its original condition!"

Rodenstock had, of course, resealed the bottle himself. As he wrote to the editor of the *VWGA Journal* in June of 1985, "I have sealed all the bottles," and the photograph Rodenstock sent along with the letter showed one of the bottles with a seal very similar to the one Rodenstock was now accusing Frericks of adding. The fall 1985 issue of the *Journal* had included the letter and photo, and would have been powerful evidence in support of Frericks, but the obscurity of the publication ensured that neither Frericks nor his lawyers discovered it.

Rodenstock had an edge when it came to media relations. Most of the important German-language wine journalists were longtime recipients of his generosity. "Hardy Rodenstock is a friend of mine," *Alles über Wein*'s Heinz-Gert Woschek said later. "It was very delicate for me to write objectively." The longer articles that appeared in wine magazines had a distinctly pro-Rodenstock bias. Urged by a mutual friend, Rodenstock reached out to Mario Scheuermann, to whom he had stopped speaking five years earlier, but who now wrote for the respected Hamburg broadsheet *Welt am Sonntag*. Scheuermann then wrote an article about the GSF results, from Rodenstock's point of view.

"For everybody in the inner circle, whatever they thought of Hardy, they thought Frericks was an unserious person," Scheuermann recalled. "His attitude was always, 'I'm the biggest.' His tastings were more of a wine carnival."

Journalists and trade members in Switzerland, where Rodenstock had bought and sold a lot of bottles over the years, were less kind to him. Franz Wermuth, an auctioneer at Steinfels in Zurich, where Rodenstock was a regular, recalled that in the 1980s, four mid-shoulder bottles of 1924 Pétrus had come up for sale. This was a wine so rare that Wermuth had never before seen it on the market. Rodenstock bought all four bottles; later, at one of his tastings in Arlberg, he served a double magnum—four bottles' worth—of 1924 Pétrus. Wermuth had also noticed that Rodenstock was more interested in bottles with low fills than in those in good condition. Wermuth aired the theory that Rodenstock was buying these heavily ullaged bottles at bargain prices, then topping them up with young wine and selling them for large profits.

"Somebody is carrying out active protection of the environment with clever bottle recycling," Wermuth suggested wryly. "At least ten books with tasting information about old wines must now be basically rewritten."

Rodenstock sent Wermuth a letter purporting to describe the

complex evidence in support of the Jefferson bottles, but which devolved into pseudoscientific gibberish:

> It is extremely important for the determination that the Jefferson wines are absolutely authentic; there were clear signs of multi-element processes for the simultaneous determination of many elements, both processes of long wave and energy dispersing Roentgen fluorescence, the expensive atom emission spectroscopy with inductive coupled plasma stimulation and the strongly provable neutron activation processes for ultra-trace elements as radio-chemical activating analysis for group element examination and as instrumental activation analysis for individual element studies.

Rodenstock had earlier suggested to *Der Spiegel* that it was possible he himself had been conned, but the editors of *Vinum,* a Swiss wine magazine, took a jaundiced view of this. They saw it as a case of Rodenstock hedging his bets "in case the scientists were to reveal the 1787 as adulterated." Pointing out that there was no proof that the two bottles in the before-and-after photographs were identical—and noting discrepancies in the engravings—the magazine scoffed at Rodenstock's protestations in the media that there was no reason for him or his supplier to add new wine to the bottle, "as if a 1787 is not worth a bit more than a 1962."

Both Wermuth and *Vinum* subsequently received a series of angry letters from Rodenstock. In one, Rodenstock spoke of "the steaming turds that you leave behind you everywhere." Another stream of letters, attacking Wermuth and *Vinum* and defending Rodenstock, arrived from one Hubert Meier, who identified himself as a sommelier in Munich. While exhibiting a detailed knowledge of Rodenstock's tastings, Meier didn't hand-sign his letters or include his address, *Vinum* was unable to locate anyone by that name and description, and no one in Munich had heard of him. And Wermuth noticed that both the Hubert Meier letters and others written under different names seemed to have been typed on the same machine, one with a raised letter *e*. Among themselves, *Vinum*'s editors jokingly referred to the apparently pseudonymous letter writer as "Hubsi," and in the magazine, they critiqued his spelling, called him "Little Darling," and otherwise mocked him.

"Naturally our buddy is upset," editor Rudolf Knoll wrote. "Hubsi, let's hear from you." When the magazine subsequently received another mysterious, unsigned, no-return-address letter, this one from "Uschi Berthold, Munich" (the same person who had written to Frericks's wife), the editors wondered, in the magazine: "Perhaps our friend has undergone a sex change. . . ."

PREVIOUSLY, WHEN HIS wines had been questioned on the basis of how they tasted, Rodenstock had been able to fall back on his unrivaled experience. How an old wine might taste was so uncertain that only the most knowledgeable could confidently assert whether a particular bottle was as it should be. In this uncertain environment, Rodenstock and Broadbent were elite possessors of occult knowledge, high priests no one dared challenge. When Rodenstock played the experience card, it was a conversation stopper. Those few who had the temerity to doubt him, Rodenstock would belittle as lacking the expertise to do so. Regarding the Jefferson bottles, he would always cite the 1985 lab test he had had performed on the 1787 Yquem.

But rival scientific evidence was something he had never before faced. He couldn't dismiss it with rhetoric. Late in the summer of 1992—with the GSF test results pointing to some kind of tampering, with Frericks telling everyone who would listen that the Jefferson bottles were "the Hitler diaries of wine," and with open derision in Swiss wine circles—Rodenstock retained Raphael Mullis, a Zurich lawyer. Mullis had attended several of his tastings, first gaining entrée by agreeing to serve as a *commis* at one of the Arlberg events, and in later years attending as a guest and serving as notary for corks and bottles. On Rodenstock's behalf, Mullis threatened legal action against both *Vinum* and the Steinfels auction house. Whenever a letter from Mullis arrived, Wermuth, the auctioneer, would instruct his secretary to address his response to "Mr. Moulis," the name of a minor Bordeaux appellation.

By now, Rodenstock had determined that he needed more persuasive evidence to make his case. Again using Mullis as his lawyer, Rodenstock gave a small bottle of "1787 Lafite" engraved with "Th.J." to the Eidgenössische Technische Hochschule in Zurich. ETH was home to Georges Bonani, a chemical archaeologist who in 1989 had used carbon dating to debunk the Shroud of Turin. On August 27, Rodenstock, Mullis, Broadbent, and Bonani assembled at ETH to open the bottle. The men gathered in a spartan meeting room with a panoramic black-and-white photograph of the Manhattan skyline on the wall. For the sake of comparison, Rodenstock had brought along an old Burgundy, a half-bottle of 1893 Pommard. As expected for a younger wine, it had a higher fill level than the "1787 Lafite." The Pommard's cork came out cleanly.

The Lafite was placed upright on a wood conference table, and Rodenstock hunched over the bottle and worked on the crumbly gray wax seal with a knife, while Broadbent sat writing his observations in one of his red notebooks. The cork, black and shrunken, crumbled as it was drawn, and appeared to be considerably older than the cork from the Pommard. Rodenstock rolled up his sleeves and loosened his tie.

Broadbent brought the bottle close to his face, then poured a small glass. He held it against the white backdrop of a notebook page, and Rodenstock and Bonani leaned in to examine it. The wine was pale. Broadbent poured a small amount into a test tube, which he then sealed, to give to Professor E. T. ("Teddy") Hall, an Oxford scientist. Like Bonani, Hall had been involved in dating the Shroud of Turin, although he had first made his name, in the 1950s, by using X-ray fluorescence to debunk the Piltdown fossils as a hoax. Hall was also "a very keen wine man," in Broadbent's words, with a substantial cellar, part of which Christie's would later sell. Rodenstock, Mullis, and Broadbent each tasted the wine. It had no fruit left, and was Madeira-like, though not so sweet. Broadbent and Mullis were both convinced the wine was old and authentic.

Afterward, Rodenstock, Broadbent, and Mullis ate lunch at a posh hotel on Lake Zurich. Later, Rodenstock would take a blue ballpoint and inscribe the back of a photograph of the bottle-opening at ETH for Mullis: "For a 200-year-old wine, very interesting." But even Rodenstock's Swiss lawyer—to whom Rodenstock revealed no more about the Jefferson bottles' provenance than he had to Broadbent—was puzzled by something: the bottle was tiny. It wasn't even as large as a half-bottle. None of the articles describing Rodenstock's find had ever mentioned tiny bottles being part of the cache.

Broadbent returned to London carrying the sample for Professor Hall. At Oxford, Hall produced a 1955 Lafite from his own cellar, and Broadbent a 1962 Lafite from Christie's cellar, for comparison. Both were opened, and a portion of each sent back to Zurich for Bonani to use as well. Hall was going to test the 1787 Lafite sample, as well as the younger Lafites. He cautioned Broadbent that while it was possible to prove that something dated from after the onset of the atomic era, there was a two-hundred-year gap before that when, because of the imprecision of carbon dating, it was nearly impossible to come up with a positive finding.

TO JUDGE BY the reports in the wine media, things soon began to go Rodenstock's way. In December, Rodenstock received Bonani's report at his address in Monaco. Bonani had used accelerator mass spectrometry, the same technology used by the University of Toronto as part of the GSF tests. Writing from Zurich on December 7, 1992, Bonani reported that his radiocarbon dating pegged the wine around 1830, with a thirty-five-year margin of error. This meant that the wine's vintage could fall anywhere between 1795 and 1865. The cork's date range, meanwhile, was between 1825 and 1895. Bonani wrote that "the radiocarbon tests carried out on the 1787 Lafite show no mixing of wine younger than 1962. The reported age of the wine and its cork fall within the confidence limits." Hall, according to Broadbent, obtained a similar result. The Oxford lab would later report that it could not find the results, a highly unusual event, according to its deputy director.

In actuality, Rodenstock had not proved his case. Although old, both wine and cork had been shown to be younger than 1787. Moreover, the 1985 lab result purporting to show that the cork in the 1787 Yquem was "original" had analyzed its chemical composition but proven nothing about the age of the wine or the cork. To the contrary, Heinz Eschnauer, a German chemist to whom Rodenstock had sent part of the cork, specifically rejected Rodenstock's contention that it was possible to confirm the wine's age based on the tests he performed. This was the same scientist who, according to a note by Broadbent in a 1986 auction catalog, had "rigorously examined" the 1784 Yquem Christie's ended up selling to Iyad Shiblaq/Dodi Al-Fayed. Most damningly, on December 14, 1992, the Munich court found that in the case of the Frericks bottle tested earlier, Rodenstock "adulterated the wine or knowingly offered adulterated wine."

Remarkably, the explicit finding of guilt went unnoted in the wine media, the science of the 1985 tests went unanalyzed, and Rodenstock and Broadbent reveled in their test result, glossing over the fact that it wasn't actually exculpatory. On December 15, 1992, writing from Monte Carlo, Rodenstock told *Rarities* co-editor Dennis Foley, who was sympathetic to the German, that the recent test had vindicated him: There was no post-1962 wine in the bottle that had just been carbon dated; moreover, "the wine couldn't be younger than 1795 on average." Rodenstock raised questions about GSF's impartiality—why had it taken a year to do the test and announce the results?—and suggested again that Frericks must have manipulated the bottle provided to GSF.

The New Year came and went. On January 7, 1993, Broadbent eagerly wrote to Kip Forbes to reassure him. "Dear Kit," his letter began, inauspiciously. "First of all, thank you for the charming family Christmas card. Always beautifully done." Broadbent went on to say that the Zurich bottle had passed "with flying colors" and that "there is no reason to doubt that any of the Jefferson bottles which emanated directly from Hardy Rodenstock's cellar have been tampered with."

He also asserted that Cinder Stanton's allegation that Jefferson never had his bottles engraved had been "disproved," citing a September 17, 1789, letter from Jefferson to John Jay that Broadbent had discovered after the original furor in 1985. (Broadbent had since amassed a substantial Jefferson library.) In a postscript regarding a shipment of wine to George Washington, Jefferson had written, "Every bottle is marked (with a diamond) with the initial letter of the wine it contains." Though the evidence related only to a single shipment of wine—a shipment to Washington rather than to himself, which included no red Bordeaux and only the generically described "Sauternes"—and mentioned only a one-initial engraving, Broadbent claimed vindication. One month later, in a letter to Margaret Kelly, the Forbes Galleries curator at the time of the original auction, Broadbent was more pointed. "The researchers at Monticello said that there was simply no evidence of Jefferson giving instructions for bottles to be identified by engraving," Broadbent wrote. "How wrong they are."

That spring, a lawyer for another owner of some Jefferson

bottles, Bill Koch, expressed concern about the Frericks dispute. Koch's office hired a Munich lawyer, Jack Schiffer, to look into it. Schiffer was satisfied by the evidence of the Bonani test, and Koch didn't pursue the matter further.

On January 21, Rodenstock gloated to Foley, who was preparing a big article on the whole affair for *Rarities,* that the minister of research who had oversight of GSF, Hans Riesenhuber, had been fired two days earlier. Rodenstock suggested that the ouster was due to mistakes related to the Frericks test, including not charging Frericks for its cost. The following month, on February 15, Rodenstock wrote to Foley again. In this letter, Rodenstock set down a few further thoughts about Pétrus large-format bottles, the Jefferson-Yquem connection, and the recent Bonani/Hall tests, and he enclosed copies of friendly letters to him from Frericks sent as recently as the late 1980s. Only "jealousy and envy," Rodenstock said, could have motivated Frericks to come forward with doubts years later. On February 23, Michael Broadbent wrote to Foley, including the 1789 Jefferson letter to John Jay mentioning diamond engraving, and concluded, "Let's hope the whole subject can now be dropped."

Rodenstock and Frericks tentatively agreed to a settlement in which they would stop denouncing one another and drop their respective legal claims, but Rodenstock couldn't help himself. "Churchill always said that it is important who wins the last battle," Rodenstock crowed. "As the experts have accepted, the wine can only be authentic. This has been proved by the exact and encompassing examinations in Oxford and Zurich. Whoever it was who poured new wine in the other bottle in an attempt to harm me, thank God he didn't succeed."

When Foley's *Rarities* article came out, it included an entirely personal tangent about Frericks, describing him as a drunk and, quoting a German newspaper, "a flathead." Frericks and Rodenstock wouldn't reach a final settlement until 1995.

∼

IN SPITE OF the scandal, Rodenstock claimed that his business had grown substantially from 1991 to 1992, and he continued to make the international wine scene. He was now often accompanied by Helga Lehner, a blond Munich actress he had married in 1991. In early 1994, Rodenstock and Georg Riedel hosted a blind tasting of French versus Napa wines, attended by twenty-four journalists, including Hugh Johnson, dean of English wine writers. The following year, in November, Rodenstock attended a lavish tasting in Ohio hosted by an ob-gyn who stored his 18,000-bottle collection in an underground bank vault he had bought and repurposed. And Rodenstock received two important new endorsements which suggested that the luster of his name had been at least partially restored by the tests in Zurich and at Oxford.

The first came from the Rothschilds, the first family of Bordeaux, whose name graced two of the five first growths. In 1994 the family acquired one of the Jefferson bottles to display at Waddesdon Manor, ancestral seat of an Anglo-Austrian branch of the dynasty and now a part-time tourist site overseen by Lord Jacob Rothschild and owned by England's National Trust. The Waddesdon Wine Cellars were opening, and Michael Broadbent, who had kept the empty pint-sized bottle from the Bonani test at Christie's on King Street, presented it to Lord Rothschild at London's Spencer House on February 15. (Château Lafite itself donated a magnum of 1870, and Philippine de Rothschild, when she saw it, made a one-upping gift of 1868 Mouton.) The following week, Lord Rothschild sent a thank-you note to Rodenstock. The bottle took its place in a Lucite case in the cellar. A few years later, at the invitation of Lord Rothschild, Rodenstock and his wife would attend a lunch thrown at Waddesdon by Gordon Getty.

In 1995, Rodenstock executed his greatest public-relations coup yet, drawing Hugh Johnson and Robert Parker to his annual tasting. Johnson normally avoided such events (two years earlier, he had written witheringly about "the awe-inspiring vulgarity of some of America's wine spectaculars"). Parker, though, was the real catch. He had, by this time, achieved an importance in the wine world unmatched by critics in other fields. It was hard for a retailer to sell a wine Parker didn't like, and hard not to sell one he had praised. Though Parker was controversial—for his power over the market, for the largely European perception that he favored "obvious," overconcentrated wines, for the silly precision of his 100-point scoring system—he was widely respected for his independence, integrity, and indifference to Bordeaux's traditional hierarchy. He had launched his newsletter, *The Wine Advocate,* with Ralph Nader as his model, did not accept advertising, and, unlike many other wine writers, eschewed junkets and gift bottles.

Parker had some experience with old-wine collectors. It had been Bipin Desai who arranged for him to first taste Margaux 1900, which Parker then awarded 100 points in *The Wine Advocate*. But for the most part, Parker steered clear of mega-tastings, and he had declined several invitations to previous Rodenstock events. Eventually the two men were brought together by Daniel Oliveros and Jeff Sokolin, the Russian-born cousin of Bill Sokolin, for whom both men had worked before launching their own rarities business, Royal Wine Merchants. Among colleagues, Oliveros and Sokolin were known as "the sexy boys," because they seemed to have an exclusive line on "sexy juice"—old bottles in large formats that nobody else offered. They were close to Parker, and they were believed to serve as Rodenstock's distributors in America.

At some events in 1994 and 1995, Parker met Rodenstock and found, as he would later tell his newsletter subscribers, that "the unkind remarks I had read about him were untrue. A man of extraordinary charm and graciousness, Rodenstock is a true wine lover in the greatest sense of the word, as well as exceptionally knowledgeable, and generous to a fault (he charges nothing for the opportunity to participate in his tastings). His passion for wine history, and of course, the world's greatest wines, is irrefutable." Parker went on to say he had been persuaded to attend Rodenstock's annual tasting in 1995 by three things: Rodenstock's conviction that Pomerol had been given short shrift by the wine media, his "obsession with finding extraordinarily old bottles of Pomerol from private cellars in Europe," and his sheer "passion and enthusiasm."

At the tasting, held at the Königshof Hotel in Munich, Rodenstock included a vertical showcasing l'Eglise Clinet, a relatively unknown Pomerol estate. Parker tasted many older vintages of the wine for the first time, and later gave them top scores. At the same event, Rodenstock pulled out all the stops with a 10:00 a.m. "pre-phylloxera breakfast," at which he served sixteen pre-phylloxera wines blind, including both an 1874 Ausone and an 1847 Rausan-Segla. Parker was the guest of honor. He called the 1811 and 1847 Yquems "the greatest Yquems I have tasted." The 1811 was "liquefied crème brûlée"; the 1847 "would have received more than 100 points if possible." A photograph captured him and Rodenstock huddled together, talking about the wines. On his flight home to Baltimore, by way of London, Parker "set a personal record for mineral water consumption," he wrote in his newsletter.

"Not only was the weekend the most extraordinary three days of wine tasting, superb eating, and wine camaraderie that I have ever experienced, but it stands as the wine event of my lifetime," Parker wrote. If he had any doubts about the authenticity of the bottles, they were laid to rest by the presence of Broadbent. "The condition of the bottles was extraordinary," Parker wrote. "No other than Michael Broadbent authenticated the age of the bottles." In the next edition of Parker's massive *Bordeaux,* his reference guide to the world's greatest wine region, the critic thanked Rodenstock and included several tasting notes from the 1995 tasting.

As the most powerful person in the wine world, someone depended on by rich neophytes unsure of their palates, Parker had just given Hardy Rodenstock an exceedingly valuable public seal of approval. Rodenstock began boasting that, before the tasting, he had bought up all the old l'Eglise Clinet on the market, confident that Parker would award high scores and send the wine's price soaring.

CHAPTER 15

"AWASH IN FAKES"

*I*N 1996 A SECRET CONCLAVE OF FIFTEEN LEADING players in the rare-wine market met in a boardroom at the Intercontinental Hotel in London. Merchants and auctioneers who normally competed with each other, they included Serena Sutcliffe from Sotheby's, a representative from Christie's, Stephen Browett from Farr Vintners, and Tim Littler, the Whitwhams merchant whose Jefferson bottle had been broken by Bill Sokolin. Sotheby's insisted that everyone sign confidentiality agreements. The topic of discussion was wine piracy.

In the last three years, fine-wine prices had exploded. In late 1993, New York State legalized wine auctions, and in 1995 and 1996, auction totals in the United States surpassed those in the UK. In 1996, worldwide wine auction sales exceeded $70 million, more than twice the amount in 1994. A lot more wine was being sold, and the center of the auction market had shifted from its historical base in England to the United States.

The profits to be made from selling trophy wines, and the relative ease of forging them, had yielded a flood of bogus bottles on the market. Invariably they were the wines with the most shocking price tags—cult labels, in cult vintages. Pétrus '61. Romanée-Conti '90. Mouton-Rothschild '45. Cheval Blanc '47. Le Pin '82. Often they were in magnums.

The prices for these rarities had seemed to soar in the 1980s, but in the 1990s they rose vertically. In 1996 a case of six magnums of '82 Le Pin fetched $47,740 at Sotheby's, while a case of '45 Mouton brought in $112,500 at Zachys-Christie's in New York. With the exception of Mouton, Cheval Blanc, and a few others, these wines had tiny productions—Pétrus, rarely more than 3,500 cases a year; Le Pin, six hundred cases on average—and their rarity only added to their cachet and market value. Yet Pétrus '82 was raining from the sky. Merchants who never used to see '45, '47, or '61 Pétrus in magnum were now being offered it every week. Littler and a few others believed the trade needed to take action.

The London summit began ambitiously. A letter was drafted, with the idea of collectively sending it to the major French châteaux and negociants asking for more-stringent anti-piracy measures: short capsules, so corks could be read; embedded codes in the labels; vintages embossed in the bottle glass. Someone from Farr, which, despite having become a well-respected player, hadn't entirely escaped its upstart reputation, mentioned the name of a Burgundy broker based in Paris: he was a major source of theirs, and they'd been encountering problems with a lot of the DRC they received from him. It was speculated that Rodenstock might get some of his wine from the broker. Farr said they'd stop using the man if everyone else would.

But self-interest and apathy conspired to kill the whole initiative. Half the room wouldn't agree to stop using the dubious source of rare Burgundy. As for the letter, a British broker predicted glumly that the French would say, "That's why you shouldn't buy from foreign negociants, only straight from the châteaux." The letter was never sent. The meeting went nowhere. Given the confidentiality agreements, it also went unreported at the time.

"Serena told me Sotheby's couldn't be seen as in association with Farr Vintners," one participant recalled, claiming that her behavior then quickly changed. "Suddenly, Serena disapproved. Two weeks later, she gave an interview to the *Times* about the counterfeiting problem." The merchant laughed bitterly. "Sotheby's does no checks at all."

IN WINE CIRCLES, talking openly about fraudulent wine remained virtually taboo, and Christie's and Sotheby's continued to disagree about the scope of the problem. Sutcliffe was singularly outspoken about its seriousness, and given to pronouncements regarding provenance, like, "If the trail goes dead, you have to drop the transaction." Two years later she would tell *Wine Spectator* that the market was "awash in fakes." Christie's Broadbent and Paul Bowker, along with Rodenstock, were dismissive, minimizing the problem as exaggerated.

Yet it was clearly expanding. Only a year after raving about the Rodenstock tasting, Robert Parker published an essay titled "In Vino Veritas?" The article focused on "the growing evidence of phony bottles" in "the gray market," meaning distribution channels outside of authorized supply chains. "[R]are wine may be the only luxury-priced commodity in the world that does not come with a guarantee of authenticity," Parker wrote. "The appearance of dishonest segments of society with only one objective, to take full advantage of the enormous opportunity that exists to make a quick buck by selling bogus wines, is not that shocking. This has always been a problem, but based on the number of letters and telephone calls I have received from victims who have been the recipients of suspiciously-labeled wines, with even more unusual contents, it is a subject that needs to be addressed."

Parker himself had seen numerous fakes, but added that all of his own experiences dealing with the gray market had been on the up-and-up. When he republished the essay in the next edition of his big book, he added a few sentences reporting that Pétrus owner Christian Moueix said that old vintages of Pétrus in big bottles, especially, should be considered suspect. Soon his fax machine was buzzing with indignant letters from Rodenstock.

REPORTS OF FAKERY, since the episode with the fabricated Warhol Mouton labels, had been sporadic prior to the early 1990s. When there were incidents, they often involved the 1982 vintage, which had drawn speculators and seen price increases unlike any other modern vintage. Near the end of 1985, French police arrested several people in the right-bank city of Libourne and seized some seventy cases of regional plonk masquerading as 1981 and 1982 Pétrus. In 1990, five cases of 1986 DRC Montrachet, sold by the Wine Merchant of Beverly Hills to a Japanese collector, turned out to be cheap Pouilly-Fumé, gussied up with fake labels.

As wine prices, especially those of luxury labels, soared in the early nineties, incidents began cropping up much more regularly. In 1995, at a dinner in Hong Kong, a merchant from England's Corney & Barrow was served a fake magnum of 1982 Le Pin. In 1996 an attempt to sell fake 1982 Le Pin was uncovered in the UK; the forger had simply relabeled and altered the corks of some 1987 Le Pin, which sold for £1,300 ($2,000) less per bottle. In the late 1990s a London customer became suspicious of a bottle of 1982 Pétrus he had bought from a New York wine merchant for $2,000. He took it to château owner Christian Moueix, who examined it in the presence of *Wine Spectator*'s James Suckling. The bottle seemed legitimate until the capsule was removed and the cork drawn; the cork had two small indentations on its sides, indicating that it had previously been removed. It also lacked a vintage mark; the old one had apparently been sanded off. Moueix and Suckling tasted the wine, which was obviously not a 1982; they speculated it was Pétrus, but a lesser and much cheaper vintage, such as 1980 or 1984. In March of 1998, Langton's, an auction house in Australia, discovered some phony 1990 Penfold's Grange, the most famous red wine Down Under.

Older fakes were a less common occurrence, in part because older wines constituted only a sliver of the market. But they were worth much more money than young wines, and easier to pull off. In 1985 two American businessmen bought a magnum of 1865 Lafite, supposedly from the legendary Rosebery cellar, for $12,000. When they opened it, at a $1,500-a-head fundraising dinner in San Francisco, several people present who had previously tasted 1865 Rosebery Lafites deemed it fake. Marvin Overton III thought it was 1911 Lafite. Robert Mondavi said the cork looked five or ten years old. One of the two businessmen who had acquired the bottle thought it tasted like a faded rosé. Then came the string of incidents involving questionable, Rodenstock-sourced bottles at megatastings in the late 1980s. And among the wines offered for sale by Christie's in Chicago, as part of the sale of Lloyd Flatt's cellar in 1990, was a bottle of 1947 Romanée-Conti that turned out to be a bottle of 1964 Échezaux with a dummied-up label. An Impériale of 1947 Cheval Blanc, auctioned at Christie's in 1997, sold for $112,500 despite doubts by both the château and a leading Swiss collector that such a bottle was ever made at the château; nonetheless, the château had given the bottle its imprimatur by providing a new label. Near the end of 1997, a bunch of low-priced, fake 1900 Taylor Fladgate and 1908 Sandeman vintage Port appeared on the London market.

Also suspicious was the prevalence of certain old vintages that had only been produced in limited quantities in the first place. The high number of cases of 1945 and 1947 Mouton sold at Christie's and Sotheby's in the previous twenty-five years raised eyebrows, given the relatively small production of those vintages. A German restaurant was reported to have served two cases a year of 1959 Pétrus for six years at tasting events; this was a wine that estate owner Christian Moueix had tasted only twice, and of which Pétrus itself owned only one bottle. By the late 1990s, Serena Sutcliffe was convinced that there were a lot of fake 1947s on the market.

AN ENTERPRISING FORGER could employ any of several methods to counterfeit wine. He might switch the contents of a case, substituting cheaper bottles for more expensive ones, confident that by the time the case was opened, years later, he'd be long gone. He could apply the same logic to bottles, soaking the label off of a more expensive wine and gluing it onto a cheaper one. When the bottle was eventually opened, he'd be forgotten, or the taster wouldn't have the knowledge or confidence to know the difference. Alternatively, instead of switching the bottle or label, the forger could switch the wine itself, siphoning out a more expensive one and replacing it with something inferior.

Old bottles, either empty or terribly ullaged, could be bought and reconditioned. A trick with DRC was to scuff the part of the label bearing the serial number, as if it had been a victim of normal handling. Labels could be reproduced with a color photocopier. Colin Lutman, an English forger of Port in the 1980s, went to more creative lengths, having apparently blasted one bottle with a shotgun to give it the pitted look of age, sprayed others with aerosolized dust, stained labels with orange juice and tea, and used sepia ink to reproduce château names on the labels.

More-sophisticated methods were also available. At the molecular level, a forger could add a proportionate amount of C-14 to simulate a vintage. To fool noses and palates, he could introduce an essence that mimicked aged oak. Émile Peynaud, the great French oenologist, once conducted an experiment in which he left a red wine and a Sauternes in a warm, damp lab oven for three weeks. At the end of the period, the red wine was undrinkable, but the Sauternes tasted like an old one and was very good. In the late 1990s, "a German sommelier with a vast knowledge of rare, old Bordeaux" offered the *Wine Spectator*'s Suckling detailed recipes for specific fakes, including a 1961 Pétrus, any mature vintage of Latour, and a 1945 Mouton. These recipes mostly involved lesser vintages of the same wine, doctored a bit, or other good wines that resembled them. Suckling didn't name the sommelier in the article, but Ralf Frenzel, Rodenstock's old sidekick, later acknowledged it had been he. "Whoever says that these great wines cannot be duplicated is not being honest with themselves," Frenzel had said, under cover of anonymity.

Wine was among the easiest collectibles to fake. As a luxury commodity—more like a Louis Vuitton bag or a Rolex watch than like a unique painting by a famous artist—a bottle of fine wine wasn't carefully tracked in its peregrinations. "This is the only product in the world," Robert Parker said later, "that you can sell for thousands of dollars without a certificate of origin." The rare-wine world, clubby and closemouthed, had allowed the problem to flourish by countenancing a gray market. And wine was made to be left alone in the dark for years, untasted and often unseen. Even when it was opened, tasting wine was rarely conclusive: few tasters were skilled enough to detect frauds, and an accused could always chalk up a strange taste to "bottle variation" or, with older bottles, the vinodiversity that characterized different merchants' bottlings of the same wine. Experienced tasters had, after all, been divided about the questionable Rodenstock wines at the 1980s L.A. tastings. The limits of science precluded analyzing the wine itself without opening the bottle, a trade-off that owners of very expensive bottles were reluctant to make.

Of course, even if you did decide, when tasting a wine, that it was fake, you had also just destroyed the evidence.

THE MOTLEY WAYS to make fake wine were matched only by the variety of clues that could lead to its detection. Sometimes, instead of asking market value for a fake, and counting on the wine's scarcity to generate demand among gray-market middlemen, a forger would make the mistake of setting a price that was too good to be true. Often the mimicry was shoddy and unresearched. In the Mouton episode in 1982, the gold lettering was neither embossed nor as brilliant as real gold leaf, the paper had a gray tinge, there were typographical errors, and the capsule lacked the real Rothschild seal. The 1981 and 1982 Pétrus faked in the mid-eighties bore wrong-colored foil capsules and stumpy, unbranded corks. The fraudsters behind the 1990 Penfolds Grange had meticulously copied the cases, packing tissue, and corks; their undoing had been spelling errors—"pour" was spelled "poor" on the label—and incorrectly colored bar codes (black instead of red).

In the matter of the five cases of 1986 DRC Montrachet arriving in Japan in 1990, the Japanese customer noticed that the labels read "Appellation Romanée-Conti Controlée" rather than the correct "Appellation Montrachet Controllée." In hindsight, given that only two hundred cases of DRC Montrachet were produced each year, a five-case allocation to a single consumer was itself suspicious.

So was the 1947 Romanée-Conti from Lloyd Flatt's cellar, since no such wine was ever produced. In 1945 the Domaine de la Romanée-Conti had belatedly yielded to phylloxera and torn up all its vines, replanting with American rootstocks; from 1946 to 1951, as the DRC waited for the newly planted vines to mature, no wines were bottled under its label. Despite this small problem, neither Flatt nor Christie's Chicago caught it; only when Christie's published the auction catalog did a rival auctioneer helpfully call up and point it out.

Sometimes it was the wine inside the bottles that didn't look right. Maybe the ullage was telltale: a fifty-year-old wine, say, that showed little or no evaporation. In the 1980s, Tim Littler, from Whitwhams, bought a Jéroboam of 1869 Mouton at Christie's London. When he got home to Manchester, he left the bottle upright on a table. Later, when he turned to look at it, he could see right through. Alarmed, he held the bottle up to the light. The fluid inside seemed far too translucent for a red Bordeaux, and, strangely, no sediment was swirling around from moving the wine by train from London. Littler opened the bottle and, sure enough, it contained colored water. He called Broadbent, who called the consignor, a Danish restaurateur who became aggressive with the English auctioneer. Littler theorized that the bottle had been drunk decades earlier, then filled with colored water for the sake of display; the restaurant had then changed hands a few times, and the new owners had no way of knowing that the bottle contained diluted ink.

In 1987, a bottle labeled as vintage Port exploded in an office at Sotheby's London. The cork shot out, hitting the ceiling, and wine sprayed all over the desk of Christopher Ross, the unlucky auction-house employee. The seal turned out to be candle wax dyed black, the contents a mix of Safeway-brand plonk and a partially fermented homemade concoction. Ross visited the consignor of the bottle, Colin Lutman, at home in Kent, and warned Lutman that he might have been victimized by a forger. Lutman had already sold several bottles at auction, including two bottles of "1924 Croft" at Christie's. Ross also warned Christie's about Lutman, and was told, incorrectly, that Lutman hadn't sold through them. Lutman tried selling again through Sotheby's, which called the police, who in turn contacted Christie's, which had itself just had another three bottles consigned to them by Lutman. When the police arrived at Lutman's home in Kent, they interrupted him in the midst of creating a new batch. He got off with a £750 fine.

In all these instances, something was visibly wrong with the wine or bottle or cork or capsule; no doubt, many more skillful fakes were simply never detected. The structure of the business was such that collectible wine often went unscrutinized, even as it was bought and sold and traded among merchants and auction houses and restaurants and collectors. Wine might be purchased at auction, sight unseen, by a telephone bidder, and then held "in bond" in a storage warehouse for decades before being resold. If it was an intact case, an auction house might never look at what was inside. Montrachet came in a wooden box girdled by a metal band that had to be cut to remove it; retailers often moved cases without ever opening them to inspect their contents. The 1981 and 1982 Pétrus wasn't detected until it reached Paris and London and the wooden boxes were opened. The boom in buying wine purely for the sake of investment had only exacerbated this phenomenon, which wine people made light of in an oft-recycled story.

"Abe bought a shipment of sardines that had already been traded many times and each time profitably," went one version. "Unlike previous buyers, Abe took the trouble of procuring a box of his purchase. The sardines were terrible. He telephoned Joe, from whom he had bought them, only to be told, 'But Abe, those sardines are for trading, not eating.'"

As CONCERN ABOUT the counterfeiting problem grew, there were fitful indications that a scientific solution might be found. A technique developed in France in the late 1980s, nuclear magnetic resonance, could not identify vintage, but could determine where the source grapes had been grown. An auction house challenged a

Champagne consignment using radiocarbon dating. The University of Seville would soon come up with a spectrometry test used to compare trace metals in wine and grape source.

But just about everyone other than the châteaux believed that the responsibility, and the only truly effective response, must lie with the châteaux themselves. The easiest problem to attack, from a château standpoint, was older vintages. As of 1990, leading châteaux had become suspicious of a wave of requests to recork old bottles, and become warier of recorking. Recorking opened a loophole for counterfeiters, both in creating an atmosphere in which nonoriginal corks and labels and unnaturally small ullage were considered acceptable, and in providing a mechanism to launder fake wine into wine with an official seal of approval. Given that châteaux had long reconditioned bottles by using different, less rare vintages to top up, the idea that an old bottle was purely what it purported to be was naïve. The practice of recorking therefore provided counterfeiters with yet another plausible argument for why an old wine might taste different from another bottle of the same vintage. Lafite, whose winemakers, starting in the mid-1980s, had regularly flown around the world to recork customers' bottles, would end the program by 2005. Yquem's Lur Saluces, who was a member of the brand-protecting Comité Colbert, banned recorking of all Yquem bottles older than 1940.

Countermeasures with regard to new vintages were slower to arrive, with many châteaux resistant to taking meaningful precautions. A few did adopt new anti-counterfeiting technology. Haut-Brion had been embossing its bottles since 1957. Starting with its 1988 vintage, Château Pétrus became one of the first winemakers to take steps specifically to combat counterfeiting, introducing a label containing a hidden code visible only under ultraviolet light. In 1996, Pétrus also began etching its name in its bottles. Margaux, too, was an early adopter, laser-etching each bottle with a château and vintage code starting with the 1989 vintage, and adding a bottle-specific random number, laser-etched in the neck, with the 1995 vintage. Margaux would also add an embossed *M* in the bottle's punt, vintage-specific corks and capsules, and anti-counterfeit labels, as well as weighing each case and encoding the poundage in a bar code stamped on the outside, so that bottle theft could be detected without removing the case's sealing bands.

"It makes their life difficult," Margaux's Paul Pontallier said of would-be counterfeiters. "You could maybe fake a few bottles, but you couldn't do it at an industrial level."

In 1996, Lafite began using engraved bottles. Lur Saluces took several steps to make it harder to fake Yquem, contracting with a printer of currency to use special watermarked paper, embedded with a signature pattern of particles visible only under ultraviolet light. He also introduced the use of a particularly adhesive glue, which did not endear him to those collectors who liked to soak labels off bottles and paste them into scrapbooks. The glass bottles, too, were embossed with certain marks. In Burgundy, the Domaine de la Romanée-Conti put a new system in place, including using embossed script on the label, changing the color and thickness of the bottle glass, and fixing labels more securely. After Langton's discovery of the fake Grange, Australia's Penfolds began laser-etching its bottles.

As an international cash business involving commodities, with little transparency in the distribution chain, rare wine seemed ripe for exploitation by organized money launderers, and the FBI and New Scotland Yard began looking into fine-wine merchants in the United States and the UK regarding possible fake bottles. The investigators spoke of Asia as a major new target of counterfeiters; while parts of the continent, especially Singapore and Hong Kong, were home to serious connoisseurs, many new-money collectors were naïve (Pétrus and Coke being a popular combination). Soon after his "In Vino Veritas?" essay appeared in *The Wine Advocate*, Robert Parker received a visit from two FBI agents; he spent a day with them, giving a tutorial in the wine business. "They led me to believe it was pretty serious and widespread," Parker recalled, "and that the Russian Mafia was involved. The question was, 'How do you prove it?'"

In 1997, a year after the secret anti-counterfeiting meeting in London, Sotheby's was presented with a fitting opportunity to demonstrate its commitment to sound provenance. A handful of other Jefferson bottles had surfaced, and Sotheby's announced that it would sell them. Though they didn't come from Rodenstock, and had a much different history, the bottles were a remarkable thing for the auction house to offer. Serena Sutcliffe had very publicly spoken of the rising problem of fake wine, and the three Jefferson bottles sold by Christie's, though she didn't say so publicly, were Exhibit A when it came to suspect old vintages.

While the seller remained anonymous—Sotheby's listed the lot of three Madeiras as "Property of a Nobleman"—the bottles seemed to have a very clear and convincing chain of ownership. Each bore a paper slip label attesting to its origin. All were Madeiras dating back to 1800, and as the auction catalog laid it out, they had been "purchased at sale of effects; President Jefferson; by Honl. Philip Evan Thomas of Maryland 1843." The labels showed the succession of owners through whom the bottles were then passed down, ending with their purchase by Douglas H. Thomas in 1890. The consignor was Thomas's great-grandson.

As Madeiras, these bottles stood a greater chance of being drinkable than eighteenth-century Bordeaux, but their conditions varied significantly. One was empty; Sotheby's estimated it would fetch between $2,500 and $3,500. One was less than half-full, its contents brown and cloudy; this was estimated at $6,000 to $8,000. The bottle in the best condition, with ullage at mid-to-low shoulder, was estimated to fetch between $10,000 and $15,000. Nonetheless, the catalog cautioned warily that all of the bottles were being "sold on the basis of their historical relevance only and purchasers should assume that the wine is not fit for consumption."

"These bottles, once belonging to President Thomas Jefferson, have miraculously survived being passed through generations and are of extraordinary historical importance," Sotheby's enthused. Beyond the slip labels, there were contemporaneous documents to back them up: an 1890 auction catalog mentioning the bottles as part of a sale of the estate of the daughter of Philip Evan Thomas, and an October 11, 1904, *Baltimore Sun* article recounting a dinner at which Douglas H. Thomas had made a toast with the Madeira. The dinner, which featured "crab flakes, Belvedere, in chafing dish" and "fancy ices," had wrapped up with the "Jefferson Madeira Vintage, 1800." The *Sun* article, from ninety-three years before, laid out the wine's pedigree exactly as the tattered slip labels did. The provenance seemed solid. Sotheby's saw no reason to contact Monticello to obtain a second opinion.

At the auction, on Friday, May 16, 1997, the bottle estimated at $10,000–$15,000 sold for $23,000. The winning telephone bidder was Barrie Larvin, wine director at the Rio Suite Hotel & Casino in Las Vegas, who oversaw a $6-million collection of some 100,000 bottles, including an assortment of Yquem worth $1 million. The year before, Larvin had shown a penchant for attention-getting bids when he bought a couple of Nebuchadnezzars of 1985 and 1989 Mouton for $33,350 each, and the following year he would place a winning bid of $20,000 for a 27-liter bottle of Dry Creek Vineyard 1995 Reserve Merlot, the largest bottle in the world. Now Larvin announced that he would open the Jefferson Madeira that July 4 or wait until the Millennium and sell sips for $100 each. Larvin also bought the empty Jefferson Madeira bottle for $6,000 as something to possibly offer in the casino's gift shop. In 1999 *Wine Spectator* identified these bottles, without qualification, as having "once belonged to President Thomas Jefferson."

As promised, Larvin offered tastes of the Jefferson Madeira on the New Year's Eve of the Millennium, though for $2,500 a pour rather than $100 a taste. When he was halfway through opening it, though, the cork crumbled, and he aborted the mission. Three days later, while in the casino cellar with a winemaker visiting from Australia, Larvin decided on the spur of the moment to open the bottle with a corkscrew.

He poured a small amount into a glass, then sealed the remainder in an airtight decanter. The wine had a dark amber color and smelled like Madeira. "The bouquet was extremely powerful," the winemaker reported. "It had hints of almonds, caramel, and burnt sugar aromas all mixed seamlessly with the rich, smooth spirit. Everything in the aroma followed through to the palate, perhaps without the same intensity, but still surprisingly well. The palate was reminiscent of raisins. The characteristic acidity of Madeira seemed to have fallen away, but the spirit made it deliciously warm to finish. I couldn't detect any fruit flavors in the wine—the palate was all about secondary bottle characteristics—as indeed one would expect after two hundred years in the bottle!"

Whether it had been in the bottle for two hundred years, however, turned out to be a question. The Sotheby's provenance had referred to an 1843 sale of Jefferson's effects, but the only such sale known to the experts at Monticello had occurred in 1827, the year after Jefferson's death. Serena Sutcliffe, informed years later of Monticello's doubts, replied that Sotheby's "research involved our book experts who analysed the paper and the handwriting. It all tallied. We were comfortable with the origin, the glass, the bottle, the writing—it all matched. A lot of work went into it." Later she added, "The origin of the Madeira was solid and totally satisfactory. Funny that any other theory was never mentioned at the time. . . . As I am sure you know, there are many 'Jefferson scholars,' just as there are many Rembrandt scholars! Not to mention the Jane Austen tribe."

It was true that the community of Rembrandt scholars had been riven by controversy regarding the authenticity of certain paintings, that specialists in Jane Austen were at odds over her sexuality, and that Jefferson experts had carried on a long debate over the paternity of Sally Hemings's children. But Sutcliffe, an auctioneer without expertise in Thomas Jefferson, was now talking about the leading center of Jefferson scholarship, Monticello, as if it were a fringe group, and treating the well-documented history of the disposition of Jefferson's estate as if it were a matter of interpretation. Her audacity would pale, though, next to that shown by Rodenstock at his next tasting.

Chapter 16

The Last Vertical

*F*OR HIS 1996 TASTING, RODENSTOCK HAD HIRED Andrea Bocelli, the blind Neapolitan tenor, to sing; for his next, he had in mind something even grander—a weeklong extravaganza devoted to a single wine. He spent two years preparing. The invitations to his Château d'Yquem Festival, mailed eight months in advance, boasted that guests would sample more vintages of the iconic Sauternes—125, from 1784 to 1991—"than anyone else in the world—including the owner." Two of these—the 1784 and the 1787—would be Jefferson bottles. The event, at Munich's Königshof Hotel, began on Sunday, August 30, 1998, and lasted seven days. When not drinking Rodenstock's wines, from the Rodenstock-designed Riedel Sauternes glass, guests could smoke his cigars; the wine dealer, now fifty-six, had recently launched a signature Hardy Rodenstock line of Robustos and Churchills, rolled in the Dominican Republic and marketed by a Hamburg manufacturer of high-end wine closets.

"This was hard work," Mario Scheuermann recalled of that

year's Ironman of wine. "It was really the final tasting. It was impossible to top this."

To the initiated, a roll call of the absent was as revealing as the guest list. None of the core members of Rodenstock's 1980s collecting circle was there, not Mr. Cheval Blanc or Herr Pétrus or Magnum Uwe. Another major German collector had finally left the fold two years earlier. The collector's enormous cellar included what was possibly the world's greatest private assemblage of DRC. He had been amassing a horizontal of 1961 Bordeaux in double magnums, and he was looking for a Super Second called Lynch-Bages. Neither the collector nor Bipin Desai, whose ability to ferret out rarities was topped only by Rodenstock, was able to find such a bottle. Two years later, Rodenstock called to say he had found *two* double magnums of the stuff. The collector told Lynch-Bages owner Jean-Michel Cazes about Rodenstock's find, and Cazes said he doubted such bottles had ever existed. The collector decided not to buy the bottles, and Rodenstock got angry. Then, in 1996, the collector was seeking an 1847 Yquem, and Rodenstock offered him a bottle at "a friendship price" of 12,000 Deutschmarks, less than one-third the market price. Again, the collector declined, and at that point became non grata at Rodenstock's tastings.

Desai, too, didn't attend the 1998 Yquem tasting. Desai had continued to associate with Rodenstock into the mid-nineties, but had gradually become more distant from him. (Among other reasons, Desai was now in touch with a Venezuelan food journalist, who, despite years of inquiries, hadn't been able to find anyone who could confirm the existence of the Caracas cellar from which Rodenstock had supposedly garnered some of his most impressive bottles.)

Most glaring, given the focus of the tasting, was the absence of Yquem's proprietor. Rodenstock had invited Lur Saluces; the count told friends he had never opened the invitation. (Elsewhere, he and Eigensatz reviewed the list of Yquem vintages served, and speculated that forty of them, many never before seen on the market, were fakes.)

Some of the changes in attendance resulted from a transformation of the wine scene. The American Group, by now, had effectively disbanded. In the early 1990s, after being diagnosed with cancer and recovering overnight in what he deemed a miracle, fifty-seven-year-old neurosurgeon Marvin Overton had become a Pentecostal evangelist, selling much of his 10,000-bottle collection and giving away the rest. "I was an excellent heathen," he said, "and now I'm an excellent Christian." In 1997, Tawfiq Khoury, now sixty-seven and moving to Hawaii, sold much of his collection at a joint Zachys-Christie's auction for $3.2 million. He kept 10,000 bottles. Lloyd Flatt, after auctioning his cellar in 1990 in the face of a divorce, had begun to rebuild, but the old days of the Group were long over.

Serena Sutcliffe, who attended the Rodenstock blowout in 1989, had signed on as Sotheby's wine director two years later. Under her direction, the department had made great gains and now was a real challenger to Christie's. In 1997, Sotheby's two-day May sale of composer Andrew Lloyd Webber's 18,000-bottle cellar brought in more than $6 million, making it the largest wine sale up to that time. In 1999, Sotheby's and Sherry-Lehman would jointly hold an auction in New York of wine from the cellar of Norwegian investor Christen Sveaas, which fetched $14.4 million. (Christie's had already sold the other half of Sveaas's cellar, billing it as "the world's most exclusive private wine cellar ever to have appeared at auction," for more than $11 million.)

Michael Broadbent couldn't stand Sutcliffe. Regal and stylish, she was the second woman ever to be certified as a Master of Wine. In contrast to Broadbent, she tended to employ gushing and fanciful descriptors for wine ("jammy wonder"; "the Cairo spice bazaar"). And, just as Keith Richards had taken out a policy on his guitar-plucking fingers, she had insured her palate. It was no empty gesture. The eminent English importer and writer Harry Waugh, late in life, had been in a car accident that threw him into his dashboard and killed his sense of smell. For someone whose livelihood depended on her nose, the idea of losing it was horrifying. Robert Parker, too, had such an insurance policy (for $1 million). But it all added up to a glittery, modern persona that chafed against Broadbent's old-school sensibilities.

Not long before Rodenstock's 1998 Yquem tasting, Broadbent had taped an interview for *Vintner's Tales,* a BBC documentary hosted by Jancis Robinson, in which he acknowledged that he refused to attend tastings where Sutcliffe would be present, explaining, "I find that there is a chemistry between people and I find, really, if you want to know the truth, her haughty and rather nose-in-the-air. The word, if you really want the word, is pretentious. They are going to kill me for this. She probably thinks I am a most tiresome person, too." Sutcliffe declined to appear in the series.

Three years later, Walter Eigensatz would host a tasting at his and his wife's spa in Bad Schwalbach, and arrange for two cars to fetch the British contingent arriving at the Frankfurt airport. One was to carry Broadbent and Robinson, the other Sutcliffe. When one of the cars broke down on the way to fetch them, the three were forced to spend a car ride together. "It was very awkward," Eigensatz recalled.

An outsider would never have guessed the extent to which Rodenstock's reputation had been tarnished. Although privately, leading Bordeaux châteaux owners and the most knowledgeable German, Swiss, and American collectors had long since become disenchanted with Rodenstock, a number of prominent wine world people still held to their opinions of him, or at least to their willingness to accept his largesse. Jancis Robinson remained dreamy about the "pre-revolutionary bouquet" of the Jefferson Mouton opened in 1986, which "was reticent at first and then built up to a great cloud of sweetness hanging over the whole room." In addition to the big books by Broadbent and Parker, the definitive studies of both Yquem and Margaux still depended heavily on Rodenstock bottles for their tasting notes for the oldest vintages.

Over the course of the weeklong Château d'Yquem Festival, the guest list ballooned from thirty people the first night to sixty at the final, black-tie dinner. Most of Rodenstock's journalist friends were there, as was his old sommelier Ralf Frenzel, who had since left the business. Broadbent came, along with crystal maker Georg Riedel. From Pomerol, Denis Durantou, of Château l'Eglise Clinet, attended; from the Piemonte came Angelo Gaja, the charismatic Italian wine pioneer. Most of the guests, though, were people new to wine, not professionally involved with it, or not deeply knowledgeable about it. There was the usual passel of German celebrities, as well as a lot of deep-pocketed collectors, many from the German-speaking countries. A few were from America, including a New Jersey food company executive named Steve Verlin, whose enormous personal collection of wine was one of the foundations of the new, celebrated New York restaurant Veritas.

The most telling new contingent was from Asia. Rodenstock had been dealing wine to Japanese industrialists as early as 1990, and by 1994 he had begun inviting Hong Kong collectors to his annual tasting. But the 1998 blowout made clear just how important the Asian market had become to his business. The roster of Hong Kong guests was impressive, and included members of the powerful Liu banking family. Henry Tang, a member of the crown colony's executive council, and James Tien, chairman of the island's Chamber of Commerce, held forth in Cantonese while placing large wagers on the identity of certain wines.

EACH DAY WAS staged with German precision. The schedule featured a morning tasting, beginning at 10:00 a.m. sharp, followed by a light lunch (meaning just two courses, one red wine, and one white wine), with a heroic dinner in the evening. At the Sunday-night dinner that kicked off the event, a young Russian tenor sang opera arias. The final evening, small-trumpet virtuoso Otto Sauter performed Baroque pieces.

Rodenstock, on the defensive, had printed booklets for each guest, containing expert analyses of the wine and glass from other Jefferson bottles in the cache. After the corks had been drawn, ever so gently, Rodenstock put them on a silver tray and showed them around the room. The tasting proceeded without much controversy, though even Broadbent found the 1858 to have an odd vanilla character. "I don't think this is right," he said aloud. "Something is wrong."

Rodenstock, for his part, said that the point of the mammoth vertical was to prove conclusively his long-voiced contention that pre-phylloxera wines were superior to post-phylloxera wines. Though this thesis dovetailed conveniently with the commercial niche of a man with a unique penchant for discovering pre-phylloxera wines, Rodenstock claimed he had made a lot of money investing in stocks and didn't need to sell wine to live. He said he was mostly retired from the wine business, and that he just wanted to win the pre-phylloxera debate. "I've said it before, and now nobody can challenge it," he crowed, between drafts on one of his namesake Robustos. "Nobody can say Hardy Rodenstock doesn't know what he's talking about, and you're all my witnesses."

To make the limited quantities of the rarer vintages go further—forty of them dated from the nineteenth century—only nine glasses were poured from each bottle, three people sharing each glass. But each person still drank a daunting amount of wine. In addition to the 125 vintages of Yquem, Rodenstock served 130 other wines during the week. He upped the ante by threatening to eject anyone caught spitting; Broadbent and *Wine Spectator*'s Per-Henrik Mansson took their chances, hiding spittoons in their laps. It was all a bit much for some. "[I]t is crazy, really," commented Jancis Robinson, who split her glass of older wines with Georg Riedel and Angelo Gaja, "to be chewing over the relative merits of such extraordinary relics."

Every night, near midnight, the Liu brothers ("Ping and Pong," as Mario Scheuermann flippantly referred to them) would come down to the lobby with $5,000-per-kilo black tea, given them by their grandmother, which had been fermented in caves for over one hundred years. The brothers said a cup of the tea would prevent a hangover. The first night, everyone kind of laughed about it. The second night, they sipped at it. The third night, people were begging for it. "The tea was very good," said a participant. "I have no idea whether it really helped."

RODENSTOCK WAITED UNTIL Friday morning to serve the Jefferson bottles. That day, he wore a royal-blue dress shirt with a white collar, a striped tie with matching pocket square, a double-breasted navy suit, and large aviator-style eyeglasses. He and his wife sat at a small round table with soccer legend Franz Beckenbauer and his wife.

Beckenbauer was given the honor of opening the 1784. The wine was decanted through a metal funnel filter. Everyone wanted a look. Angelo Gaja peered intently at the engraving. Georg Riedel posed with it for photos.

Jancis Robinson tasted both Jefferson wines and was convinced they were old. "They were the deepest of deep browns with a slightly greenish rim. At first they smelled slightly moldy," she recalled later, "but then the miracle of great old wine began to work, and the scent of the wines themselves came through. The 1784 had a gentle, distinctly feminine fragrance of roses, with a great persistence of flavor that reached a peak about fifteen minutes after the wines were poured. The more assertive, longer-lasting 1787 had chunkier, richer, distinctly autumnal aromas of burnt sugar and undergrowth."

To *Wine Spectator*'s Mansson, a correspondent based in Switzerland, the 1784 "tasted as if it were decades younger, perhaps from the mid-1800s," while the 1787 "was clean but showed the passage of two centuries in its faded fruit flavors and a dry, tart finish."

ONE OF THE lasting mysteries of the Jefferson bottles had been the exact number Rodenstock started out with. Though he told friends, at the time of the discovery, that there were twenty-four of the bottles, he had always been vague when speaking with journalists. The most exact he would get was to say there were "more than a dozen." Even Michael Broadbent had been led to believe there were only "thirteen or fourteen bottles in all." Friends explained this fuzziness away as a shrewd businessman's tactic, saying it was easier to make something seem rare if one didn't mention that there were twenty-three more where that came from. Skeptics saw the reticence as one more question mark around the bottles' authenticity, countering that it was easier to indefinitely come up with new bottles if there wasn't a record of how many there were to begin with.

At least one other Jefferson bottle had turned up, its origin unclear. In Jerusalem, a restaurateur named Moise Pe'er, who ran a place that was popular with politicians, boasted of owning a Jefferson Margaux from 1789, a year Rodenstock had never publicly claimed was represented in the cache.

In opening the two Jefferson bottles at this tasting, Rodenstock told some people that these were the last of his Jefferson Yquems, though he told Jancis Robinson he still had "one or two" left. The number of Jefferson bottles out on the market was anyone's guess. Rodenstock claimed that he didn't "know who exactly owns Jefferson bottles. . . . The journalists have written so much nonsense on the Jefferson bottles that I have crossed that subject off long ago." Rodenstock had now opened four at his big tastings, "a couple of half bottles" privately, the Yquem at Yquem, and the Mouton at Mouton. He had traded another Yquem to Lur Saluces, a Lafite to Lloyd Flatt, and sold a Lafite 1784 and a Lafite 1787 to Frericks. In a late-1992 interview, he mentioned having just sold a 1787 Jefferson Yquem; he provided a half-bottle of 1787 Lafite for analysis in Zurich; and two years after that he provided the Zurich lab with a second bottle for analysis, a 1787 Yquem (the results were no more conclusive than the lab's first test). Besides the three bottles sold by Christie's (to Forbes, Shanken, and Shiblaq/Al-Fayed), and the five bottles sold by Farr (one to Sokolin, four to Koch), there were another two bottles (a 1784 and a 1787) in the collection of the Swiss wine merchant Badaracco. This amounted to twenty-five plus "one or two," not including the bottle supposedly in Jerusalem. With more than two dozen bottles drunk, broken, sacrificed to science, or ensconced in collectors' cellars, Rodenstock's Jefferson saga seemed finally spent.

The subculture in which the bottles had flourished had also largely come to an end. Partly this was because there were fewer pre-phylloxera first growths around; 1864, 1865, and 1870 Lafites, to name just three, appeared only rarely in auction catalogs now. Many of the bottles simply didn't exist anymore. Partly the change came about because of soaring prices; the people who could afford the rarities now tended to be rich status-seekers rather than wine obsessives. And partly the era ended because of the dispersal of Rodenstock's generation of tasters. There was no way to improve on the Yquem marathon. "If ever you have a chance to taste like this, you are lost," Scheuermann said. "You never will have a chance to come back to common taste." Scheuermann and his friends had lived through a golden age that could not return.

For these few, the normal quality scale didn't apply. Was a 100-point wine some barrel-tasted, right-bank upstart anointed by a self-styled arbiter in Monkton, Maryland? No, for these people it was an 1865 Lafite, a 1900 Margaux, a 1945 Mouton, a 1947 Cheval Blanc. "People who haven't tasted these wines should refrain from judging on a 100-point scale," Scheuermann said. "They should judge up to 90 or 95. One hundred points means the greatest wines ever produced for us to taste. Boys and girls who haven't tasted these should refrain from judging." He paused, as it dawned on him how this sounded. "On the other hand, that's arrogant."

Others simply appreciated their experience for what it was and moved on to more commonplace wines. Talking about the rarities wasn't just arcane, it was obnoxious and boring. People who had shared an intense experience they could discuss only with each other, they kept quiet. "The 1871 Yquem, my favorite, I drank four times," Otto Jung recalled. "Only about fifteen people in the world have done that. You can't talk to your normal friends about it."

It appeared that the full truth about the Jefferson bottles would never be revealed. Thirteen years had passed since they first made news. Circumstantial arguments aside, there was no definitive proof that they had belonged to Jefferson, and none that they hadn't. When it came to sensory evaluation, the authority on old wines, Michael Broadbent, had deemed the six he tasted to be authentic, while other tasters had expressed skepticism. A scientific test had established that at least one bottle contained young wine, but another test a year later had seemed, at least in the eyes of the wine media, to rebut the idea that all the bottles might be affected. The second test had also thrown into question who had tampered with the bottle from the first test. Every answer had given way to new questions. It seemed unlikely that another scientific test could break the tie. The most famous of the bottles had, after all, been compromised before the eighties were up, the Forbes bottle through its cork slippage, the Sokolin bottle by being broken at the Four Seasons. And the Jefferson bottles were so expensive as to create a strong disincentive for the owner of one, even if skeptical, to destroy it for the sake of . . . what? Barring an uncharacteristic revelation by Rodenstock, or the unexpected emergence of a previous owner of the bottles, the secret looked as if it would die with Rodenstock.

CHAPTER 17

~

KOCH BOTTLES

O N A WEDNESDAY IN SEPTEMBER OF 2005, NEARLY twenty years after the Forbes family made wine-auction history, their bottle reposed on lower Fifth Avenue, in a suite on the second floor of the Forbes Building. There, amid the hushed sounds of clicking keyboards and chirruping phones, the galleries' staff was busy with its curatorial mission, which increasingly meant getting rid of things.

Fifteen years after Malcolm's death, the Forbes children had deaccessioned many of their father's collections in order to raise funds. In 1993 they auctioned off the Orientalist art that had adorned his palace in Tangiers. Over the next several years they sold his collection of toy soldiers, an Edward Hopper painting (to Steve Martin, the actor, for $10 million), and, through Christie's, sixty-two American paintings and sculptures. At the time, the *New York Times* reported that, "given the Forbes provenance," prices could greatly exceed estimates and quoted the chairman of Christie's in America as saying, "We're hopeful, but who knows? It's a great name." In 2002 the Forbeses sold a number of their historical manuscripts. Economic pressures that year also led to job and benefit cuts at the magazine, and in 2003, over the objections of Kip, his siblings sold off the Victorian painting collection he had lovingly assembled over many years. At the sale at Christie's London, which Kip reportedly stayed away from because it would be "too sad," a fan illustrated with a drawing by Charles Keene was snatched up by none other than Michael Broadbent, who had been collecting the nineteenth-century artist's work since the 1950s. In 2004 the Forbeses sold off their most famous possession, a 180-piece collection of jeweled eggs and other *objets* from the House of Fabergé.

The Forbes brand continued to stand for expert collecting and connoisseurship. *Forbes* magazine published an annual collectors' issue, and for the preceding three years the company had published a collecting newsletter. The articles didn't shy away from the issue of counterfeit collectibles in general ("Spotting Fakes"), or fake wine in particular ("In Vino Falsitas," "Château Faux"), but they did omit the Forbeses' own susceptibility to being duped. The articles failed to note that a painting by the American artist William Aiken Walker, *Levee at New Orleans,* which Kip Forbes had purchased for more than $50,000, had turned out to be a forgery.

Even now, their Jefferson bottle continued to pop up in the news and on Internet boards, both because twenty years on it still held its world record, and because it remained a compelling example for those who saw it as the ultimate in human folly. Just a month earlier, the London *Times* had recalled the bottle's ignominious end in a squib headlined "Blunders of the World."

On this day in September, Bonnie Kirschstein, who presided over the galleries, wore a black pantsuit. She reached into a box of pristine white cotton gloves, removed two, and put them carefully on her hands, pulling them snug. Then she moved toward a closed door. Standing squarely in front of a security keypad, making it invisible to anyone behind her, she punched in a code and turned the handle. The door opened.

Stepping inside, she flicked a switch, and fluorescents clicked on above her. It was a small, windowless room with a linoleum floor. The temperature and humidity were carefully controlled, and the air was cool and dry. To the right, reaching almost to the ceiling, stood four beige metal bookcases, the kind that have giant dials on the end and slide along tracks to make the most efficient use of limited space. Kirschstein went to the second-to-last case, turned the dial, and wheeled the unit toward the door, exposing the last case.

The room was a way station for objects not yet cataloged, in between exhibits, or waiting to be moved to a deep-storage warehouse. On one shelf of the now-exposed case was a scuffed leather milliner's box containing Abraham Lincoln's black stovepipe hat. On the shelf above it was a white plastic auction paddle, printed with the word CHRISTIE's and the number 231. Beside it was a *New York Post* article mounted on a plaque, headlined "What a Corker!" and a yellowing piece of paper, mounted on a board, with a faded indigo scrawl. It was a letter from Thomas Jefferson to Joseph de Rayneval, a diplomat. Behind that, toward the wall, was a black Lucite cradle for displaying the bottle. Next to it, on a three-by-three-foot chocolate-colored piece of silver cloth, was the greenish-brown thing designated in the Forbes curatorial system as Object 85054: the Jefferson bottle. It rested on its side, stored as wine should be.

Since its purchase in 1985, the bottle had emerged from storage only occasionally—to be displayed in the Forbes Galleries, or to be photographed by Christie's as a prop for wine accessories, or for Jefferson-related promotions. When the Jefferson Hotel in Washington, D.C., opened a new restaurant in 1990, the Forbeses lent the bottle to be displayed for two months.

Now Kirschstein gently retrieved it and brought it out of the room. On a round table, she spread out the cloth, and set the bottle upright on it. The front was clean, the back veiled with a clinging gauze of dust and grit. The black liquid within came only up to the shoulder, a dramatic difference from 1985, when the wine came within an inch and a half of the base of the cork. A black wax seal remained, but the cork, which eighteen years before had been bobbing in the liquid, was nowhere to be seen. If it was an eighteenth-century relic, it seemed out of place in the artificially bright, dun-carpeted offices.

BILL SOKOLIN, WEARING thong sandals and his wife's teal bathrobe, was sitting in his house on Long Island, where he had moved in 1996 after giving up the Manhattan storefront. Three years later, he retired. He spent much of his time by the pool out back, and his skin was mottled from the sun. His son David had taken over the business and now ran it almost entirely as an Internet and telephone operation from a climatized, million-bottle-capacity warehouse here in Southampton. In Bill Sokolin's home, the bookshelves contained volumes about Jefferson. Plaques from Margaux and Lafite were displayed on a credenza. Behind the house, a neighbor's patch of vines hugged the property line. Long Island wines were thriving. Margaux's Paul Pontallier was a consultant to a Long Island winery, and Dave Sokolin was a partner in two vineyards, Bedell and Corey Creek.

Bill Sokolin had been trying to get rid of his broken Jefferson bottle for years. Twice a prospective buyer had offered to exchange a house for it, according to Sokolin. One was in New Jersey, one in Southampton, both in the $250,000–$300,000 range, but Sokolin's lawyer advised him that it wouldn't be considered a trade-in-kind and he would be clobbered with taxes. In January 1991, Sokolin tried selling the bottle at auction, through Guernsey's in Manhattan. "We are ready to set the record for a broken empty wine bottle," auction house president Arlan Ettinger said at the time. The pre-sale estimate was $20,000–$30,000, and the catalog stated that "it is now generally conceded that the bottles found did indeed belong to Thomas Jefferson." The bottle didn't sell.

In 1995, with the movie *Jefferson in Paris* about to be released, Sokolin saw another opportunity. In a letter to customers that whimsically proposed to "Re-elect Jefferson in '96" and announced that he would donate his Jefferson bottle to Monticello, Sokolin touted a $150-a-case, private-label "Thomas Jefferson Chardonnay" made by a Virginia winery, as well as a limited-edition book, *The Jefferson Legacy,* for $495. He said the broken 1787 Margaux bottle was now worth $750,000, "according to an article in the *New York Observer*" (which had gotten its estimate from Sokolin). Monticello wouldn't take Sokolin's bottle, and he couldn't persuade the Smithsonian's National Museum of American History, in Washington, D.C., to let him donate the bottle or to exhibit it. Briefly, according to Sokolin, the William Jefferson Clinton Library expressed interest in obtaining the bottle. In 2002, Sokolin announced that he was looking for the right charity to which to donate the bottle; he had lowered its valuation to $700,000. Early in 2005, Sokolin gave the American Jewish World Service the right to offer the bottle on eBay "to help raise money for tsunami relief and reconstruction." The bottle didn't sell. Finally, in the summer of 2005, Sokolin succeeded in giving the bottle to Love Our Children, a Manhattan charity. When its director came to pick the bottle up, Sokolin got a bit shaky, but now he was glad it was gone.

THE THIRD JEFFERSON bottle known to be in the New York area lay in a triangular, glassed-in room in the reception area of *Wine Spectator*'s midtown offices. Marvin Shanken displayed his trophy alongside such other legendary wines as a 1945 Romanée-Conti, an 1847 Yquem, and an 1870 Lafite in magnum.

The last two decades had shown Shanken to have chosen a good business. Between 2002 and 2005, Riedel Crystal had tripled its business in the United States, selling 8 million stems annually. In July the annual Gallup Consumption Habits poll reported that, for

the first time, wine had eclipsed beer as Americans' favorite alcoholic drink. (Thirty-nine percent of respondents said they'd prefer
a glass of wine, compared with 36 percent for a glass of beer.)
And the wine they were drinking had changed; for the first time in
memory, red outsold white in America's supermarkets. It was a vin-
dicating moment for Shanken, who in purchasing his magazine a
quarter-century earlier had gambled on an American wine boom.

Wine Spectator's paid circulation had risen every year, and stood
now at 380,000 copies a month, for an annual price of fifty dollars.
It had subscribers in two hundred countries. In 1992, just when the
American tobacco industry was entering its death spiral, Shanken
had founded Cigar Aficionado. It had been a surprising success.
Famous people who didn't talk to the press lost their shyness when
it came to cigars; General Tommy Franks, Michael Jordan, and
Francis Ford Coppola were among those who graced the cover.
The magazine now had a circulation of 250,000. Shanken also published several other trade publications, as well as staging big events
like the Wine Experience and a cigar equivalent, the Big Smoke,
plus "lifestyle seminars" on connoisseurship of everything from
cheese to chocolate. When people referred to Shanken Communications as "a publishing business," Shanken would correct them: he
was in the education business. Cigar Aficionado had taught people
how to select, cut, light, smoke, evaluate, enjoy a cigar. Wine Spectator had introduced its readers to new wines and new winemakers
and new regions.

Enabled by the wealth that accompanied his success, Shanken
had done a lot of crazy things since his out-of-control bidding
against Kip Forbes. The craziest, perhaps, was bidding on a walnut
humidor once given to JFK by the comedian Milton Berle, at the
1996 dispersal of Jacqueline Kennedy Onassis's estate. At the well-
publicized New York auction, lines wrapped around the block. The
humidor was just one of hundreds of lots. Shanken thought it might
go for up to $30,000, but he told his wife he really wanted it. He

was more prosperous now, and this time it was he who, with Yablonian self-assurance, would be "going to pick up the humidor."

Shanken sat out the first few bidding rounds, watching in some astonishment as the number quickly shot up in $10,000 increments to $200,000. Five people were competing for it. At $250,000, Shanken made his first bid. Soon the bidding was at $400,000, and Shanken and a telephone bidder were the only two remaining bidders, still going up in $10,000 increments. When the other man bid $440,000, Shanken decided to end this once and for all. He held up five fingers. "Four hundred fifty thousand?" the auctioneer asked. Shanken shook his head and spread the five fingers wider. "You mean $500,000?" the auctioneer asked. Shanken nodded. "And this piece of shit goes to five ten," Shanken recalled later of the rival bidder. Shanken bid $520,000, but was ready, or so he would claim, to drop out if the other man outbid him again. The man, a commodities broker in Chicago, did not. Shanken won.

By the time the buyer's commission and sales tax were added, the total amount he paid for the humidor was $622,000. Shanken briefly considered having it sent to a friend or relative in New Jersey to skirt the sales tax, but thought better of it. And his accountant wouldn't let him take it as a business expense, because it wasn't a depreciable asset. He framed the bill and hung it in his office. His wife had been with him but feeling under the weather; he later got mad at her for not having stopped him, but at least now he could afford it. The humidor took its place in a display cabinet in a conference room at his offices, where his other humidors included one given to Winston Churchill in 1941 by the Cuban government, and another signed by Fidel Castro *"Para Marvin."*

THE BEST OPPORTUNITY since the 1985 Forbes exhibition for the general public to see a Jefferson bottle came in September 2005, when the Boston Museum of Fine Arts announced that it would put on an exhibit featuring the eclectic collections of Bill Koch, the six-foot-four fossil-fuel heir who had bought four of the Jefferson bottles in the late 1980s.

Since that time, Koch had patched things up with his brothers, or at least one of them, and had come into his own with a long-shot victory in the America's Cup in 1992. He owned a privately held energy company called Oxbow, which was a major trader of petroleum coke as well as being the operator of a low-sulfur coal mine in Colorado. He divided his time mainly between homes on Cape Cod and in Palm Beach.

Koch was as passionate as ever about wine. Despite having pruned his cellar by 3,400 bottles through a 1999 sale at Christie's New York, Koch now owned about 35,000 bottles. It was one of the largest collections in the world. The bottles had cost him $12 million, a lot in wine terms, but a fraction of the $30 million he had paid for the Modigliani above his fireplace, which was just one of many expensive works of art he owned. He bought both broadly (more than 1,400 different wines) and deeply: 60 percent of his wine was Bordeaux, and 35 percent Burgundy. He bought favored wines in quantity, including eight cases and thirty magnums of Latour 1961, and ten cases of 1945 Mouton, and he served $500-a-bottle 1996 Latour at his third wedding. In the glossy coffee-table book published to accompany the Boston MFA show, Koch explained "why I love great wine so much. Not only does it taste beautiful and wonderful and makes you feel great when you're drinking it—you can also really taste the love the vintner had in making the wine, which is an art form."

Koch could sometimes seem unserious about the collection. He bought just about any new book on wine, while admitting that he hadn't read many of them. He liked to take out his bottles and show them off, and once, after producing his Jefferson bottles for a visitor's benefit, he clinked one against another, chipping off part of the wax seal. "Oh shit!" he said. "Dammit. Oh, *c'est la vie*. They can fix it." In the summer of 2000, he and his then-wife saw a couples therapist to discuss his drinking. The *New York Post* reported that in Palm Beach Koch had openly talked about checking into rehab. He had since remarried.

But his interest in wine went beyond the usual rich man's accumulation. When buying at auction, Koch often placed the phone bids himself. In 1991, when he was gunning for the America's Cup, he relocated his wine collection with him to San Diego during trials. Not long after buying the first of his Jefferson bottles from the Chicago Wine Company, Koch had invested $1 million in the firm. He had a bathroom in his house decorated with corks, labels, case ends, and bottle bases from much of the wine he had drunk. And his enthusiasm for wine colored other of his collections: He owned a Greek drinking cup from 470 BC, as well as a marble head of Dionysus.

He also attended wine events, such as the exclusive 2000 Christie's tasting in New York, a Latour vertical, where he had his one encounter with Rodenstock. He recalled the encounter as having been limited to his saying hello and nodding. (He had been seated next to Matt Dillon, the actor, but then Dillon moved away. Koch remembered this self-deprecatingly, as if Dillon had found him wanting in some way.)

Koch had obtained a Ph.D. in chemical engineering from the Massachusetts Institute of Technology. To win the America's Cup, he had spent $68 million and hired a team of MIT scientists to build a better boat—with lighter sails, a sleeker hull, and a more hydrodynamic keel. He brought the same rationalistic, free-spending approach to wine. In 1996 he installed a $10,000 state-of-the-art computer system in his 1,750-square-foot primary cellar in Cape Cod. He could walk into his cellar, choose a wine using the touch screen, and get a printout of a map showing exactly where in the cellar to find a particular bottle. A bar code was affixed to every bottle, and as Koch exited the cellar with a bottle in hand, he could swipe it past a scanner, which would automatically update his digitized inventory. Similarly, when decanting older wines, Koch eschewed the traditional candle in favor of using laboratory equipment—including a vacuum pump and a chemical filter. Many connoisseurs consider such filtering anathema, on the theory that it can strip wine of essential qualities, but Koch didn't buy that argument.

By 2005, 20,000 of his bottles had moved with Koch to Palm Beach, where he had purchased a 36,000-square-foot oceanfront mansion. The new 1,300-square-foot cellar, designed by an Austrian architect and completed in 2001, seemed styled after a European castle—full of salvaged-brick vaults, iron grillwork, Roman mosaics, and candelabra. Sixteen years after Koch had first bought them, the seven eighteenth-century, Rodenstock-sourced bottles remained the centerpiece of his wine collection, and his new Palm Beach cellar included a mirror-backed cage to showcase them.

Though in person he could come off as folksy, awkward, and even shy, few wine collectors of Koch's magnitude were as publicly proud of their holdings. The show "Things I Love: The Many Collections of William I. Koch," which opened in Boston on August 31, 2005, promised to include at least one of the four Jefferson bottles. The coffee-table book produced to accompany the show, its covers lined with a photo collage of trophy-wine labels from Koch's collection, contained images not only of that quartet—Lafite and Mouton, in both 1784 and 1787 vintages—but also of his three other eighteenth-century vintages of Lafite (1737 and 1771) and Latour (1791).

A visitor wandering through the exhibit, expecting to see the bottles, came first upon Koch's collection of miniature models of every boat that had won or lost the America's Cup. There were Sitting Bull's bead belt and breastpiece, Custer's hunting rifle, and the revolver that killed Jesse James. There were Impressionist paintings, sculptures by Rodin and Botero, and ancient coins. As Koch put it, "My brother Charles collects money. David used to collect girls, but not anymore. Fred collects castles. And I collect everything."

The wine, or rather the wine bottles, were displayed in the low-lit, high-ceilinged Torf Gallery. There were ten of them, all empty, ranging from an 1865 Latour to a 1921 Pétrus in a big bottle to a Nebuchadnezzar inscribed "America's Foundation/America's Cup 1992." A caption, painted in white on the gray wall in the glass case, announced: "With more than thirty thousand bottles, Bill Koch's wine collection includes Château Pétrus, Château Latour, and Château Mouton, just to name a few. He is particularly proud of bottles of Mouton and Lafite thought to have been purchased in France by Thomas Jefferson. Some of Koch's life accomplishments, such as the victory of America[3] in 1992, have been commemorated by specifically designed bottles."

Strangely, the Jefferson bottles were nowhere to be seen.

CHAPTER 18

GHOST PARTICLES

PROUD AS BILL KOCH WAS OF HIS JEFFERSON bottles, he had grown increasingly concerned about their provenance. During the same period when Koch was assembling the verticals that anchored his wine cellar, he had had a fateful experience involving some rare coins. It began in 1984, when, flush with his buyout money, he acquired for $3.2 million what were believed to be the rarest coins ever found: 1,700 ancient Greek pieces, including thirteen silver decadrachms, in a clay pot unearthed by three prospectors in a field in southern Turkey. Koch thought he could make an easy profit by selling some of the coins, while still retaining the greatest hoard in the world.

Even before Koch bought the coins, there were clues that the Turkish government might be looking for them. (Turkish authorities had been tipped off to the find after one of the peasant treasure finders "bought a Mercedes or did something similarly intelligent," according to a warning letter sent by a Swiss coin dealer to the Boston MFA classical-art curator who was authenticating the coins for Koch.) In a move he would later regret, Koch satisfied himself with warranties from the Turkish and German dealers that the coins were unencumbered. After a decade-long legal fight with the Turkish government, Koch settled, returning the coins to Turkey in exchange for a plaque to be displayed with them, thanking him.

Now sixty-five, Koch wanted to ensure that there would be no repeat of his decadrachm experience. The MFA had asked him to supply provenances for every object in the show, but with only weeks to go before it opened, the prospects for guaranteeing the authenticity of the Jefferson bottles were dim. In March, Brad Goldstein, his spokesman, had had an initial phone conversation with Susan Stein, the curator at Monticello, that got his antennae up. When Goldstein told Koch of Monticello's doubts, Koch "was not a happy camper."

Koch could have been forgiven, at this point, for choosing to leave well enough alone. It must have been tempting simply not to know, to continue to believe he possessed a treasure that might have belonged to Thomas Jefferson. He risked embarrassment if it were revealed that the bottles he had paid so much for and taken such pride in were not what they seemed. He must have known that this was strictly a rich man's problem, though, as likely to arouse schadenfreude as sympathy.

He also was painfully aware that he made a soft, fat target for the press. When he had subpoenaed his eighty-two-year-old mother, all the jackals could focus on was the stroke she'd had a few months earlier, totally disregarding that she sided with his brothers in the fraternal feud. Yes, he'd wanted to compel her testimony, but after all, he hadn't known about the stroke at the time; once he found out about it, he abandoned his effort. When he had expelled his mistress from a $2.5-million condo he owned at the Boston Four Seasons, the media harped on how she was a single mother and the eviction had taken place on Christmas Eve so that he could throw a party in the 3,700-square-foot spread, never mind that he could have evicted her thirty days earlier. When he was arrested for domestic violence after his second wife accused him of punching her in the stomach and "[threatening] to beat his whole family to death with his belt," the hacks were all over it, neglecting to point out that witnesses to the altercation had disputed his wife's account and that she later recanted it. (The charges were ultimately dismissed.) Although a court issued a restraining order against Koch, his Palm Beach estate was spacious enough that he was able to stay in a beach house on the property and still be in compliance.

Koch's darker side was mitigated by a disarming willingness to introspect in public—about his years in psychoanalysis, say ("For a long time I didn't think I was worth shit"), or his short fuse ("I could be a really nasty prick. . . . [In later years] I would go up to my secretary [and say], 'You dumb shit, why'd you make that mistake?' I was that kind of guy"). But the candor didn't always help his case. A 1994 *Vanity Fair* profile, written with Koch's masochistic cooperation, had been a mutilation without anesthetic, likening his paranoia to Richard Nixon's and his dissembling to Bill Clinton's and saying Koch is "a man whose closet is free of skeletons in large part because they all seem to be turning somersaults in his living room."

Worst of all was the Boston press, which delighted in quoting from naughty love letters between Koch and his "X-rated Protestant princess," as the evicted mistress styled herself. ("My body parts are like moist orchids in bloom," she wrote in one fax. Koch, somewhat less steamily, described his ardor as "beyond calculation by the largest computers.") Boston reporters almost uniformly deemed the MFA show crass and egotistical. *Boston Globe* columnist Alex Beam was especially caustic, gratuitously noting that Koch "rhymes with joke" and disinterring the moldy beat-his-family-to-death-with-a-belt threat allegation. With Koch talking about a lawsuit, the *Globe* subsequently ran a fairly groveling editor's note acknowledging the conflicting evidence. But who reads editor's notes? Koch felt he could not get a fair shake.

On the other hand, Koch couldn't stomach feeling taken advantage of. In 1985, after deciding that his brothers had cheated him in their settlement, Koch had gone back to court. What followed, Bill Koch said later, "would make *Dallas* and *Dynasty* look like a playpen." There were private detectives and wiretaps and room bugs and body mikes and stolen garbage bags and scurrilous whispering campaigns. There was even a mysterious Israeli "security consultant" whom Koch's own employees later accused of taping their calls at Koch's behest (a charge Koch denies). Many more lawsuits followed. *Fortune* called it "perhaps the nastiest family feud in American business history."

The same mix of traits that had mired Koch in ruinous litigation and led him to victory in the America's Cup—contrarian determination, a belief in technology and professional investigators, scads of money, a profound need to win, and an impish glee at sticking it to the man (or, it sometimes seemed, the straw man)—would prove equally useful when it came to the Jefferson bottles. In the end, Koch decided to get to the bottom of the matter, and the person he charged with investigating it was a former FBI agent named Jim Elroy.

Elroy had crossed paths with Koch in the 1980s, when Koch, in the midst of the eye-gouging brawl with brothers Charles and David, blew the whistle on their alleged theft of oil from Indian reservations. Elroy served as an investigator for the Senate Select Committee on Indian Affairs, which looked into the accusations and found them to have merit, and Koch was impressed by his work. Elroy, who went by the e-mail sobriquet SEAWOLF410, also happened to share Koch's interest in sailing.

Now one of Elroy's men went to Charlottesville, Virginia, and spent several days at Monticello doing his own research into the bottles' Jefferson connection. Among the people he met was Cinder Goodwin Stanton, who was now the Shannon Senior Research Historian. Twenty years before, she had found the entire matter unpleasant. Her attitude had since mellowed into bemusement. She had no new theories about the bottles, and hadn't read her own report on them in two decades. When she reexamined it now, she was embarrassed to see that she had written that Hardy Rodenstock was a man "of unquestioned knowledge and integrity." Her Jefferson research had since led her in other arcane directions; just now she was working on an article about Jefferson's moldboard plow. As Koch's investigator retraced the steps taken by Stanton in 1985, he found the same gaps and omissions in the Jeffersonian record as she had. Which is to say almost none. "Jefferson was *anal,*" Elroy recalled.

As Bill Koch's team expanded their inquiry, they noticed that a lot of people were nervous. Monticello refused to give Goldstein a copy of Stanton's 1985 report. When a deputy of Elroy's contacted Farr Vintners, he was referred to the firm's solicitors. After Elroy spoke with Count Alexandre de Lur Saluces and learned about the Frericks controversy, he began to wonder whether the Jefferson bottles were even real. Lur Saluces told Elroy that, as far as he knew, the document Rodenstock claimed was a page from Yquem's ledger—showing an order by Jefferson of the 1787 vintage— hadn't come from Yquem's archives.

Elroy was drifting straight toward the same morass of subjectivity that had bedeviled all previous challenges to the bottles—the arguments about bottle variation, the blind street of Rodenstock's reticence, the how-would-you-know-what-it's-supposed-to-taste-like posture, Monticello's skepticism versus the impossibility of proving a negative, the inadequacy of existing radio-dating methods, the sensory validations by such luminaries as Broadbent and Jancis Robinson, not to mention the disincentive for Koch to sacrifice a bottle that had cost tens of thousands of dollars for a test that might not be definitive. The odds were against his coming to any more certain a conclusion than had the few people before him who had questioned their bottles.

Then, cruising the Web, Elroy discovered some papers written by a French scientist who had recently invented an unusual device he called a germanium detector.

THOUGH HE LIVED outside of Bordeaux, Philippe Hubert was an unlikely person to have become the world's leading expert on anything having to do with wine. He had spent his career first as an experimental nuclear physicist, and more recently as a specialist in the ghostly subatomic particles called neutrinos. Unlike Bipin Desai, a theoretical physicist whose main activity outside of work was rare vintages, Hubert was a casual mealtime drinker. It was happenstance that led him to wine.

In the late 1970s, when the 8-mile Fréjus road tunnel was being constructed on the French-Italian border, a group of scientists had recognized a rare opportunity. Particle physicists are always on the lookout for bigger and better isolation chambers. So tiny and quiet and subtle are the particles and reactions they are measuring that it is impossible to detect them unless the world's light and noise and tumult are shut out. With the tunnel being built, the scientists seized the chance to drill through the side of it into the alpine massif and hollow out the deepest underground lab in Europe, more than a mile beneath the summit. The location of the Subterranean Laboratory at Modane, accessible only from the Fréjus tunnel, made for some hairy circumstances, including the need to play Frogger when parking inside the tunnel and crossing the road to the lab entrance without being run over.

The other part of lowering "the background," as physicists call it, is using lab equipment fabricated from materials with the lowest possible radioactivity. Around 1990, Philippe Hubert and some fellow scientists set about isolating the best materials; to do so, he in turn needed an exquisitely sensitive detector to identify *them*. This was how he came up with the germanium detector.

It consisted of a supercooled metallic crystal sheathed in "archaeological lead" salvaged from a Roman ship sunk two thousand years earlier off the coast of Brittany. The hypersensitive crystal was capable of detecting the subtlest radioactive signals, while the inert lead blocked out other particles that might be distracting. By measuring the pulses generated in the crystal when it was put near radioactive material, it was possible to detect both the amount and kind of radioactivity.

In the late 1990s, Hubert began to wonder if there might not be other uses for his detector. He shared a more modest, less sensitive detector, on the campus of the University of Bordeaux, with the French agency charged with *"répression des fraudes."* Bernard Medina, an analytical chemist who ran the regional lab for the agency, spent his time testing food products—mainly wine—to assure both their authenticity and, post-Chernobyl, their lack of contamination. Medina and his colleagues studied chocolate, coffee, prunes, salt. They analyzed regional *cepes,* and sniffed out an imposter batch from abroad. Once, Medina helped solve a murder case by establishing that a vinegar stain on a shirt came from a particular bottle.

He and Hubert were often in the lab at the same time, and the two hit it off. "Like two guys at a garage," Medina recalled. "He had a brand-new Lamborghini; I had a beat-up Ferrari. We each needed spare parts." Over the next few years, the Bordeaux native Medina taught the Brittany native Hubert about wine, and Hubert taught Medina about radioactive physics. As they traded notes, Medina wondered if the germanium detector could help to date wine.

With a bottle of wine, using the detector wasn't as simple as putting the bottle next to the crystal. The shape of the bottle, the radioactivity in the glass, and the dilution of the datable material in water combined to make it unlikely that gamma rays emitted by the material would be strong enough for the detector to sense. Opening the bottle and reducing the wine to ashes would, on the other hand, yield a workable sample. At the underground facility in Modane, Hubert tested three bottles of wine, from three different vintages, and found that the concentration of cesium-137, a radioactive isotope, varied with each vintage.

He and Medina were surprised, and they decided to expand the experiment. They gathered bottles from various well-known modern vintages—not an easy task, even though they were in Bordeaux, because of the high prices—and tested them. Each of these, too, revealed its own distinctive cesium concentration. Hubert plotted a chart, showing the levels of cesium in these wines from 1950 up to the present.

Like tritium, the element present at 1962 levels in Hans-Peter Frericks's Jefferson bottle, cesium-137 is man-made. It didn't exist in nature in significant concentrations prior to the first hydrogen bomb test, in 1952. It then rose rapidly until the 1963 atmospheric test-ban treaty, after which it declined. It spiked again in 1986, following Chernobyl. Hubert now had a yardstick for dating wine, at least wine made since 1952.

In 2001, Medina presented Hubert with a real-world test of the wine-dating technique. In 1999, conveniently just in time for Millennial celebrations, an improbable number of bottles of 100-year-old first growths had flooded the French and Belgian markets. People in Bordeaux were skeptical. The negociant Barton & Guestier tipped off Château Margaux, which went to the fraud office. The fraud office then obtained six bottles each of "Lafite 1900" and "Margaux 1900," and Hubert administered his cesium test to one of each. He did this in Modane, which took six hours, two planes, and a train to reach. He didn't destroy the wine, but poured each into a container surrounding the crystal. Within ten minutes, in each case, he knew it was fake, because the distinctive cesium curve on his computerized spectrum revealed it to date from the modern era. The two bottles showed different levels of cesium, though. At this point Hubert sent two more of the bottles to be carbon dated. The results were almost identical, confirming the validity of the cesium test. But the different levels of cesium between the Margaux and the Lafite puzzled Hubert.

He thought it a pity to reduce potentially priceless wine to ashes, and a pity to pour it into a container, as he had been doing. Either way meant opening the bottle. Testing a closed bottle of wine was a less sensitive method, but he and Medina decided to give it a try. To their surprise, it worked. They tested the remaining bottles without opening them. All had different cesium levels. It was clear that the forger was mixing different wines, but for his base wine he had chosen the worst possible vintage from a radioactive standpoint: 1963, the year with the highest concentration of cesium in history. When the man, a Belgian national, was arrested, he claimed he had merely topped up true 1900 wine with younger wine from the same château.

Having solved that crime, Hubert developed something of a reputation for his wine-detection skills. The Bordeaux trade group was concerned at first about all this public talk in which the word *radioactivity* appeared in the same sentence as their sublime product. But ultimately they supported Hubert's dating work. Hubert was only a year away from retiring, and he enjoyed the new and unexpected sideline he had stumbled into so late in his career. It brought him into contact with a whole new group of people and a whole new subject.

He had lived with the curse of a job that could not be explained to others or, at least, understood by them. Once, with a group of journalists, he was embarking on an explanation of his field by saying that "a neutrino is a particle that——" when someone interrupted to ask what a particle was. Neutrinos might be interesting, people would say, but how useful were they? Wine, on the other hand, everybody understood, and everyone was interested in. It was also a lot easier to get funding for. Commercial interests hinged on this work. And if, along the way, it was a palatable way to introduce people to a little thing called the neutrino, well, Hubert couldn't argue with that.

WHEN JIM ELROY learned of Hubert's work, he realized that there was, after all, a way to test Koch's bottles without opening them. In

April of 2005, Elroy contacted Hubert, who leaped at the opportunity. He didn't ask to be paid, or even want to be paid. A scientist to the core, Hubert welcomed the chance to put his method to such a test. He had never heard of Bill Koch, but if he could prove that the wine in the most famous bottles in the world was actually young, it would be a ringing endorsement of his work.

The following month, Elroy flew to France, changing planes in London, where he quipped to the Heathrow security guards inspecting his luggage: "You just can't get a good bottle of wine on the airplane." He arrived at the Saint-Exupéry Airport in Lyon on the afternoon of May 24. It was the same date that Jefferson had arrived in Bordeaux two centuries earlier. Elroy was carrying two small bullet-proof suitcases lined with molded foam, which contained all four of Koch's Jefferson bottles as well as the 1771 Lafite and 1791 Latour that had come from Rodenstock. Philippe Hubert had driven eight hours from Bordeaux and was there to meet Elroy.

They drove two hours southeast to Modane, going straight to the lab and beginning parallel tests in two germanium detectors. Knowing that the sheer price of the bottles would spook the lab's administrators, Hubert hadn't asked for permission to run the measurements. He and Elroy stayed in Modane for the next five days, sleeping at a small hotel nearby, where Hubert was close with the owners. During the day, they were in the lab. Elroy wasn't interested in doing any tourism, and stayed close at hand as Hubert performed his tests. The other scientists and technicians present in the lab that week all wanted to see the bottles.

To Elroy's dismay, Hubert's tests on the bottles were inconclusive. While the wine in them was not modern (or, at least, younger than 1952), it was impossible to say how old it was, as its age fell somewhere in the two-hundred-year gray area (1750–1950) that wouldn't yield its secrets to carbon dating.

Elroy had intended to fly straight back to the States, but during the week in Modane, he and Hubert noticed that one of the bottles of Lafite was leaking slightly through the wax. Elroy changed his plans, and on Sunday, May 29, he packed the bottle-bearing suitcases in the trunk of Hubert's car, and together they drove across southern France to Bordeaux to see about getting the bottle recorked. On Monday they went to Lafite, only to be told that the château, because of the fragility, value, and possible historical significance of the bottle, would not recork it for them.

Hubert offered to do a longer test of the Jefferson bottles in the detector in the fraud lab at the University of Bordeaux. While it was a less sensitive device, it offered two advantages: it was big enough to accommodate all four Jefferson bottles at the same time; and it was available for tests of much longer duration. Elroy and Medina agreed, and Elroy left the bottles there for the next two months.

Like many who had crossed paths with the Jefferson bottles, Hubert found himself becoming interested in the Founding Father. He read a book on Jefferson's European travels. He also read a book about Yquem in which one of Jefferson's handwritten letters was reproduced in the original French, and was impressed by Jefferson's command of the language.

The longer test again revealed no significant presence of Cs-137. Although Hubert wouldn't send Elroy his official report until October, it was clear that his method, which had seemed so promising, was not going to resolve the mystery. At the end of July, Elroy returned to Bordeaux to pick up the bottles and bring them back to Florida. For their troubles, Hubert and Medina were left with a couple of souvenirs. Koch sent Hubert a book about his America's Cup victory, and Elroy, who had programmed his cell phone to ring the whistled tune from *The Good, the Bad and the Ugly*, gave Medina an FBI baseball cap.

THE MADDENING INCONCLUSIVENESS of the tests only caused Elroy's questions to multiply, and as he learned more about

Rodenstock, Elroy ramped up his inquiry into a full-blown investigation. He had a global network to call on, the far-flung fraternity of ex-agents from Scotland Yard, the FBI, and other police and intelligence organizations, and he assigned men to several different areas of research. In California he reached out to an FBI alumnus named Stanley Los, whose claim to fame had occurred when he was off duty and chased a serial killer down his Santa Barbara cul-de-sac. In London, Elroy called on Richard Marston, a thirty-three-year veteran of Scotland Yard with a penchant for flamboyant red bow ties and an expertise in international money laundering and commercial fraud; Marston had previously been stationed in Florida, where he worked with the FBI going after Caribbean con men. In Germany, Elroy used an outfit called Investigations and Forensic Services, a division of PriceWaterhouseCoopers, and in Hong Kong he tapped another ex-FBI colleague. Within Koch's office, publicist Brad Goldstein got into the spirit, too, embracing the chance to revive his former career as an investigative reporter; back then, his journalistic crusades had been directed more at governmental corruption than at the lifestyles of the rich and famous.

Stanley Los was tasked with making contact with Rodenstock. On September 2, Los sent Rodenstock a fax, asking him to confirm that Koch's Jefferson bottles came from Rodenstock's collection and that they came from a Paris home once occupied by Jefferson, inquiring what steps Rodenstock had taken to authenticate the bottles, and asking for any scientific or other records supporting the attribution. "Based on your knowledge and research," Los asked, "do you believe that the above bottles were owned by or bottled for Thomas Jefferson?" Los concluded on a wryly ambiguous note, writing: "Your reputation in the wine world is without equal, and your information confirming the authenticity of these bottles would mean much to Mr. Koch."

Three days later, Rodenstock responded. Though he was "finished with the subject Jefferson bottles," which had been amply covered by "the press (serious and unfortunately also unserious)," Rodenstock said that because he had "met Mr. Koch about five years ago personally at a fantastic Château Latour tasting and found him very kind and competent, I will answer your questions nevertheless."

Rodenstock's letter betrayed a lingering anger: "The nonsense written by many journalists in the matter of Jefferson proved that many scribblers were not really concerned about the matter, but only interested in a primitive gutter press report." He then laid out Broadbent's well-worn circumstantial arguments about Jefferson and wine, mentioning Christie's authentication of the bottle and the engraving, and sharing, unbidden, his opinions about Jefferson. "One can't pay enough tribute to [him] . . . ," Rodenstock wrote. "He was a great connoisseur. . . . Jefferson's wine knowledge should be recognized much more in the U.S.A." Rodenstock cited the Zurich/Oxford carbon datings, and said, alluding to the Frericks episode, "in that case, envy, malevolence and intrigues have been at work."

"I hope," Rodenstock continued, "that Mr. Koch isn't one of these wine lovers who collect wines during half their life to compose a great wine cellar and then unfortunately put all the wines up for auction one day. That would be sad (and Mr. Jefferson would surely turn in his grave), since the *Maître du chai* has produced the wine to be drunk. It shouldn't be a speculative object. . . . It is always an indescribable experience to drink such old wines. It literally gives you 'gooseflesh.' Alone the thought that Jefferson and Washington have also drunk these wines (1784, 1787 . . .) makes you have a minute of silence when drinking these wines. You just drink history! And therefore one shouldn't only collect, but also draw the cork of the bottles now and then. Mr. Koch has certainly already opened a Jefferson bottle or will do this some day."

A LOWER-TECH EXAM, in the end, was what settled the matter.

After the disappointment of Philippe Hubert's tests, Jim Elroy had been running his fingers over one of the Jefferson bottles when it occurred to him to have the engraving analyzed. Elroy had the bottles examined by two experts, one an engraver who worked near the Corning Museum of Glass in upstate New York, the other a former tool-mark specialist with the FBI, who scrutinized the inscriptions much more thoroughly than the Christie's ceramics and glass department had in 1985. These experts had access to pedal-driven eighteenth-century engraving equipment, and Elroy bought some old bottles to experiment on. They tried to reproduce the engravings.

The size of the apparatus required for wheel-engraving drove home the fact that the "Jefferson bottles" would have had to be sent to an expert engraver, which didn't fit neatly with the narrative of offhanded bottle-marking long conjured by Broadbent and Rodenstock. More damning, the experiments made it clear that the Jefferson bottles couldn't have been engraved using a pedal-driven copper wheel, which would have resulted in more-ragged lines. Instead, the bottles had clearly been engraved by a modern method: a power tool with a flexible shaft.

Probably a dental drill.

"We believe Rodenstock did the drilling himself," Brad Goldstein said. "It's easy. *Jim* did it."

CHAPTER 19

TAILING MEINHARD

*I*T WAS JUST BEFORE CHRISTMAS 2005, AND BILL KOCH sat at a table in his fourteenth-floor corner office in West Palm Beach, quietly cocky as he described his planned response to his investigators' findings. "I don't like lawsuits," Koch said, "but they can be a good tool."

The room featured views of the water and souvenirs from his America's Cup win. Koch often wore conservative suits lined with psychedelic vintage Pucci silk—a sartorial expression of what he considered to be his hidden wildness—but on this day, with his baggy dark brown khakis, striped button-down shirt, and mop of white hair, he looked like a suburban Midwestern dad. A recent knee replacement had left him with a temporary limp, but he was as aggressive as ever.

His doubts mounting, Koch had decided to yank his bottles from the MFA show, at the last minute changing the catalog wording to "reputedly purchased by Thomas Jefferson." But pulling the bottles from the MFA show only motivated him to further expand the investigation.

By now, Jim Elroy had zeroed in on Hardy Rodenstock, search-ing for any and all biographical information about the elusive German. As with Koch's lawsuits against his brothers and his prepa-ration for the America's Cup, when he deployed frogmen and spy helicopters to gather intelligence, Koch availed himself of a range of investigative tactics. His team, led by Elroy, had tracked Roden-stock to Hong Kong. Among the facts the investigators learned was something Ralf Frenzel had stumbled upon twenty years earlier: "Hardy Rodenstock" was a fictitious name. Hardy Rodenstock was really Meinhard Görke.

Frenzel had been eating at a restaurant in Essen in the 1980s when the waiter said, "You work with my father." The waiter's last name was Görke, and he informed Frenzel that he was the son of Meinhard Görke, better known as Hardy Rodenstock. This was the first Frenzel had heard of Rodenstock not being Hardy's real name, of his being a father, and of his having been previously married. The name change didn't strike Frenzel as a big deal. In the German music business, stage names were common. Rodenstock's girlfriend, Tina York, and her sister Mary Roos had been born Monika and Rose-marie Schwab, and Jack White, a Berlin music producer who was a regular at Rodenstock's tastings, had changed his name from Horst Nussbaum. It was the secrecy about Rodenstock's real name—and his family—that made an impression on Frenzel. When he men-tioned the encounter with the son, Rodenstock seemed unsettled.

Two decades later, Koch's investigators, who viewed the name change in a more sinister light, were discovering other interesting things as well, including the fact that Rodenstock owned a company that manufactured perfumes and essences. And they had obtained the sealed court documents from the Frericks dispute. They were amazed to learn that, contrary to all the press reports at the time, a court had decisively sided with Frericks (when the Munich court, on December 14, 1992, found that Rodenstock "adulterated the wine or knowingly offered adulterated wine"). The investigators' findings now filled a fat spiral dossier and two CD-ROMs.

ELROY WAS EMPLOYING some "very clever" methods in his investigation, Koch said now at his office as he stood up to go to lunch. Koch drove a visitor, along with Oxbow's publicist, Brad Goldstein, and general counsel, Richard Callahan, in his Maybach to the Palm Beach Yacht Club. The car featured a flat-screen TV on the back of each seat, puffy headrests, and four different cell phones positioned around the wood interior. At lunch, Koch sat with his back to the water. He reported that Broadbent was backpedaling now, saying the wine "tasted like a wine of that period" and retreating from the assertion that it was definitely Jefferson's. He said he was about two months away from being ready to sue.

Koch told a story about a nationally prominent appellate lawyer who had stayed at his house and was discovered trying to abscond with $70,000 of Koch's wine in his suitcase. He told other stories about wine merchants he'd sued over undelivered wine, and a wine consultancy he had funded that had become, without his knowledge, a party to tax evasion. And he and Goldstein described how Goldstein had approached *Wine Spectator* to offer it an exclusive on the story of a spectacular fraud. Although *Wine Spectator* had covered several episodes in the Jefferson bottles' history, despite Marvin Shanken's ownership of one, the editors now demurred, saying it was "a sensitive subject." That was the Goldstein/Koch version of events, anyway. Later, Thomas Matthews, the magazine's executive editor, wouldn't recall Goldstein specifying that the bottles at issue were the Jefferson bottles; the magazine had been covering counterfeit wine for years, and according to Matthews, Goldstein had demanded that Koch himself author the article. "We don't let a collector write his own story and make allegations we haven't investigated,"

Matthews says. In any case, all these experiences had soured Koch on the wine world.

Nor were any of the chief members of his legal and investigative team likely to have leapt to the defense of that world. Callahan, Koch's lawyer, allowed somewhat sheepishly that he ordered cardboard boxes of wine from a Massachusetts chain retailer and kept them in his basement. Goldstein, compact and pugnacious, seemed intimidated when it came to wine. In general, he brought the native cynicism of a former investigative reporter to his work: although he had no evidence to back it up, he suspected that Hardy Rodenstock and Michael Broadbent had a hidden financial relationship. He assumed Bill Sokolin had been an insurance scammer. He was quick to question whether even documents signed by Rodenstock had actually been written by him. He spoke with a hardboiled swagger, saying things like "We'll keep going until that man feels my breath on the back of his neck."

For all his anger, Koch also seemed energized by the pursuit, and he and Goldstein were convinced they were living a real-life caper film. "This is *National Treasure*," Goldstein kept saying. In the car back to the Oxbow office, they amused themselves by speculating who might play them on the big screen. Koch had skirted the edges of the entertainment business. In the early nineties he had made a ham-fisted play to buy MGM; he called the film studio "Metro-Golden-Mayer" in a press release he claims was unauthorized, misidentified then-owner Crédit Lyonnais as "French Lyonnais," antagonized industry powerbroker Michael Ovitz, and was laughed out of Hollywood. More recently, he had wed Bridget Rooney, of the Pittsburgh Steelers–owning Rooneys, who was the mother of actor Kevin Costner's son. Now someone suggested Michael Caine could play Koch, and everybody laughed.

MUCH REMAINED FOR Koch's team to do before filing a lawsuit. Some was legal preparation. Koch had bought the bottles more than fifteen years earlier, and they needed to determine whether the statute of limitations for fraud had run out. Koch's lawyers advised him that the statutory clock only started ticking once a victim became aware of a potential fraud. Even though Koch had paid a Munich lawyer a few thousand dollars in April of 1993 to look into the Frericks-Rodenstock dispute, Koch now said he didn't remember doing so. After Rodenstock and the Munich lawyer disputed this, and records disproved Koch, he said that the lawyer had reassured him of the bottles' authenticity, and that he first heard of Monticello's doubts during the run up to the Boston MFA show in 2005. Koch said he had never read the *New York Times* or *Wine Spectator* articles that publicized Monticello's skepticism years earlier.

Koch and his lawyers still needed to decide whom to sue (Rodenstock, Christie's, Broadbent, Farr Vintners?), where (Germany? England? America?), and whether to seek out other plaintiffs. Koch initially sought allies in his cause, and Kip Forbes seemed amenable. The Forbes family had already decided to sell their bottle through the books and manuscripts department at Christie's in May 2006 as part of a dispersal sale of their historical American documents collection. But they withdrew the bottle from the sale, citing restrictive New York laws governing the sale of alcohol. The other reason was that Kip had been contacted by Koch, and he wanted in.

To build a strong case against Rodenstock, Koch knew that it was necessary to amass overwhelming evidence, and the investigation proceeded along several parallel tracks. One was to methodically create a paper trail linking Koch's bottles to Rodenstock. In early January, Koch himself faxed Rodenstock from a family-owned apartment in New York, asking the German to affirm that he was the source of Koch's Jefferson bottles and that he believed they had belonged to Thomas Jefferson. Faxing Rodenstock from New York was deliberate. Koch's lawyers viewed it as a favorable venue for their lawsuit, and communications routed through New York would help to justify it as the proper jurisdiction.

A week later, Rodenstock bit, responding with a fax sent to the New York number. Rodenstock said he had already answered the questions posed by Stanley Los, reiterating his and Broadbent's case for a Jefferson attribution and the story of the carbon-dating test he had commissioned. He ended with a cheery postscript: "I have heard that you have bought many fantastic wines at the spectacular Zachys auction. Congratulations!"

All this was the groundwork necessary for Koch to make his case about the Jefferson bottles. But what mattered to him, ultimately, was not just the Jefferson bottles, but the integrity of his entire collection. Accordingly, in March 2006, Elroy was dispatched to Château Pétrus in Pomerol. His mission: to authenticate two Rodenstock-sourced magnums of 1921 Pétrus. Koch had bought one of them at the "spectacular" Zachys auction for $33,150 and said he knew it came from Rodenstock because the consignor, a San Francisco tech entrepreneur named Eric Greenberg, had told him so. (Greenberg, who was reputed to have 70,000 bottles in his cellar, would later deny this.) Now, with a lawyer present, Pétrus officials found eight faults with the bottles. They called the Rodenstock-Greenberg-Zachys bottle "a very impressive fake made by a master forger of wine . . . the cork was too long and the metal cap and label on the wine appear to have been artificially aged."

Elroy had brought his glass experts with him on this trip, and the men, along with Philippe Hubert, visited Château d'Yquem to inspect the two Jefferson bottles, one full and one empty, in its possession. As with Koch's four Jefferson bottles, the experts determined that the engravings on these two had also been made with a modern power tool. Later they would reach the same conclusion about the Forbes bottle.

Elroy then let Hubert take a gamma-ray reading from the Pétrus magnums. The wine inside showed no trace of cesium-137, but the bottle glass itself emitted a post–World War II level of radioactivity.

On April 10, Koch faxed Rodenstock again. This time he asked for a meeting "over a good glass of wine, at a place of your choosing. . . . A short exchange of information face-to-face will accomplish more than a number of faxes and telephone calls." A month later, writing "from the sunny Kitzbühel," Rodenstock responded. He was testier this time, saying that "the matter is settled. From a legal point of view the purchase and the sale are barred by the statute of limitation." He denounced "the yellow press" for covering the Frericks dispute—"that farce"—"in a very primitive way." Legally, he said, it was Farr Vintners with whom Koch should be speaking; he saw no point in a discussion, and in any event "my English is unfortunately also not so good to speak with you about all the things I have already told you in writing." He claimed that he had "had all of the faxes I have sent you translated from German to English." For the first time he offered a detail about his supposed Parisian source: "The person from whom I have bought the bottles at the time was about sixty-five years old. I don't even know if the seller of the bottles is still alive today."

After all this, his amiable tone returned: "As said, if you would like to drink some fantastic wines with me in a nice circle of wine friends at a trip to Europe, I will gladly organize a wine tasting in your honor. Is there a wine you always wanted to drink but you don't have in your wine cellar? I would be glad to fulfil you that wish if I should have this wine in my cellar."

KOCH EXPANDED HIS investigation to the contents of his entire cellar, and hired David Molyneux-Berry, the former Sotheby's wine director who had first deemed the Frericks bottles fake, to vet his collection. The Englishman spent weeks in Koch's cellars, in Palm Beach and on Cape Cod. The weather was poor, and he worked from nine in the morning to six in the evening without surfacing for sun or air.

Simultaneously, another collector joined Koch's cause. A Boston entrepreneur named Russell Frye had recently sold his cellar through Sotheby's for nearly $8 million, the auction house's second-largest wine sale ever. But Sotheby's had rejected a lot of Frye's older bottles as fraudulent, and had put him in touch with Molyneux-Berry and Koch.

Molyneux-Berry examined hundreds of Koch's bottles, taking one at a time and comparing it with others. Because Koch's collection was so encompassing, Molyneux-Berry often had the luxury of comparing the same wine in the same vintage in multiple bottlings, even fifteen or twenty bottles of the same kind. All might look right except, say, three, which would look wrong in exactly the same way. It could take up to an hour to examine each bottle, but Koch insisted that Molyneux-Berry take the time necessary to assess the cellar.

"One, he's very rich," Molyneux-Berry said during a break from his work. "Two, he's absolutely pissed off at being defrauded."

Molyneux-Berry had worked up a list of thirty-two indicators of authenticity. They ranged from the shape of the bottle to the color of the glass, to the label material, to the label's coloration, to the importer's "slip" label, to the pontil scars and mold marks and ullage and capsule and cork and color of the wine and sediment. He would tick them off one by one.

Among the fakes he found was a magnum of Lafite 1945 that was in a bottle of a sort only created in 1964. A batch of 1950s La Tâche just purchased by Koch at auction had suspiciously high fills. Other bottles bore labels that had clearly been copied. Those were the easy ones. More difficult were instances where the bottle was correct, the label was good, the slip label seemed right, but Molyneux-Berry just had a feeling at first, and on closer scrutiny found some more definitive clue.

Molyneux-Berry made a point of not wanting to know the

source of any bottle before he had made an assessment of its authenticity. He didn't want to have an unconscious bias. "I don't want to know the provenance," he said. "That could color my own opinion. I'm just picking up each bottle, writing down what I think: fake . . . real . . . I don't want to be like a jury told of a prior criminal record."

In July, Molyneux-Berry took a break from cataloging, flying to Moscow to judge a sommelier competition before returning to the United States to resume his work in the Koch cellars. Molyneux-Berry had left the paper trail to others in Koch's organization, and as they narrowed down the channels—not easy, given the compartmentalized information structure of the rare-wine market—news filtered back to him that several of the bottles he had deemed fake had come from Rodenstock.

Regarding Michael Broadbent, his old rival, Molyneux-Berry was split. He respected Broadbent's success and his talent. He thought less of the lengths to which Broadbent was willing to go in order to win. "He told me," Molyneux-Berry recalled, "'My major weakness is I'm a salesman. I have to cut the deal.'"

Looking back now on the original Christie's catalog featuring the bottle bought by the Forbes family, Molyneux-Berry noted that Broadbent hadn't even mentioned Monticello (Molyneux-Berry had consulted with them first thing upon being offered the Frericks consignment in 1989): "There's a fear in the way it's cataloged. I suspect he was sick as a parrot about the authenticity, but he couldn't resist the opportunity. It was the juiciest carrot he'd ever got."

Molyneux-Berry wasn't losing sleep over Rodenstock's fate, which he thought might be worse than losing a lawsuit. "One or two of these guys are ferocious," he said, referring to Rodenstock's Hong Kong customers. "They will chop his head off, not ask for their money back. If we find a torso that looks like Hardy Rodenstock's, we'll know they've gotten their revenge."

FOR NOW, AN intact Rodenstock was still making the society scene. In early 2006 he appeared with Prince Albert of Monaco at an event where Rodenstock made a donation to one of the prince's charities. In May, Rodenstock attended Riedel's 250th-anniversary celebration in Kufstein. But there were indications that he was getting nervous. In August he reached out to Walter Eigensatz, Mr. Cheval Blanc, who hadn't spoken to him in years. Rodenstock called him and asked after his health, speaking of the good wines they had shared and suggesting they get together sometime. Eigensatz was measured in his response, leaving Rodenstock with the stark warning that he should "be careful." It was clear to Eigensatz that Rodenstock was trying to make nice with his enemies. "A year ago he was telling people he hoped I'd die," Eigensatz said a month later.

Michael Broadbent, pedaling blithely into the gloaming, seemed only mildly concerned by what was happening. "He was reluctant to tell me where he got them," Broadbent told a guest in late 2005, speaking in Room Number 7 of the London headquarters of Christie's. The room, its walls lined with red fabric, was one of a suite of tiny, windowless compartments on the ground floor that were reserved for specialists to meet with clients. Broadbent and the visitor were seated at a small square table. The former head of the wine department wore a pin-striped suit. Gold cuff links peeked out from the sleeves.

Broadbent's tasting notes now exceeded 85,000, and he had only two blank red notebooks left. The manufacturer had changed the color to black, but Broadbent didn't expect to have to make the change. "I'll be dead by then," he said. For a seventy-eight-year-old man who had devoted his life to alcohol, Broadbent looked fantastic. His face bore none of the exploded capillaries of the vodka-dependent; his liver functioned properly; his waistline remained in check; his mind was still acute.

"He was reluctant to tell me where he got them," Broadbent was recalling. "That's the only big question. And I said to Hardy, I said, 'Look, if you tell me where you got these, and I'm happy, my Christie's clients will be happy that I'm satisfied.'" Two decades on, to Broadbent's unceasing irritation, Rodenstock had still not obliged him.

Broadbent had recently been fielding all kinds of inquiries about the bottles, including one from a woman who ran the New York charity to which Bill Sokolin had donated his broken Jefferson bottle. She had contacted Broadbent in an effort to ascertain its provenance. Broadbent, in turn, had put the question to Rodenstock. On August 21, Broadbent had received a fax from Rodenstock, who had just attended the Salzburg music festival, where he reported that he had had "a lovely time."

Broadbent had begun to get nervous, as the possible repercussions of a full-fledged investigation began to dawn on him. In a handwritten fax to Rodenstock on October 4, he wrote:

> Dear Hardy,
>   Jefferson bottles. You and I are bored stiff with this subject. Unhappily, more pressure from the USA. I had a huge file, including Frericks, but neither I nor my secretary can find it. I seriously need all the filing you have on the Bonani/Hall analyses, and anything else relevant. It is important that I produce the evidence, again, for your reputation, Christie's, and mine is at stake.
>   Warm regards as always,
>   Michael

Rodenstock faxed a reply six days later, saying that he had been contacted by Koch's investigator. Rodenstock promised to send copies of the before-and-after photos he had presented as evidence in the Frericks case, which he falsely claimed "clearly show that the bottle has been tampered with after it has left my cellar. Frericks certainly had fiddled about with the wine himself. The sealing wax is without any doubt no longer identical with the sealing wax the bottle had when Frericks had bought it from me."

Now Broadbent's nervousness seemed to have receded and been replaced by weariness. Talk turned to Sotheby's, toward which Broadbent's hostility had hardly abated. "Of course, I hate her," Broadbent said now of Serena Sutcliffe. "I find her totally pretentious." He continued, "But the great joy was, Serena is incredibly proud of her lingual abilities. Philippine de Rothschild was having a lunch party in London, and Serena was being over-the-top about something: her father was in the war, and I never had any relations in the war or killed in the war, things like that. She was just being absolutely obnoxious. And Philippine de Rothschild leaned over and said, 'Serena, I cannot abide the way you speak French.' And Serena was knocked back." Broadbent did his best impression of Sutcliffe looking astonished. "And I said, 'Tell me, what is it about her speech?' Philippine said, 'First of all, it's very pretentious. She's trying to speak in what she thinks is the French upper-class accent, and she's using words that went out of favor years ago, and she just misses it.'" Broadbent grinned, clearly enjoying himself.

"I can tell you endless stories about her pretentiousness, silly mistakes she makes," he said. "But I won't. But she is very bright. She's known as Pushy Galore in America. Some American told me that. She is pushy. I mean, she's a hand-presser, particularly in Bordeaux, and she charms them all, but some people there can't stand her, either." He paused. "But she's done a great deal and put Sotheby's on the map. Whereas they were lagging hopelessly before."

The conversation grazed other topics, then Broadbent said, "It's terribly hot in here. Let's go and have a drink." King Street was still slick from the morning rain. The world headquarters of Christie's was situated in the heart of St. James, a neighborhood of bespoke shirtmakers, old-line wine merchants, and private men's clubs dating to the time of Britain's seventeenth-century glory.

Broadbent's club was Brooks's, one of the oldest. At the bar upstairs, he ordered a glass of Tio Pepe sherry, one of his preferred tipples. That morning, as on many others, he had begun the day with a buck's fizz, as the British call a cocktail of Champagne and orange juice. Even in his old age, he exuded a winsome boyishness, and his varied enthusiasms could distract him from the topic at hand. He might be mid-conversation at his ninth-floor riverside flat when suddenly he'd leap toward the window to point out some passing boat on the Thames that he'd never seen before. Or he'd be having lunch in a restaurant when he'd stop, mid-sentence, his attention caught by an attractive young woman, and murmur, "Dishy little Indian."

Broadbent and his guest repaired to Brooks's dining room for lunch. Broadbent ordered potted shrimp to start, followed by roasted grouse. "Pink," he told the waiter, "but not bloody." He ordered a small carafe of Macon-Lugny, a pleasant white Burgundy, followed by a half-bottle of a delicious blended red from Lebanon called Château Musar. He didn't need to look at the wine list; he had previously sat on the club's wine committee.

"Like me," Broadbent said, returning to the Jefferson bottles, "Hardy is sick of the subject." He sipped at his Musar. "Very drinkable, don't you think?" His note on it would have to wait until later; Brooks's discouraged the mixing of business and pleasure by forbidding papers in the club. Broadbent was fed up with Richard Marston, Koch's British investigator, who had called him several times. "If they want anything further from me," Broadbent said, "Mr. Koch himself can call me." He pronounced *Koch* like *Bach,* with a throaty scrape on the final consonants. Broadbent dismissed the inquiries as "malicious." Jim Elroy was an "FBI bore."

BILL KOCH WAITED for months to see whether Kip Forbes would join him as a coplaintiff. In the end, although Forbes wanted to, his brothers argued against it, and Koch and Russell Frye decided to go ahead without him. Then the FBI approached Koch, saying they had their own investigation under way and asking him to delay his suit against Rodenstock until they could, in Brad Goldstein's words, "lure him into the U.S." Koch demurred. Waiting for the FBI would be "like watching a glacier melt," Goldstein recalled.

On the last day of August 2006, a Thursday, Koch sued "Hardy Rodenstock, aka Meinhard Goerke," in federal court in Manhattan. Koch had decided not to sue Christie's or Farr, in the hope that they would become cooperating witnesses instead. Simultaneously, in federal court in San Francisco, Russell Frye filed suit against a California merchant, the Wine Library, and its owners, brothers Edward and Carl Gelsman. Koch's complaint laid out his evidence regarding the Jefferson bottles, and also singled out the magnum of 1921 Pétrus that had come from Rodenstock. The complaint noted that 1921 Pétrus had been given a perfect score by Robert Parker, and that the critic had first tasted the wine at the 1995 Rodenstock tasting he attended.

Koch's complaint mentioned that Russell Frye had been told by the Wine Library that Rodenstock was the source of many of the bottles he believed to be fake (Frye's complaint likewise cited two fake magnums of 1921 Pétrus). Describing Koch as "one of Rodenstock's many victims," the complaint stated: "[Rodenstock] is charming and debonair. He is also a con artist."

CHAPTER 20

THE FINISH

$\mathcal{F}$OR A MAN SEEKING TO LEAVE HIS PAST BEHIND, Germany is a hospitable place. Although it has less than a third as many people as the United States and is smaller than Montana, privacy laws there make it almost impossible to trace a person who is set on reinventing himself.

Nonetheless, with Koch's fat bankroll and well-connected team of law-enforcement veterans, the investigation yielded tantalizing glimpses of Rodenstock's past. Besides learning of Rodenstock's name change, which occurred in the mid-1970s, they gleaned other facts: he was born not in Essen but in Marienwerder, a village in northern Poland that was now named Kwidzyn. His father, Alfred Görke, had been stationed there with the German army and it was there that he met twenty-year-old Lydia Ristau, whom he married in 1940. Meinhard was born the next year.

Alfred, working on the railroad supply chain for the eastern front, had to stay in Marienwerder, while Lydia fled west, by horse and handcart, with her infant son. They settled first in a refugee camp in Hanover, then traveled by bicycle to Gelsenkirchen, a small town in northwestern Germany.

In 1945, Alfred rejoined the family and went to work for the civilian railroad in Essen. Though his son would later boast that Alfred "ran" the regional railway, he spent his career as a general clerk. Meinhard attended the Alma high school, where he was an unexceptional student, and then a technical school, where he studied surveying. He married young, to a hairdresser named Gisela, who gave him two sons, Törsten and Oliver. Meinhard never rose higher than "apprentice land surveyor" for the regional railway, and, contrary to his later assertions, never held teaching positions or published academic papers. He also had a younger brother named Gisbert, who lived near Essen, and whom the investigator, with cutting thoroughness, reported to be "a very small-sized man."

Curiously, though none of Rodenstock's wine friends knew of the brother, Gisbert appeared to share a passion for the grape. In 2000, without mentioning their relationship, "Gisbert Görke" had written to *Welt am Sonntag* to applaud a pair of articles penned by Hardy Rodenstock. Around the same time, the Hamburg-based food magazine *Der Feinschmecker* received several letters from Gisbert Görke, all praising Rodenstock and his friends and attacking the magazine's independent-minded editor, Madeleine Jakits. And in 2004, Gisbert Görke had written a letter to the magazine *Vinum* in response to an item about how to tell whether a 1928 Latour was real or fake.

Koch's investigators interviewed the Görke brothers' mother, as well as Rodenstock's old girlfriend Tina York. York, whose relationship with Rodenstock had lasted for close to a decade, revealed that Rodenstock had told her he was a member of the well-known Rodenstock clan, that he had kept the fact that he had two sons hidden from her, and that once when she had put a bowl of potato salad in his wine cellar to chill it Rodenstock "just flipped out." And the investigators, led by Secret Squirrel, as Brad Goldstein had taken to calling the stealthy and ubiquitous Elroy, were still sleuthing at full speed.

"You know that movie *Catch Me If You Can?*" Goldstein said. "That's what I want. I want the lab where he makes the bottles. I want the printing press."

Goldstein soon came close to getting what he wanted. In October, two months after Koch filed suit, his office received an e-mail from a German financial planner named Andreas Klein. Klein's wife's family had been Helga Lehner's landlords since 1968 and Hardy Rodenstock's since he married and moved in with Lehner in 1991. The house, on Ostprcussenstrasse in Munich, was a small, conspicuously modern twin with bright orange siding; the Rodenstocks lived in one half and, starting in 1997, Klein and his wife lived in the other, sharing a thin wall with their neighbors.

The Rodenstocks weren't home much—they moved freely among their apartments in Monte Carlo, Bordeaux, Kitzbühel, and Marbella—and over the years the Kleins' contact with them was polite but limited. Andreas Klein found Rodenstock bizarre. When they spoke, Rodenstock would invariably mention, apropos of nothing, "my friend" Franz Beckenbauer or Gerhard Schröder or Wolfgang Porsche or Mick Flick (the Mercedes-Benz heir). The name-dropping was so insistent that Klein was left with the strong impression that Rodenstock lacked self-confidence.

Occasionally, Rodenstock would give the Kleins a bottle of wine—always accompanied by a request of some sort. Once, Rodenstock asked the Kleins to stop barbecuing out back because the smell was seeping into his first floor. Another time, Rodenstock requested that the Kleins walk more softly going up and down stairs because he could hear the sound through their shared wall. At one point, he gave Klein a pair of slippers he had bought in southern Spain, to encourage softer walking.

The Kleins were more tolerant of the noise Rodenstock made. When he was home, they often heard a banging sound coming from the direction of his basement. It sounded distinctly like wood being hammered against wood, and at first Andreas Klein assumed

Rodenstock was doing carpentry or making furniture. But Roden-stock was not a visibly handy person—he always hired people to mow his grass and do other housework—and something about the sound suggested to Klein that Rodenstock was assembling wooden wine cases. The Kleins knew that Rodenstock bought and sold wine, but couldn't understand why he would personally be ham-mering the cases together.

The shared attic had a mold problem, and in 2001, the Kleins decided to have their leaky roof replaced and a new attic flat con-structed. Under German law, the Kleins needed permission from their tenants, but Rodenstock, after initially saying he would go along with it, started demanding increasing amounts of money and lease concessions.

The Kleins and the Rodenstocks ended up in court. Because of the mold, the Rodenstocks temporarily moved out of the house and into an expensive penthouse apartment in a posh nearby neighbor-hood, but they left much of their furniture and possessions behind and at the same time stopped paying rent on the Klein house. Rodenstock now told the Kleins it would cost them 150,000 euros for him to give up his tenant rights, and in the court case, according to Klein, Rodenstock fabricated evidence, at one point presenting the court with a copy of a letter to Klein's mother-in-law, the tech-nical landlord, which he had patently, but carelessly, backdated: the address on the letter contained a postal code which had not existed at the time of the date on the letter.

The case dragged on. The Kleins had two young children, were living in a house without a proper roof and with mold on the walls, and couldn't afford protracted litigation, but in the meantime the court wouldn't permit them to evict Rodenstock or proceed with their renovation.

At a loss for how to get rid of their nightmare tenant, the Kleins began to devise more creative methods. They thought maybe Rodenstock had been using their house as an office, which would be a lease violation, but that year, 2002, Rodenstock moved all his files to another apartment nearby. Klein went to look at the apartment and saw that the buzzer said Rodenstock/Görke. He assumed Görke must be the name of Rodenstock's business.

Then Klein hit on another idea. As part of their case, the Kleins had argued that the planned renovation shouldn't pose any problem for the Rodenstocks, since they were hardly there anyway. Rodenstock had countered, in testimony to the court, that his other homes were just vacation apartments and that Munich was his primary residence. It occurred to Andreas Klein that Rodenstock probably didn't pay German taxes and that the German tax authorities would be very interested to learn that Rodenstock was now claiming Munich as his place of residence. Klein gave a copy of Rodenstock's court testimony to the tax authorities.

In December 2004, nearly three years after the Kleins had submitted their tip, they received a visit from the tax police, who just wanted to confirm that Rodenstock was no longer living there. They apologized for the delay in following up on the tip, citing delays in foreign countries; they were interested in his apartments elsewhere in Europe. They now had a list of addresses associated with Rodenstock and were apparently conducting coordinated raids on them. The Rodenstock/Görke office flat was around the corner, and Klein watched as the tax authorities drove away from it with three carloads of documents. Three days after the tax raid—and a full three years after the court case had begun—Rodenstock finally agreed to move out of the Kleins' house in exchange for a relatively small payoff of about 15,000 euros.

After Rodenstock at last moved his belongings out of the house, in 2005, Klein went into the vacated basement. In one corner of a small room, he found a stack of what appeared to be unused wine labels, with no type on them, as well as a pile of old-looking corks. In the cellar's bigger room, Klein found a few dozen empty wine bottles, and something stranger: Rodenstock had laid a carpet down on the concrete floor, and on top of the carpet was a large mound of dirt (with a dead frog in it); the carpet and the dirt were covered in mold. The room stank, making Klein wonder how the scent of an occasional barbecue could possibly have bothered Rodenstock. The Kleins thought back to all those times they had heard the sound of hammering. Though they couldn't prove anything, Andreas Klein would later learn about Bill Koch's suit from a German tabloid and write that upon seeing the cellar, "we were absolutely sure that he prepared the bottles in the smaller room and made them older in the bigger room. It was too obvious."

THOUGH THE LAWSUITS would take time to play out, it was likely that Hardy Rodenstock, as an entity in the wine world, was finished. Hans-Peter Frericks had posed his challenge to the bottles in pre-Internet days. The news about Bill Koch's investigation spread much faster and farther. Now it would be impossible for Rodenstock to count on most customers being unaware of the accusations against him. And the accusations were, this time, far more conclusive.

Rodenstock's options were limited. Koch was in this for justice and for sport. He wasn't going to settle with the German on terms any less humiliating than the Treaty of Versailles had been to an earlier generation of his countrymen. If Rodenstock confessed to having faked the bottles, or to having knowingly sold fakes, he would open himself up to countless other civil suits and criminal prosecution. He could fight Koch head-on, of course, but Koch had demonstrated an ability to maintain a fight for decades, and to all appearances Koch had a lot more money. (He had already spent more than $1 million on this investigation, and three weeks after the lawsuit was filed, the new edition of the annual Forbes 400 list pegged Koch's personal wealth at $1.4 billion.) It would be an ugly war of attrition. In any case, fighting Koch would require that

Rodenstock offer a persuasive counternarrative, something he had never been able to muster in two decades of accusations.

When a major German collector faxed a *Wall Street Journal* article about the Koch and Frye suits to some friends, one of them reported back to Rodenstock, who sent the collector an angry fax from his apartment near Bordeaux. The collector hadn't spoken to Rodenstock in ten years, and wrote back, "If you think this isn't of interest to wine collectors, you are mistaken. And if you think the issue of fakes is overrated, you are mistaken."

Rodenstock, nonetheless, was already cranking up his fog machine. He threatened journalists. He made unverifiable statements and legalistic arguments. He attacked the characters of his accusers. He blustered. In an assertion that hardly smacked of an innocent man unjustly accused, Rodenstock said that even if the bottles were fake, the statute of limitations for a fraud lawsuit had expired. He said he had bought the bottles without actually seeing the cellar, contradicting what he had written to *VWGA Journal* editor Treville Lawrence in 1986. He even claimed that he still had some Jefferson bottles in his possession, and that he had received new orders for them *since* the filing of the Koch suit. After some obviously fake Jefferson bottles went on sale on eBay in late September, Rodenstock bought one and said the bottles were evidence of just how many fakers were out there.

Surrogates, meanwhile, posited far-fetched arguments. Perhaps, they said, Koch himself had traced over the "original" engravings with a drill. Why? Because Koch was "a neurotic maniac." Rodenstock suggested that Koch was upset because, at the 2000 Latour tasting where the men had had their only meeting, Rodenstock had made a comment to the effect that Koch was a prestige collector, rather than a true connoisseur. Specifically, Rodenstock recalled uttering the expression "the last shirt has no pockets," the German equivalent of "you can't take it with you." Now, he theorized, Koch was avenging that remark. To the glossy society tabloid

Bunte, Rodenstock dismissed Koch with a pearl of Bavarian trash talk: "The oak tree is not concerned with the pig that is scratching its back against the roots."

THOSE WHO HAD vouched for the bottles over the last two decades varied in their responses. Jancis Robinson was quick to put news of the suits on her website, writing that "I should perhaps have smelled a rat," but pointing out that she had mentioned the questions about the authenticity of Rodenstock's bottles in a late-1990s newspaper column. Alexandre de Lur Saluces, who in 1986 had called Rodenstock "my friend" and said he saw "no reason to doubt the authenticity" of the Jefferson bottles, now stated that he had always been skeptical of the bottle he tasted in 1985. Winespectator.com, in the awkward position of belonging to someone who owned one of the bottles, stayed silent. Decanter.com published a story that dealt with the role of Broadbent, despite his being one of its star columnists. Robert Parker's opinion of the non-Jefferson Rodenstock bottles he drank in 1995 hadn't changed: "[T]he wines I tasted were great wines—real or fake." Robinson handled the delicate matter of her old friend Broadbent's role by not mentioning it in her write-up of the scandal, instead leaving that work to a reader's post she published on her site. "I knew he'd had a tough time in the [newspaper]," Robinson later explained. "I suppose I was being a bit protective of him."

Those who had sold the bottles began pointing fingers, all in the same direction. Farr Vintners, which had sold more of the bottles on Rodenstock's behalf than anyone else, emphasized that it had been a mere conduit. "Our position," Farr's Stephen Browett wrote in an e-mail, "is that we made it clear to our buyers at that time that we were not guaranteeing the quality of the bottles and made it absolutely clear that Mr. Rodenstock was the source of them. We just took a commission. At that time the wines had been authenticated by Michael Broadbent of Christie's who was regarded as the world's leading expert." In another e-mail, Browett added, "I don't think that anyone would have bought or sold these bottles without his expert opinion."

"Looking back, more questions could have been asked" was the gentle bureaucratese used by Christie's North America wine head Richard Brierley as he threw his department's venerable, seventy-nine-year-old chairman emeritus under the bus. The auction house told the *Wall Street Journal* that Broadbent wasn't available to comment.

Privately, Broadbent was shaken by the news of the lawsuits, if not enlightened. A few days after they were filed, he said Rodenstock was "an absolute fool for not revealing where he got the bottles," as if there were still possibly a legitimate answer to that question. In Koch's lawsuit and the subsequent news coverage, Broadbent saw "an obsessive witch-hunt."

There was a general sadness among Broadbent's many admirers, who could not deny that the affair had left him, as one collector put it, "very damaged." His old-vintage bible, which continued to be quoted from liberally in every new Christie's auction catalog, was riddled with tasting notes from Rodenstock bottles. Nearly all of the rarest wines, in a book premised on its comprehensiveness and inclusion of wines almost no other living person had tasted, Broadbent had drunk courtesy of the German. Any number of others had been drunk courtesy of friends of Rodenstock, and had likely come from him.

With his 2002 edition of his big book, far from quietly cutting back on the number of notes derived from Rodenstock tastings, Broadbent strewed them throughout. No one collector appeared as often as he, and Broadbent wrote of Rodenstock's "close friends, among whose number I am lucky to count myself . . . Hardy is a remarkably modest man, but jealous of his sources, though many of his rare wines have been bought at Christie's. Through his immense generosity I have not only had the opportunity to taste an enormous

range of great and very rare wines, but have met a very wide circle
of enthusiasts and collectors, becoming one of the privileged fix-
tures at Hardy's events." Unlike the previous edition, in this one
Broadbent included no special appendix delving into the provenance of the Jefferson bottles.

No one was suggesting that Broadbent had had criminal intent,
but only that he had put on salesman's blinders. And again the Hitler
diaries came rushing back with their striking parallels. One of the
reputations that suffered most in that earlier scandal had been that
of the Oxbridge historian Hugh Trevor-Roper, who authenticated
the diaries. Trevor-Roper's misguided authentication, however, evaporated in a matter of days. Broadbent continued to insist that the Jefferson bottles were legitimate for more than twenty years, through
many Rodenstock bottle sales, innumerable tastings of Rodenstock
wines, and multiple editions of his increasingly Rodenstock-reliant
book.

"I think he felt vulnerable," Jancis Robinson said later. "This has
been a very important part of what he has done, but I think even
today he has been convinced that he has enough evidence."

And Broadbent wasn't giving up the fight. Twenty years before,
the *New York Post* had reported that the real buyer of the 1784 Jefferson Yquem purchased by the "teetotaler" named Iyad Shiblaq was
Dodi Al-Fayed. Broadbent knew otherwise. Following the 1986
auction, he and his wife had dined with Shiblaq at the Jordanian's
gambling club in London. Shiblaq himself had been the purchaser of
the bottle.

Now Broadbent tracked him down and persuaded him to lend
his bottle to Broadbent so he could have his own experts examine
the engraving. Afterward, Broadbent declared that Christie's had
commissioned the new examination and that "we can confirm that
the engraving is exactly correct, French and of the period," but a
Christie's spokesman disavowed knowledge of the reappraisal, and
Broadbent wouldn't allow independent inspection of the experts'

report. In a chatty fax to Rodenstock in November, Broadbent revealed that the new appraisal had been done by Hugo Morley-Fletcher, the former head of Christie's ceramics and glass department, who had done the original appraisal of the 1787 Lafite back in 1985; he was now a consultant who served as an expert on the TV program *Antiques Roadshow UK*. Koch's team remained confident that the Shiblaq bottle was as fake as all the others.

In January, Broadbent underwent major heart surgery. Afterward, he cut down on his public appearances. When he attended an event honoring a Bordeaux winemaker in London, Jancis Robinson thought he looked "very frail." In early May he retired from Christie's board of directors, though he remained a senior consultant to the wine department.

THE RARE-WINE POOL was indelibly tainted. "Whoever's doing this," Bipin Desai had said of fakes, the month before Koch filed his suit, "they have to be caught. They're spoiling the old wine market—slowly, steadily destroying it like a cancer." Estimates of the number of fakes in circulation were usually given as 5 percent of the market, but ran much higher for certain cult bottles. Suddenly the flashier offerings of some merchants began to seem almost ridiculous. There was the provenanceless 1784 Lafite advertised in the catalog for Christie's September auction in New York, which the auction house yanked from the sale at the last minute. There was the 1787 Yquem sold earlier in the year by the Antique Wine Company in London to a private American collector for $90,000. Rumors were rife that some collectors were knowingly unloading fakes from their cellars at auction.

Koch's lawyers now sent letters to Christie's, Zachys, Farr Vintners, Royal Wine Merchants (the company of Jeff Sokolin and Daniel Oliveros), a Washington State importer named Bordeaux Wine Locators, which had been the consignor of many of the questionable bottles Koch had bought at auction, and collector Eric Greenberg, among others, warning them not to destroy any documents. Koch's attorneys were getting ready to serve a raft of subpoenas. "That's the day a lot of assholes are going to pucker," said Brad Goldstein, who seemed invigorated by the whole affair.

Goldstein snidely referred to Greenberg, who had been invited by Steven Spielberg to join the Survivors of the Shoah Visual History Foundation and then been given its Ambassadors for Humanity award, as "Mr. Shoah." Goldstein was practically salivating at the prospect of deposing Rodenstock: "It will be a show trial." The aggressive newsmagazine *Stern* was "like the Gestapo," Goldstein said approvingly. A German journalist who seemed to be falling prey to Rodenstock's misdirection, on the other hand, was wasting his time "separating fly shit from pepper."

A lot of stones were about to be overturned. Numerous wine-world icons—Shanken and *Wine Spectator*, Parker and *The Wine Advocate,* Rodenstock, Robinson, Broadbent and Christie's, Farr Vintners, Riedel—had been touched by the affair. Scores of tasting notes would need to be reconsidered, if not discarded. Jancis Robinson hopefully suggested that the whole thing could be "cathartic" for the business. She had always considered the Jefferson bottles "an intriguing and suspicious mystery," she said later, but when she now asked Rodenstock exactly how many of the bottles had been in his original find, and he answered "about thirty," she was struck by his vagueness about such valuable objects.

Robinson found herself becoming more cautious. When she was asked to conduct a tasting in March at the Palais Coburg in Vienna, which would feature a '34 Romanée-Conti, she asked for a complete list of where the hosts had obtained the wines. "It was probably looking a gift horse in the mouth, and I felt bad doing it," she said later, "but I didn't know them."

The same month, the *Wall Street Journal* reported that the FBI's art fraud unit had opened an investigation into counterfeit wine, and that a grand jury in New York was hearing evidence. Subpoenas had been sent to Christie's, Sotheby's, and Zachys.

In Bordeaux, where for years most châteaux had done little to stanch the problem, some owners were jubilant, or at least ready to face the problem head-on. "We are very pleased," said Christian Moueix of Château Pétrus, "that this has finally become a scandal." When Robinson traveled to Bordeaux in April for the annual *en primeur* barrel tastings, the first thing that Château Margaux owner Corinne Mentzelopoulos said to her was "Now, what are we going to do about this fake business?"

If any person or business was going to benefit from the mess, it was Sotheby's, and more than one observer saw a subtle Sotheby's revenge plot playing out. Christie's had long been aligned with Rodenstock, and not only through Broadbent. When Christopher Burr, who briefly headed Christie's wine department after Broadbent, helped put together a tasting in Paris in 2001, he later wrote that it had been a challenge "assembling the best of these wines from unquestionable provenance, no mean task, but fortune and some visionary wine men helped, such as Hardy Rodenstock—a legendary wine collector." It was entirely possible that the bottles were all real, but if Rodenstock's name stood for one thing, it was questionable, not unquestionable, provenance.

Serena Sutcliffe, meanwhile, had spent the last fifteen years positioning the Sotheby's wine department as the discriminating auctioneers, the house that didn't sell Rodenstock's bottles and that was vocal about the rising problem of counterfeit wine. While still lagging behind Christie's wine department overall, Sotheby's had pulled ahead of it in the important North American market. Koch, having used Christie's when he sold part of his collection in 1999, had since seemed to subtly shift his allegiance to its rival. In early 2006 he was scheduled to host a wine event with Sotheby's North American wine director, and it was a former Sotheby's wine head, David Molyneux-Berry, whom Koch hired to vet his cellar as part of the investigation. It was also Sotheby's that tipped off Russell Frye to the problems of his cellar and put him in touch with Molyneux-Berry, through whom he joined forces with Koch. As if to cosmically rub the turn of fortunes in Broadbent's face, five weeks before Koch filed suit, France, in recognition of her promotion of its wines, made Serena Sutcliffe the first member of the British wine trade to be awarded the Légion d'honneur.

"Sotheby's must be gleeful!" Broadbent remarked bitterly after Koch's suit was filed.

IN JUNE 2007, nearly a year after Koch sued, Rodenstock found a way, at least temporarily, to wriggle free. He had hired a German lawyer at a New York firm to defend him and endured months of pretrial motions and preliminary discovery. On June 1, Rodenstock's lawyers received a stack of discovery documents from Koch, including the e-mail correspondence between Koch's office and Andreas Klein, Rodenstock's former Munich neighbor and landlord. Later that same day, Rodenstock sent a fax directly to the judge overseeing *Koch v. Rodenstock* and pled his case. Koch, he said, was "a psychopath."

"You will surely understand that I don't want to have dealings with such a person," Rodenstock wrote, adding that "the quarrel with him has come up to a more than primitive level I don't want to bear any longer."

Later, Rodenstock informed the court that he had spent more than $150,000 in legal fees and was not able "to continue to participate in the proceeding." His lawyer petitioned the court to withdraw as Rodenstock's counsel, and Magistrate Judge Debra Freeman scheduled a teleconference with Rodenstock's and Koch's lawyers and Rodenstock himself. Rodenstock, however, refused to take part, saying through his lawyer that he "cannot accept the friendly offer of a telephone conference, for which he thanks the court."

The court was not moved by his gratitude. "Contrary to Mr. Rodenstock's prior understanding," Judge Freeman wrote in a June 22 order, "the Court is not extending him a 'friendly offer' to participate in a conference. Rather, the Court is *ordering* Mr. Rodenstock to appear on July 5, in person or by telephone, *and he is cautioned that his failure to appear may result in the imposition of sanctions against him.*"

Rodenstock asked for and was granted a week's reprieve, and in the meantime his Munich lawyer sent a letter to Andreas Klein—and to Klein's mother-in-law and former employer (from whose e-mail server Klein had written to Koch)—threatening a libel suit. The New York case conference finally took place on July 11, in a courthouse in lower Manhattan, only one block from City Hall, where Rodenstock had married Helga Lehner in October 1991 (on that occasion, he had given his father's name as "Alfred Görke Rodenstock"). It was a strangely disembodied affair. Both Koch and Rodenstock dialed into the courtroom's speakerphone, with an interpreter hired by Rodenstock's New York lawyer standing by to translate Rodenstock's testimony. Rodenstock said that because he had no residence in the United States, and hadn't sold bottles to Koch directly, he had been "sued in an illegal way" and was not subject to the New York court's jurisdiction. He no longer intended to pay for counsel, or even to take part in the suit. In short, and after several warnings from the judge, he stated his intent to default. He would fight Koch in The Hague, if necessary, Rodenstock said. Judge Freeman asked if Rodenstock wished to say anything else. "Thank you very much for everything and for the phone conference," Rodenstock said.

Rodenstock's default meant that Koch would receive a U.S. court judgment in his favor. His challenge then would be to collect from Rodenstock, which would mean navigating the uncertain terrain of international conventions and German civil procedure. "He's fucked" was Brad Goldstein's legalese. "I think we can attach liens under The Hague and in Germany." Koch was also contemplating filing a second suit against Rodenstock, this one dealing not with the Jefferson bottles but with all the other fakes in his cellar that Koch had been able to link to Rodenstock.

Even if Koch was able to collect the $500,000 he now claimed he had paid for the Jefferson bottles—a questionable figure, given that a Farr Vintners invoice showed Koch to have paid just £116,000 (about $200,000) for three of the four bottles—it was a fraction of what he had spent on the investigation and lawsuit. But Goldstein continued to insist that it had never been about the money for Koch. "If the court says this guy's a fraudster," Goldstein said, "it's a victory."

It didn't end the appetite to buy or sell Jefferson bottles. The Antique Wine Company, which had sold the 1787 Yquem the year before, persisted in offering implausible rarities. In the spring, the firm rolled out "The Great Antique Chateau Lafite-Rothschild Collection," forty-eight vintages including a 1787. Antique Wine Company managing director Stephen Williams made much ado about having subjected the wine to "molecular" and "chemical" analysis, even though such tests could prove only that the wine's age predated the nuclear era. In late July, the firm offered "Chateau d'Yquem—the greatest ever cellar." This collection was not marketed publicly, on the firm's website, but announced in a message sent to a private e-mail list. In addition to numerous early-nineteenth-century vintages, the Yquems included four eighteenth-century vintages. One of them was a 1787 Jefferson bottle, priced at $156,100. Although the Antique Wine Company billed the collection as being of "impeccable provenance," when pressed as to the Jefferson bottle's origin, a representative said, "This bottle was found in a private cellar in the United States. We do not have full information on how it got there or its previous ownership. It appears to be one of several bottles sold by Hardy Rodenstock, the discredited German wine dealer."

THE JEFFERSON BOTTLES were *the* example of how people turned suggestible when it came to wine. It was precisely the fact that drinkers brought their own interpretations to wine that led subjects in a University of Bordeaux study to mistake white wine for red, and that led impressionable consumers to decide they liked a wine because Parker did, to buy first growths because they were first, and to detect notes of sweet Cuban tobacco only after someone else had.

The bottles were never about what was in them. The people who bought them weren't the geeks who got off on comparing the respective degrees of deadness of a 1787 and a 1791. Kip Forbes didn't pay $156,000 for a taste experience worth $156,000. All those who bought the bottles did so after significant doubts had been aired. And all later learned about the serious challenge posed by the Frericks case: Forbes was notified by Broadbent; Koch had contacted Rodenstock; Shanken's magazine had run an article about the case. Nor was Rodenstock, evasive and defensive when challenged, ever particularly convincing.

But each buyer had wanted his own piece of frozen history. It was enough that Thomas Jefferson's initials were right there on the bottles, that the bottles said Lafite and Margaux and Branne-Mouton and Yquem, and that Michael Broadbent had stamped them with his approval. A standard of plausible confirmability had been met. "Let me tell you something," Bill Sokolin said. "As far as I was concerned, that bottle was real because I believed it. And," Sokolin added, "because I tasted it, and it was garbage. It was garbage. So I said, 'Jesus, maybe it's real.'"

As with all successful cons, the marks and the grifter had been collaborators. One sold the illusion that the others were desperate to buy. But the marks had grown up. Now Asia and Russia were the preferred playing fields for Rodenstock and other purveyors of dubious bottles. It was the once-gullible Americans bringing a European manipulator to justice, a rare comeuppance for two centuries of Old World snobbery.

No one would have shaken his head so sadly at the affair as the author of the Declaration of Independence, whom Koch misidentified, when eulogizing "the mystique" of the bottles, as a framer of the Constitution. In the last years of his life, Jefferson was reduced to drinking lesser wines. He abandoned his earlier habits of ordering straight from the châteaux, instead employing an agent in Nice and asking for simple wines of that region, even expressing a willingness to buy an imitation-Bordeaux merchant's blend. Thomas Jefferson was drinking cheap table wine, and very happily so.

For anyone wishing for some kind of smoking corkscrew, or at least a judicial comeuppance, Koch's investigation and lawsuit, in the two years after he filed it, delivered little satisfaction. The FBI was reported to be continuing its investigation into wine forgery, but no video of Hardy Rodenstock slapping labels on bottles surfaced. He didn't make a tearful confession. He wasn't subjected to a perp walk or a punishing jury award.

Koch's legal claim against Rodenstock made fitful progress. Although Rodenstock had said that he would default, it was his good fortune that the court, in January 2008, finally accepted his lawyers' argument that New York did not have jurisdiction and threw out the suit. The dismissal was only temporary. Koch beefed up his complaint and refiled it, and in the fall the court cleared the way for the case to proceed. In all likelihood, Koch would finally get his default judgment against Rodenstock—and then face the challenge of how to collect on it.

In the meantime, Koch had opened several more fronts in his war against the rare-wine establishment. In the fall of 2007, he sued Eric Greenberg, the collector, and the auction house Zachys. The suit accused Greenberg of having knowingly sold eleven fake bottles through Zachys in an October 2005 auction and Zachys of having knowingly or negligently passed them on to Koch. Another eight bottles bought by Koch at Zachys in 2004, according to the suit, were also fake. The total value of the nineteen bottles was $340,000.

The following March, in Illinois, Koch sued the Chicago Wine Company and the Julienne Importing Company. He accused the Chicago Wine Company of having sold him the fake 1787 Branne-Mouton Jefferson bottle and of having sold him another fourteen fake bottles, between 1987 and 1990, worth $50,000. Julienne had imported nine of these.

One month later, in New York, Koch sued Acker Merrall & Condit, alleging that at least five bottles of wine he had bought through its auctions in 2005 and 2006, for $78,000, were fakes. Koch's suit demanded that Acker henceforth obtain a third-party expert validation of any pre-1962 bottles before selling them. Koch starkly revealed his motivation as nonfinancial when he rejected offers by both Acker Merrall and Eric Greenberg to make him whole.

During the same two-year period, the problem of counterfeit wine received unprecedented coverage in newspapers and magazines, and merchants whose mantra had always been "caveat emptor" furiously tried to at least appear more responsible. (The catalog for a spring 2008 auction at Zachys was, atypically, a model of transparency, disclosing the exact date and source of purchase for a significant number of lots.) Collector Russell Frye, after reaching a confidential settlement with Wine Library, launched a website, WineAuthentication.com, designed to serve as a clearinghouse and forum for anxious collectors.

But if Koch hoped that his litigation might have a sobering effect on the market, he was given little reassurance when, only two days after he sued Acker Merrall & Condit, the auction house had to interrupt a sale at the New York restaurant Cru; auctioneer John Kapon announced that twenty-two lots of red Burgundy from Domaine Ponsot, a noted producer, were being withdrawn from the sale. It seemed that proprietor Laurent Ponsot had informed Kapon that a number of the vintages couldn't possibly be authentic; the Domaine hadn't bottled them. Some of the other bottles were cosmetically suspect, bearing seals or labels that Ponsot immediately recognized as fraudulent. The winemaker flew to New York to make sure the bottles, estimated to be worth more than $600,000, were pulled from the auction. The consignor of the bottles was a willfully mysterious young collector named Rudy Kurniawan, who had rapidly ascended to prominence in Los Angeles collecting circles over the last decade.

Although Hardy Rodenstock continued to host the occasional several-thousand-euro-per-head tasting in Hamburg, he was now entirely marginalized in the wine world, his name synonymous with wine fraud. Near the end of 2008, *Stern* published a damning exposé. The magazine's reporters had doggedly tracked down a printing company in Bad Marienberg, where Rodenstock lived in the 1970s and '80s; several employees testified that Rodenstock had frequently commissioned the firm to reprint old wine labels. More incriminating, *Stern* obtained labels from bottles served at one of Rodenstock's recent commercial tastings, including a 1945 Mouton Rothschild, and showed them to experts in France. The director of Mouton Rothschild pegged one of the labels as obviously fake on sight, and Bernard Medina, who had been involved in the dating of Bill Koch's bottles, conducted a chemical analysis that showed that a label said to be from the 1900 vintage was backed by a modern synthetic glue not invented until years later.

But as late as the summer of 2008, Michael Broadbent seemed unable to admit, even to himself, that the Forbes bottle could have been phony. While he acknowledged that the record-setting sale had, over time, become "an embarrassing farce" and now claimed that he had never "authenticated" the Jefferson bottles, he continued to insist that Monticello scholars had misinterpreted the historical record and, with the continued backing of former Christie's expert Hugo Morley-Fletcher, that the engraving was truly old.

The scandal's greatest gift, in the end, might have been all the questions it raised about where, exactly, the value of a wine resides. In a Stanford/Caltech study by neuroeconomists, published in January 2008, subjects were given several glasses of the exact same wine, each with a different price tag. Believing that they were drinking different wines, the subjects described the "more expensive" ones more favorably. Moreover, brain scans showed the subjects to actually experience more pleasure from the nominally pricier stuff.

Esteemed authorities such as Jancis Robinson and Robert Parker had attended Rodenstock tastings and come away raving about them and believing the wines they tasted to be legitimate. This suggests an oenophile's twist on the old Zen koan: If a fake wine is served at a tasting and no one notices, would it have mattered if it was real?

Notes

All quotations not cited here or in the text are drawn from interviews I conducted or incidents I observed. In these notes, I use several abbreviations: *Papers,* for *The Papers of Thomas Jefferson,* edited by Julian Boyd, et al. (Princeton: 1950–); *WS* for *Wine Spectator; VWGJ* for the *Vinifera Wine Growers Journal; MAZ* for *Münchner Abendzeitung; NYT* for the *New York Times;* TJ for Thomas Jefferson; and JMB for J. Michael Broadbent. Currency conversions are based, in each instance, on contemporaneous exchange rates.

1. Lot 337

For the bid steps and saleroom dialogue in chapters 1 and 6, I relied on a report, "A Piece of History," published in *The New Yorker'*s Talk of the Town section on January 20, 1986.

2   *more than twice as big*   "Wine," *Financial Times,* August 17, 1985.

2   *more than 160,000 copies*   Simon Loftus, *Anatomy of the Wine Trade* (New York: Harper & Row, 1985), 154.

2   *When he arrived at a wine gathering*   Jancis Robinson, *Tasting Pleasure* (New York: Penguin Books, 1999), 170.

3   *"black as Egypt's night"*   JMB, *The New Great Vintage Wine Book* (New York: Knopf, 1991), 63.

3   *reminded him of Sophia Loren*   Robinson, *Tasting Pleasure,* 183.

3   *"schoolgirls' uniforms"*   Ibid.

3   *oldest authenticated vintage red wine*   "Oldest Bordeaux? Yes; Jefferson's? Maybe," *NYT,* October 30, 1985.

5   *a historical researcher in America*   Ibid.

5   *the snow horse of*   Robinson, *Tasting Pleasure,* 146.

5   *he opened the bidding at £10,000*   This is according to the contemporaneous *New Yorker* account; Broadbent recalls opening the
bidding somewhere between £3,000 and £5,000.

6   *Only after Kip Forbes bid £50,000*   "Passion vs. Reason in Wine
Collecting," *WS,* February 28, 1998.

6   *The previous record*   "Record Wine Prices," *WS,* May 31, 1988.

2. INCOGNITO

7   *an order for 250 bottles of Lafite*   Letter from TJ to Pichard, February 22, 1788, *Papers* XII, 617–8; translation in John Hailman's
definitive *Thomas Jefferson on Wine* (Jackson: University Press of
Mississippi, 2006), 148.

8   *legendary in the City of Light*   James M. Gabler, *Passions: The Wines
and Travels of Thomas Jefferson* (Baltimore: Bacchus Press, 1995), 22.

8   *"a savage of the mountains of America"*   Marie Kimball, *Jefferson:
The Scene of Europe* (New York: Coward-McCann, 1950), 15.

8   *a powdered wig and a topaz ring*   Hailman, *Thomas Jefferson on
Wine,* 12, 213.

8   *His mansion on the Champs-Élysées*   Gabler, *Passions,* 30–31.

8   *a household staff that included a* frotteur   Howard C. Rice, Jr.,
Thomas Jefferson's Paris (Princeton: Princeton University Press,
1976), 40.

8   *Jefferson hosted frequent dinner parties*   William Howard Adams,
The Paris Years of Thomas Jefferson (New Haven: Yale University
Press, 1997), 19.

8   *Franklin, for one, kept a substantial cellar*   Hailman, *Thomas Jefferson on Wine,* 75.

8   *"proof that God loves us"*   Ibid., 76.

9   *he justified the trip*   Letter from TJ to James Madison, January
30, 1787, *Papers* XI, 92–97.

9   *"your voyage is rather for your pleasure"*   Letter from Martha Jefferson to TJ, March 8, 1787, *Papers* XI, 203–4.

9   *first part constructed*   Hailman, *Thomas Jefferson on Wine,* 38.

9   *One story, passed down among Jefferson's slaves*   "Once the Slave of Thomas Jefferson," *New York World,* January 30, 1898.

9   *first planted vines*   Hailman, *Thomas Jefferson on Wine,* 372.

9   *encouraged an Italian immigrant*   Ibid., 47.

10   *a single trunk*   Letter from TJ to Madame de Tott, April 5, 1787, *Papers* XI, 271.

10   *Wanting to experience the real France*   Letter from TJ to Chastellux, April 4, 1787, *Papers* XI, 261–62.

10   *he traveled incognito*   Letter from TJ to William Short, March 15, 1787, *Papers* XI, 214–16.

10   *basked in the scattered ruins*   Letter from TJ to Madame de Tessé, March 20, 1787, *Papers* XI, 226–28.

10   *talked his way into people's homes*   Letter from TJ to Lafayette, April 11, 1787, *Papers* XI, 283–85.

10   *closely studied . . . the techniques of wine making*   TJ, "Notes of a Tour into the Southern Parts of France, &c.," *Papers* XI, 455–56.

10   *compulsively inquisitive . . . spoke French well enough*   Ibid., 455–57.

10   *luxuriated in the southern sun*   Letter from TJ to Willam Short, March 27, 1787, *Papers* XI, 246–48.

10   *soaked his aching wrist ten times a day*   Letter from TJ to William Short, April 7, 1787, *Papers* XI, 280–81.

10   *ate the tiny thrushes called ortolans*   TJ, "Notes of a Tour," *Papers* XI, 454.

10   *for nine days, Jefferson left the road*   Letter from TJ to William Short, May 21, 1787.

10   *trees full of nightingales*   Letter from TJ to Martha Jefferson, May 21, 1787, *Papers* XI, 368–69.

10   *loved traveling this way . . . wheelless atop the barge*   Letter from TJ to William Short, May 21, 1787, *Papers* XI, 371–73.

11   *wouldn't write a single letter to her*   E. M. Halliday, *Understanding Thomas Jefferson* (New York: Harper Perennial, 2001), 69.

11   *corn, rye, and beans . . . nothing but grapevines*   TJ, "Notes of a Tour," *Papers* XI, 454.

11   *glass windows*   Letter from TJ to William Short, May 21, 1787, *Papers* XI, 371–73.

11   *"those seaports with which we trade"*   Letter from TJ to William Carmichael, February 18, 1787, *Papers* XI, 164–65.

12   *The place was booming*   Hugh Johnson, *The Story of Wine—New Illustrated Edition* (London: Mitchell Beazley, 2005), 138, 145; Arthur Young, *Travels in France & Italy During the Years 1787, 1788 and 1789* (J.M. Dent & Sons/E.P. Dutton, 1915), 57–59.

12   *checked into the Hôtel de Richlieu*   TJ, *Papers, Second Series: Jefferson's Memorandum Books* (edited by Bear and Stanton), 668.

12   *a portable copying press*   Letter from TJ to William Stephens Smith, January 15, 1787, *Papers* XI, 46.

12   *had been released from debtor's prison*   *Jefferson's Memorandum Books* I, 668n.

12   *"on acct. of . . . Marocco [sic] mission"*   Ibid.

12   *bet him a bottle of Burgundy*   Letter from TJ to William Short, June 1, 1787, *Papers* XI, 395–96.

12   *visited the ruins*   TJ, "Notes of a Tour," *Papers* XI, 454–55.

12   *day trip southwest to Château Haut-Brion*   Ibid., 457.

13   *On his third night in the city*   *Jefferson's Memorandum Books* I, 668.

13   *The girls who danced and sang there*   Young, *Travels in France,* 57–58.

13   *enjoyed meals . . . admired the procession of elms*   TJ, "Notes of a Tour," *Papers* XI, 455.

13   *The quay*   Young, *Travels in France,* 56–57.

13   *cream-colored oxen*   TJ, "Notes of a Tour," *Papers* XI, 454.

13   *Increasingly the wine was going*   André L. Simon, *Bottlescrew Days* (Boston: Small Maynard & Company, 1927), 161.

13   *recent reinvention of the cork and the glass bottle*   Johnson, *Story of Wine,* 104–6.

13   *the development of cylindrical bottles*   Ibid., 164.

13   *"fury of planting"*   Nicholas Faith, *The Winemasters of Bordeaux* (London: Prion, 1999), 29–32; Johnson, *The Story of Wine,* 140.

14   *a specific hierarchy*   Simon, *Bottlescrew Days,* 157–58.

14   *"of fine quality"*   Letter from TJ to Bondfield, January 24, 1786, *Papers* IX, 210–11.

14   *two livres each*   Gabler, *Passions,* 132.

14   *the quality pyramid . . . 150,000 bottles annually*   TJ, "Notes of a Tour," *Papers* XI, 454–56.

14   *Pepys*   Faith, *Winemasters,* 17.

15   *Locke*   Ibid., 24.

15   *the* London Gazette *was announcing*   Ibid., 26.

15   *The Duc de Richelieu*   Faith, *Winemasters,* 43–44; Cyril Ray, *Lafite* (New York: Stein & Day, 1969), 20–21.

15   *By the time of Jefferson's visit in 1787*   "Notes of a Tour," *Papers* XI, 456.

15   *Falernian*   Johnson, *The Story of Wine,* 36.

15   *Steinwein*   Ibid., 155.

15   *finest available year*   TJ, "Notes of a Tour," *Papers,* XI, 457.

15   *"the best vintage . . . in nine years"*   Letter from TJ to Alexander Donald, February 15, 1788, *Papers* XII, 594–95.

15   *252 bottles of 1784 Haut-Brion*   Letter to TJ from Feger, Gramont & Cie., June 2, 1787, and footnote, *Papers* XI, 396–97.

16   *"I cannot deny myself the pleasure"*   Letter from TJ to Francis Eppes, May 26, 1787, *Papers* XI, 378–79.

16   *personal taxonomy of wine*   "Jefferson's Tasting Vocabulary," R. de Treville Lawrence, III, ed., *Jefferson and Wine* (The Plains, Virginia: The Vinifera Wine Growers Association, 1989), 108–13.

16   *resolved to make it his standard practice*   Letter from TJ to John Bondfield, December 18, 1787, *Papers* XII, 434.

16   *"it is from them alone"*   Letter from TJ to Alexander Donald, September 17, 1787, *Papers* XII, 132–34.

17   *Dutch merchants dosed claret*   Faith, *Winemasters,* 14.

17   *the Bordeaux negociants*   Ibid., 67–71.

17   *The Pardoner warned his listeners*   Rod Phillips, *A Short History of Wine* (New York: Ecco, 2000), 109.

17   *"Trade morality has come to such a pass . . ."*   H. Warner Allen, *The Romance of Wine* (New York: Dover, 1971), 243.

17   *"the Golden Age of Wine Faking"*   Ibid., 238–40.

17   *"coloured to resemble claret"*   Faith, *Winemasters,* 69.

17   *Paris officials analyzed*   Phillips, *A Short History of Wine,* 199.

17   *spoke with a broker named Desgrands*   "Notes of a Tour," *Papers* XI, 457.

17   *"I would prefer to receive it directly"*   Letter from TJ to d'Yquem, December 18, 1787, *Papers* XII, 435; translation in Lawrence, *Jefferson and Wine,* 70–71.

18   *On September 17, 1789, Jefferson hosted*   Gouverneur Morris, *A Diary of the French Revolution,* edited by Beatrix Cary Davenport (Boston: Houghton Mifflin, 1939), vol. 1, 219–23.

18   *chilly out . . . a fire crackled*   Ibid., 221.

18   *a spare, half-empty look*   Adams, *The Paris Years of Thomas Jefferson,* 21.

18   *much of the contents had already been crated*   Ibid.

18   *what he thought would be a six-month leave*   Ibid., 22.

18   *guards be posted outside*   Rice, *Thomas Jefferson's Paris,* 117.

18   *his house had been robbed*   Ibid.

18   *candlesticks*   Adams, *The Paris Years of Thomas Jefferson,* 291.

18   *sat down to eat at four-thirty*   Morris, *A Diary of the French Revolution,* vol. 1, 219–23.

19   *James Hemings had learned French cooking*   Rice, *Thomas Jefferson's Paris,* 40.

19   *eighty-six packing cases*   Rice, *Thomas Jefferson's Paris,* 122.

19   *hampers full of various wines*   "List of Baggage Shipped by Jefferson from France," *Papers* XV, 375–77.

19   *two containers earmarked for John Jay and George Washington*   Letter from TJ to John Jay, September 17, 1789, *Papers* XV, 436–37.

19   *Gouverneur Morris bet William Short*   George Green Shackelford, *Jefferson's Adoptive Son* (Lexington, Kentucky: The University Press of Kentucky, 1993), 43.

19   *majordomo was left to dismantle*   Letter from TJ to William Short, March 12, 1790, *Papers* XVI, 228–30.

19   *Amid the growing chaos*   Letter from William Short to TJ, August 15, 1790, *Papers* XVII, 392–97.

19   *One hundred twenty-five bottles of 1784 Haut-Brion*   Letter from John Bondfield to TJ, xber 6, 1788, *Papers* XIV, 336–37.

19   *never arrived*   Letter from TJ to John Bondfield, May 17, 1788, *Papers* XIII, 171–72.

19   *short one box of assorted wines*   Letter from TJ to James Brown, January 3, 1790, cited in Hailman, *Thomas Jefferson on Wine,* 202.

3. TOMB RAIDER

Michael Broadbent vividly recounted the story of his first big auction in "The Anatomy of a Sale," in *Christie's Wine Companion,* edited by Patrick Matthews (Topsfield, Massachusetts: Salem House Publishers, 1987), 121–31. Four key sources on the development of the Bordeaux wine trade, and of English claret drinking, were Nicholas Faith's *Winemasters;* Hugh Johnson's *Story of Wine;* Edmund Penning-Rowsell's book *The Wines of Bordeaux* (London: Penguin, 1989) and his article "The First Growths of Bordeaux," published in the 1987 *Christie's Wine Companion.* A useful article on the history of Christie's and wine auctions was JMB's "A Brief History of Wine Auctions," *VWGJ,* Fall 1986.

25 *seventy gallons to an acre*   Robert M. Parker, Jr., *The World's Greatest Wine Estates* (New York: Simon & Schuster, 2005), 132, 214.

25 *just one glass of Yquem*   Richard Olney, *Yquem* (Boston: David R. Godine, 1986), 35.

26 *20,000 gold francs*   Ibid., 46.

26 *Gladstone, himself a claret man*   Asa Briggs, *Haut-Brion* (London: Faber and Faber, 1994), 92.

26 *Haut-Brion had only four hogsheads*   Letter from John Bondfield to TJ, xber 6, 1788, *Papers* XIV, 336–37.

26 *"it admits of a doubt"*   Christopher Fielden, *Is This the Wine You Ordered, Sir?* (London: Christopher Helm, 1989), 124–25.

28 *Disraeli*   Ray, *Lafite,* 65.

28 *That first season*   "A Brief History of Wine Auctions," *VWGJ,* Fall 1986.

28 *By 1978 the numbers*   "The Wine Auction Market," *Christie's Wine Review* (1980), 12.

28 *Before Christie's Rosebery sale . . . launched its own wine department* Loftus, *Anatomy of the Wine Trade,* 145–46.

30 *the price of old wines*   "The wine auction market—1966–1971," *Christie's Wine Review* (1972), 25.

31 *"certainly the largest quantity of any one vintage"*   "Wine," *Art & Auction,* February 1986.

31 *"upwards of 100 loads of Good Hay"*   "Out-of-Town and Overseas Sales," *Christie's Wine Review* (1980), 35.

31   *"sexy* demi-mondaine"   JMB, *Vintage Wine* (New York: Harcourt, 2002), 33.

31   *"middle-aged lady"*   Ibid., 58.

32   *"the strenuous efforts of our competitors"*   "Introduction," *Christie's Wine Review* (1979).

32   *"pure propaganda"*   Loftus, *Anatomy of the Wine Trade,* 148.

32   *"not a very healthy step"*   "Changing Times,"*Decanter,* 1984.

32   *"of infinitely better quality"*   "Premium Policy," *Decanter,* August 1984.

32   *"essentially a piece of ephemera"*   "Premium Fallacies," *Decanter,* 1984 or 1985.

32   *"Sepulchral hollow laughter"*   "The Last Laugh," *Decanter,* August 1986.

32   *"The lack of enthusiasm shows"*   "In Britain It's All Business," *WS,* May 31, 1988.

32   *Sotheby's was the quality auctioneer*   Ibid.

33   *"the largest quantity [of cases of port]"*   "Port Prices Show Gains," *Decanter,* 1984.

33   *A magnum of 1864 Lafite*   "Time in a Bottle," *Connoisseur,* February 1992.

33   *American demand was the chief reason*   "Wine," *Financial Times,* August 17, 1985.

33   *Before leaving France in 1789, Jefferson shipped*   Letter from TJ to John Jay, September 17, 1789, *Papers* XV, 436–7.

33   *As secretary of state, Jefferson*   Letter from TJ to Joseph Fenwick, September 6, 1790, *Papers* XVII, 493–94.

33   *Jefferson's congratulatory letter*   Letter from TJ to James Monroe, April 8, 1817, Library of Congress collection.

33   *"No nation is drunken"*   Letter from TJ to J. G. Hyde de Neuville, December 13, 1818, Library of Congress collection.

33   *who regarded Jefferson as a fop*   John Hailman, *Thomas Jefferson on Wine* (University Press of Mississippi, 2006), 213.

34   *"We could . . . make as great a variety of wines"*   Letter from TJ to Lasteyrie, July 15, 1808, Library of Congress collection.

34   *Jefferson claimed, patriotically*   Letter from TJ to John Adlum, October 7, 1809, *Papers, Retirement Series* I, 586–57.

34   *America's first "exquisite wine, produced in quantity"*   Letter from TJ to William Johnson, May 10, 1817, Library of Congress collection.

34 *"There was, as usual, the dissertation upon wines"*   David McCul-
lough, *John Adams* (New York: Simon & Schuster, 2001), 587.

34 *three to four and a half glasses of wine*   Letter from TJ to Vine
Utley, March 21, 1819, Library of Congress collection.

34 *His sizable library included*   "The Wine Books in Jefferson's
Library," *Wayward Tendrils Quarterly* 11, no. 2 (April 2001).

34 *"wine from long habit has become"*   Letter from TJ to Fernandez
Oliviera, December 16, 1815, Library of Congress collection.

34 *By the turn of the twentieth century*   Peter Meltzer, "America Collects," *Christie's Wine Companion* (1987).

35 *the 1959 vintage*   Kathleen Bourke, "Rise of the American Connoisseur," *Christie's Wine Review,* 1976.

35 *The debut Heublein auction*   JMB, "Heublein and the US Wine
Auction Scene," *Christie's Wine Companion,* edited by Pamela
Vandyke Price (Devon, England: Webb & Bower, 1989).

36 *$31,000 . . . $38,000*   "'It Doesn't Make Sense,'" *WS,* January
1986.

36 *110 degrees Fahrenheit*   JMB, "Heublein and the US Wine Auction Scene," *Christie's Wine Companion,* 1989.

36 *as of 1980 a national poll*   "23% of wine consumed in U.S. 'on
the rocks,'" *WS,* May 1–15, 1980.

37 *10,000 bottles in his cellar*   "Taking Wine Off the Pedestal," *Food &
Wine,* April 1985.

37 *30,000-bottle wine collection*   "Wine," *NYT,* June 13, 1982.

37 *65,000 bottles*   "What Motivates a Super Collector?" *WS,*
October 31, 1991.

38 *Australian study of wine judges' teeth*   R. Georgiou, "A review of
the dental effects of regular wine tasting," *Wine Industry Journal* 12
(1991), 294–95.

38 *"I feel a genuine sadness"*   "A Glass Half-Full," *The Underground
Wine Journal* 19, no. 7.

38 *as early as 1973*   Edmund Penning-Rowsell, "Growth of the
Wine Auction Market," *Christie's Wine Review,* 1977.

39 *an "extraordinary recrudescence"*   Ibid.

39 *Berry Brothers had unearthed*   "Heitz Sale Slows Pace," *WS,*
August 31, 1990.

39 *Ten Broeck Mansion*   "30,000 rare bottles go on the block," *WS,*
April 15, 1978; "Heublein promises the rare," *WS,* May 1–15, 1980.

39   *Some bottles at the 1980 Heublein auction*   "Wine from the sea bed—is it drinkable?" *Decanter,* date unknown; "Heublein promises the rare," *WS,* May 1–15, 1980.

4. Monsieur Yquem

41   *"took a look at the cellar"*   "Jefferson's Paris Wines: Comparing the Questions with the Facts," *VWGJ,* Spring 1986.

41   *a hundred bottles*   "Man with a nose for a rarity," *The Times* (London), December 15, 1990.

48   *"Not since lunch"*   "Worst Wine Moments," *Decanter,* January 1991.

52   *"America's first wine expert"*   *Decanter,* August 1984.

52   *Rodenstock himself had written a long article*   "Château d'Yquem: Die Geschichte des Berühmtesten Weissweines der Welt," *Alles über Wein,* no. 3, 1983.

53   *"had no meaning to me at first"*   "400,000 Mark—beim teursten Wein der Welt hört die Freundschaft auf . . . ," *MAZ,* February 28, 1991; "Jefferson's Paris Wines: Comparing the Questions with the Facts," *VWGJ,* Spring 1986.

53   *"This suite of events"*   Richard Olney, *Yquem* (Boston: David R. Godine, 1986), 152.

53   *"dark in color"*   "Jefferson's Paris Wines Found in 1985," R. de Treville Lawrence, III, ed., *Jefferson and Wine* (The Plains, Virginia: The Vinifera Wine Growers Association, 1989).

53   *"tremendous long finish"*   "Jefferson's Paris Wines Found," *VWGJ,* Fall 1985.

53   *"historic event"*   Ibid.

54   *"I have sealed all the bottles"*   Ibid.

54   *"Questions will no doubt arise"*   Ibid.

54   *"the entire act of making love occurs"*   "Mann, da ist im Gaumen die Hölle los," *Der Spiegel,* no. 7, 1988.

54   *"a deep, luminous old gold colour"*   "Record Prices," *Decanter,* February 1987.

55   *Christie's had never sold*   "Oldest Bordeaux, Yes . . .", *NYT,* October 30, 1985.

55   *Soon after, Broadbent flew to Munich*   This is according to an October 2005 interview with JMB; in a June 30, 2008, letter to author, JMB offered a different story, saying that the Munich flight

occured in 1986, when he went to pick up the 1784 Yquem in an aluminium briefcase, and that he received the 1787 Lafite from Rodenstock at the 1985 tasting at Die Ente in Wiesbaden.

5. PROVENANCE

59   *Göring . . . placed an order*   Don and Petie Kladstrup, *Wine and War* (New York: Broadway Books, 2001), 68.

59   *outright fabrication of wines*   Edward Penning-Rowsell, *The Wines of Bordeaux* (London: Penguin, 1989), 116.

59   *Louis A. Feliciano was arrested*   "Counterfeit Wine," *Vintage Magazine,* October 1982.

60   *"appears to be original"*   Christie's Sale Memorandum 314.

60   *"the wine had an excellent constitution"*   Christie's Finest and Rarest Wines auction catalog, December 5, 1985.

61   Jefferson and Wine   Vinifera Wine Growers Association, 1976.

61   *"It's wine"*   "A Tasting of Lafites," in Frank J. Prial, *Decantations* (New York: St. Martin's Griffin, 2001), 254–57.

62   *"a meaty little wine, faded but fascinating"*   JMB, *The Great Vintage Wine Book* (New York: Knopf, 1981), 35.

62   *"crystallized violets and clean bandages"*   JMB, *New Great Vintage Wine Book,* 18.

62   *"incredibly awful creosote, tarry smell"*   Ibid., 15.

62   *"Tasting old wine is like making love to an old lady"*   JMB, *Vintage Wine,* 22.

63   *in response to an inquiry by Broadbent*   "The Jefferson Bottles," *The New Yorker,* September 3 & 10, 2007.

65   *more than 10,000 plundered bottles*   Kladstrup, *Wine and War,* 203.

65   *the only time he felt intimate*   Albert Speer, *Inside the Third Reich* (New York: Simon & Schuster, 1997), 427.

65   *half a million bottles of wine*   Kladstrup, *Wine and War,* 1–2.

65   *culled the 20,000 best bottles*   Ibid., 42–44.

6. "WE DID WHAT YOU TOLD US"

In addition to "A Piece of History," in *The New Yorker* (January 20, 1986), I also benefited from lingering BBC footage of the auction and from a first-person account by Marvin Shanken, "Passion vs. Reason in Wine Collecting," which appeared in the February 28, 1998, issue of *WS*.

67 *last in his class* "The Man Who Knows What Everyone's Drinking," *NYT*, February 16, 1986.

68 *two-bedroom smoking lounge* "He Did It His Way," *Fortune*, May 2, 1994.

71 *seemed to pine for a bygone world* Christopher Winans, *Malcolm Forbes* (New York: St. Martin's Press, 1990), 88–89.

77 *He planned to celebrate* "Record Bid Brings Jefferson Wine Home," *Baltimore Sun*, December 6, 1985.

77 *"Well, Pop, . . . I did what you told me"* Malcolm Forbes, *More Than I Dreamed* (New York: Simon & Schuster, 1989), 213.

77 *Malcolm dropped the phone* Ibid.

78 *"The Forbes family would be far better off"* Ibid.

7. Imaginary Value

The investigation by Lucia (Cinder) Goodwin (now Stanton), which is the basis for much of this chapter, was detailed in her "Research Report: Château Lafite 1787, with initials 'Th.J.,'" dated December 12, 1985.

82 *sold some furniture* James A. Bear, Jr., "Furniture and Furnishings of Monticello," *Antiques*, date unknown.

82 *gave a draft of the Declaration* Silvio A. Bedini, *The Declaration of Independence Desk: Relic of Revolution* (Smithsonian, 1992), 34.

82 *"If these things acquire a superstitious value"* Ibid., 34–36.

83 *walking stick . . . watches* Marc Leepson, *Saving Monticello* (New York: The Free Press, 2001), 14.

83 *ten clippings of his hair* "Last Few Days in the Life of Thomas Jefferson," *Magazine of Albermarle County History* 5, no. 32 (1974), 76n.

83 *40,000 letters* Leepson, *Saving Monticello*, 14.

83 *the silver went to his daughter* "Thomas Jefferson's Silver," *Antiques*, September 1958.

83 *"130 valuable negroes"* Notice in *Richmond Inquirer*, January 9, 1827.

83 *grandchildren bought a lot of the furniture* Leepson, *Saving Monticello*, 15.

83 *"desist from such trespasses"* Ibid., 17.

83 *Most of Jefferson's books* Ibid.

83 *art collection was shipped to Boston* Ibid., 16.

83 *paintings were severely damaged* Jane Blair Cary Smith, *The Carys of Virginia,* diary excerpts in Cary Papers, University of Virginia Archives, courtesy Thomas Jefferson Foundation, Inc.

83 *only one sold* Leepson, *Saving Monticello,* 16.

84 *"Superstitions! Imaginary value!"* Bedini, *The Declaration of Independence Desk,* 40–43.

84 *brass coal scuttle* "Jefferson Relic Stolen," *NYT,* June 8, 1904.

84 *marble punch bowl* "Bryan Has Jefferson Relic," *NYT,* December 19, 1904.

84 *In 1930, Jefferson descendants consigned* "Descendants Offer Jefferson Relics," *NYT,* October 26, 1930.

84 *In the 1940s a New York antiques dealer* Provenance recorded in file on 1827 effects sale in special collections of Jefferson Library, courtesy Thomas Jefferson Foundation, Inc.

85 *original wooden models* "Jefferson Relics Are Found in Paris," *NYT,* February 23, 1947.

85 *The Jefferson table lent by* "Provenance of Dining Table," Maryland Historical Society.

85 *more than fifteen pieces of the original silver* "Thomas Jefferson's Silver," *Antiques,* September 1958.

85 *586 bottles left in his cellar* Hailman, *Thomas Jefferson on Wine,* 369.

86 *the curator of Monticello traveled* "Monticello Is Seeking Wine Bottles of 1800," *NYT,* February 22, 1966.

86 *a shard of glass bearing the seal of Lafite* "Monticello Wine Glass Archaeology," *VWGJ,* Spring 1988.

86 *16,000-odd letters* Sarah N. Randolph, *The Domestic Life of Jefferson* (New York: Harper & Brothers, 1871), 381.

87 *he would swear on his deathbed* Letter from TJ to Nicholas Lewis, July 11, 1788, *Papers* XIII, 342.

90 *couldn't be expected to "note every vintage and source"* "Jefferson's Paris Wines: Comparing the Questions with the Facts," *VWGJ,* Spring 1986.

91 *he had written to John Jay* Letter from TJ to John Jay, September 17, 1789, *Papers* XV, 436–37.

91   *"led astray and raised doubts"*   "Now it's the Broadbent 1787,"
     Decanter, April 1986.

91   *a copy of what appeared to be*   "Jefferson's Paris Wines: Compar-
     ing the Questions with the Facts," *VWGJ,* Spring 1986.

91   *"one's dubious and unfounded remarks"*   "The Jefferson Bottles,"
     The New Yorker, September 3 & 10, 2007.

92   *"Did I hear somebody murmur 'Piltdown Man'?"*   "Was it worth it?"
     Decanter, March 1986.

92   *"I don't question its authenticity"*   "Forbes to Son: You Paid How
     Much?" *WS,* January 1–31, 1986.

92   *Count Alexandre de Lur Saluces came next*   Colin Parnell, "Authen-
     tic Yquem," *Decanter,* 1986.

92   *"I cannot imagine anyone in the late eighteenth century"*   "Lafite
     Again," *Decanter,* July 1986.

93   *"for each year of the life"*   "157,500 buys wine meant for Jeffer-
     son's cup," *The Times-Picayune,* December 6, 1985.

93   *"[turning] over in his grave"*   *Daily Progress* (Charlottesville, VA),
     December 7, 1985.

94   *"the major event of the wine season"*   *Christie's Review of the Season,*
     1986 (Phaidon/Christie's), 495.

94   *"the most expensive wine"*   "Guinness Factfile," *Daily Mail,* Novem-
     ber 9, 1986.

94   *rundown of the 1980s*   "80 Greats," *Life* (special issue), Fall 1989.

94   *Rodenstock would claim*   "The World's Wildest Collector," *WS,*
     December 15, 1988; "Mann, da ist im Gaumen die Hölle los," *Der
     Spiegel,* no. 7, 1988.

8. The Sweetness of Death

The primary texts I relied on in reconstructing the tasting at Mouton
were contemporaneous accounts by Michael Broadbent ("No more
doubts," *Decanter,* September 1986), Jancis Robinson ("Sweet Taste of
Legend at £5,000 a Sip—Tasting 199-year-old claret," *The Sunday Times*
(of London), June 15, 1986; "Jefferson's 1787 Mouton," *Decanter,* September 1986), and Heinz-Gert Woschek ("Die Rechte Zeit, Der Rechte
Ort," *Alles über Wein,* no. 3 [1986]); as well as recollections published in
JMB's *Vintage Wine,* 11, and Robinson's *Tasting Pleasure,* 175–78.

96   *cork bobbing in the liquid*   "Unspoiled Treasure of Lafite 1787,"
     Decanter, February 1993.

98   *sent fifty bottles of the 1846 Lafite*   Dewey Markham, *1855: A
     History of the Bordeaux Classification* (New York: John Wiley & Sons,
     1997), 113.

100 *famously serving curry*   *Winemasters,* 202.

100 *the early-1970s price spiral*   Penning-Rowsell, "The First Growths
     of Bordeaux."

102 *he refused to meet with the Germans*   Author interview with JMB,
     November 16, 2005.

9. SALAD DRESSING

For the account of the auction of the 1784 Yquem, three reports were
indispensable: James Suckling, "Rare 1784 Yquem Brings $56,000," *WS,*
January 31, 1987; Francis X. Clines, "1784 Wine Fetches $56,000," *NYT,*
December 5, 1986; and "The Thirst for Vintage Thomas Jefferson Leads
to a Record $55,800," Associated Press, December 5, 1986. My account
of the auction of the 1784 Margaux owes a debt to Suckling's "Publisher
Buys 1784 Margaux,"*WS,* August 31, 1987, and JMB's *Vintage Wine,* 11.
Lloyd Flatt's Lafite tasting, both the planning and the execution, was vividly
memorialized in two *WS* articles: Peter Meltzer, "Planning the Lafite Tast-
ing," December 15, 1988; and Terry Robards, "Lafite Lives Up to Its
Name," December 15, 1988. Some details come from two other articles by
Meltzer ("America Collects," and "Celebrated Collector Lloyd Flatt
Rebuilds His Cellar, and Focuses His Buying Strategy," *WS,* March 31,
1995) and a report by Frank J. Prial, "Wine," *NYT,* October 19, 1988.

107 *the only bottle "of its kind"*   "Record bid brings Jefferson wine
     home," *Baltimore Sun,* December 6, 1985.

107 *"One now supposes"*   "That Lafite 1787," *Decanter,* June 1986.

108 *"perfect in every sense"*   Christie's Finest and Rarest Wines auc-
     tion catalog, December 5, 1985.

108 *a buyer in the front row*   "Sale room: 1784 Wine Fetches
     £39,600," *Times* (of London), December 5, 1986.

109 *his precocious connoisseurship*   "Jefferson: A Shrewd and
     Demanding Connoisseur," *NYT,* September 15, 1976.

109   *Virginia's wine industry*   "Virginians Enjoy Some Down-Home Wine Tasting," *WS,* July 31, 1991.

110   *122 in 2006*   "Virginia: Jefferson Sipped Here . . . And So Can You," *Washington Post,* June 3, 2007.

110   *Jefferson's epistolary mention*   TJ to Miromenil, September 6, 1790, Library of Congress collection, translation in J. M. Gabler, *Passions: The Wines and Travels of Thomas Jefferson* (Baltimore: Bacchus Press), 172.

113   *a sock over the bottle*   "Jefferson wine flies Concorde," *Times* (of London), September 3, 1987.

114   *"Slight ullage"*   JMB, *Vintage Wine,* 11.

114   *"Yes . . . , Now go away"*   Ibid.

117   *"three atrocious vintages"*   Ibid., 37.

117   *"a penance"*   Ibid., 58.

119   *Robards had observed*   "Suspicions Still Surround Rodenstock Lafite," *WS,* September 30, 1992.

120   *"An ullaged bottle"*   JMB, *Vintage Wine,* 10–11.

120   *told Bill he wasn't welcome*   "Wild Bill Koch," *Vanity Fair,* June 1994.

120   *$470 million*   "The Curse on the Koch Brothers," *Fortune,* February 17, 1997.

120   *a hedonistic tear*   "Wild Bill Koch," *Vanity Fair,* June 1994.

121   *Koch had been interested in wine*   "Raising America's Cup," *WS,* August 31, 1996.

121   *deep verticals of four iconic wines*   Ibid.

121   *33 vintages of Hennessy Cognac*   "Oil, Water and Wine," *WS,* November 15, 2005.

122   *"They don't exist now"*   "Taking time to talk and taste," *Baltimore Sun,* December 4, 2002.

10. A Pleasant Stain, but Not a Great One

125   *"an incorrigible hypemeister"*   "The Adventures of an Incorrigible Hypemeister in the Wine Trade," *New York Observer,* November 21, 1994.

125   *wrote to thank the editor*   "Hype Is Ripe," *New York Observer,* November 28, 1994.

128   *found wines recorded . . . to be subpar*   John Tilson, "Another View," *Rarities* 1, no. 1 (First Quarter, 1991).

129   *"It would positively have killed Bill Sokolin"*   William F. Buckley, Jr., *Miles Gone By* (Washington, D.C.: Regnery Publishing, 2004), 43–5.

132   *$394,000 . . . $519,750*   "Wine Is Spilt; Some Tears Ensue," *NYT,* April 26, 1989.

132   *a quarter of all Pétrus*   "How Château Pétrus Became Bordeaux's Most Coveted Wine," *WS,* February 15, 1991.

132   *half of the production of the Domaine de la Romanée-Conti*   "Beware of Bogus DRC Bottles," *WS,* November 30, 1990.

135   *Forty minutes into Sokolin's birthday*   "Wine Is Spilt . . . ," *NYT,* April 26, 1989.

136   *"What a Plonker!"*   *Daily Star,* April 26, 1989.

136   *"It's a pleasant stain"*   "Matt," *Daily Telegraph,* date unknown.

137   *"looked like chocolate-brown goo"*   "Oops! A New York Wine Merchant Turns a 1787 Château Margaux Into the World's Most Expensive Puddle," *People,* May 15, 1989.

137   *"worth maybe $10 million"*   "Case of the Broken Bottle," *WS,* date unknown.

137   *"what it is to be a William Sokolin"*   "Some Special Occasion," *NYT,* April 27, 1989.

11. THE DIVINER OF WINES

140   *the wine to be drunk at his funeral*   "Old Wine in New Glasses," *WS,* December 15, 1999.

140   *When Thomas Jefferson was alive*   "A Brief History of Glass," *WS,* November 30, 1992.

141   *they got rid of all their old glasses*   "Old Wine in New Glasses," *WS,* December 15, 1999.

142   *"The palate recognised a heroic wine"*   H. Warner Allen, *The Romance of Wine* (New York: Dover, 1971), 45.

143   *Rodenstock went so far as to suggest*   Richard Olney, *Yquem* (Boston: Godine, 1986), 144.

144   *a Taiwanese company*   "The World's Wildest Collector," *WS,* December 15, 1988.

144   *The publicity from the Forbes sale*   "Jefferson's Paris Wines: Comparing the Questions with the Facts," *VWGJ*, Spring 1986.

144   *an Yquem he said he had obtained in Leningrad*   "Ein Sammler Shreibt Weingeschichte," *Falstaff* no. 3, 1988.

145   *"The rarest of all these rarities"*   Jancis Robinson, *Tasting Pleasure* (New York: Penguin, 1999), 180.

145   *"these glasses of unctuous history"*   Ibid., 181.

145   *Rodenstock spoke of a confederate*   "The World's Wildest Collector," *WS*, December 15, 1988.

145   *He told friends that he had found another trove*   Ibid.

145   *"similar powers of discovery to water diviners"*   Edmund Penning-Rowsell, *The Wines of Bordeaux* (London: Penguin, 1989), 190.

145   *a tax exile*   "Germans call for tax on the big spenders," *Sunday Times* (London), August 8, 1999.

146   *the regional railway director*   "The World's Wildest Collector," *WS*, December 15, 1988.

146   *"the youngest such person"*   "Ein Sammler . . . ," *Falstaff* no. 3, 1988.

146   *Rodenstock was a Sagittarius*   Ibid.

146   *blank checks . . . "all hell is breaking loose on my palate"*   "Mann, da ist im Gaumen die Hölle los," *Der Spiegel*, no. 7, 1988.

150   *a fortieth-birthday gift*   "Verborgene Keller," *Der Spiegel*, October 28, 1991.

151   *"grand occasion wines"*   "Six of the Best," *Decanter*, December 1989.

151   *Peppercorn agreed with her*   "'Vintage' wine," *The Times* (of London), December 15, 1990.

1 2 . A BUILT-IN PREFERENCE FOR THE OBVIOUS

154   *drinking 1964 Lanson Champagne*   Jancis Robinson, *Tasting Pleasure* (New York: Penguin, 1999), 181.

155   *"horror machine"*   "Eisiger Schock," *Der Spiegel*, no. 42, 1988.

157   *snarled to his diary*   Albert Givton, *Carte Blanche* (Vancouver: Turnagain Enterprises, 1999), 55.

157   *"a built-in preference for the obvious"*   Quoted from May 1987 *Decanter* in "Buying by Numbers," *Decanter*, October 1987.

157   *Givton was suspicious . . . "He seems too sleek"*   Givton, *Carte Blanche*, 111.

158   *Troy was certain . . . that the wine was a fake*   Geoffrey Troy, "Another View," *Rarities* 1, no. 1 (First Quarter, 1991).

158   *Among the bottles . . . were two from Rodenstock*   "Tasting 44 Years of Elegance," *WS,* January 31, 1988.

159   *"vanilla-chocolate-mint aroma"*   Edward M. Lazarus, "A Taste of History . . . or the Stench of Fraud?" *Rarities* 1, no. 1 (First Quarter, 1991).

159   *his Venezuelan haul*   "Michael Broadbent's Tasting Notes," *Decanter,* October 1987.

160   *struck many participants as atypical*   Bipin Desai, "Another View," *Rarities* 1, no. 1 (First Quarter, 1991).

160   *"a complete fraud"*   "A Taste of Deception," *WS,* May 31, 1998.

160   *Rodenstock, put on the spot*   Desai, "Another View," *Rarities* 1, no. 1 (First Quarter, 1991).

160   *auction house subsequently reported*   "Editor's note," *Rarities* 1, no. 1 (First Quarter, 1991).

160   *Rodenstock said he had made a mistake*   Desai, "Reply to the Editor's note on Hardy Rodenstock's 1905 Ch. Figeac," *Rarities* 1, no. 2 (Second Quarter, 1991).

160   *an assemblage of Pétrus*   "A Taste of History . . . ," *Rarities* 1, no. 1 (First Quarter, 1991).

161   *old merchants' catalogs*   "A Taste of Deception," *WS,* May 31, 1998.

161   *argued that all the skeptics*   Ibid.

161   *"stupid assertion[s]"*   Fax from Rodenstock to author, July 22, 2005.

161   *three pre-phylloxera vintages*   Lazarus, "A Taste of History . . . ," *Rarities* 1, no. 1 (First Quarter, 1991).

161   *Four experienced tasters thought*   "Seemingly Ageless Latour Sparks Controversy," *WS,* March 31, 1990.

162   *The tasting notes of Givton*   "A Taste of History . . . ," *Rarities* 1, no. 1 (First Quarter, 1991).

162   *"a Rolex bought in Hong Kong"*   "Seemingly Ageless Latour . . . ," *WS,* March 31, 1990.

162   *"What are we to conclude from all this?"*   "A Taste of History . . . ," *Rarities* 1, no. 1 (First Quarter, 1991).

163   *a recipe for how to fake*   Geoffrey Troy, "Another View," *Rarities* 1, no. 1 (First Quarter, 1991).

164　*Broadbent defended the German*　　"Michael Broadbent of Christie's Writes," *Rarities* 1, no. 2 (Second Quarter, 1991).

165　*"rarity following a burglary at the château"*　　"Fine wine prices remain firm," *Decanter,* December 1987.

165　*"red wine believed to have belonged to Julius Caesar"*　　"Record Price for Caesar Bottle," *WS,* April 1, 1989.

166　*June 28, 1990, sale at Christie's London*　　This was reported in an August 31, 1990, *WS* article, "'61 Bordeaux Still Tops in London." According to JMB's records, only one nineteenth-century bottle was for sale, and it went for £370.

168　*"He became Molyneux-Berry when he went to Sotheby's"*　　Molyneux-Berry says that he has always been called Molyneux-Berry.

168　*Frericks had paid only*　　"Streit um alte Flaschen," *Stern,* April 18, 1991.

169　*Rodenstock had sold eighty bottles to Frericks*　　Ibid.

169　*150,000 marks*　　"400 000 Mark—beim teuersten Wein der Welthört die Freundschaft auf . . . ," *MAZ,* February 28, 1991.

169　*They included, besides the two Jefferson bottles*　　"The Mystery of the Lafite 1787," *Decanter,* October 1992.

170　*"significant doubt as to [the] origin"*　　"Streit um alte Flaschen," *Stern,* April 18, 1991.

13. RADIOACTIVE

A number of details from the GSF bottle opening and analyses came from the report *"Weinprobe auf Wissenschanten-Art,"* and accompanying photographs, published in the institute's newsletter, *gsf aktuell,* vol. X, June/July 1992; and two GSF research reports: H. Y. Göksu, D. F. Regulla, and A. Vogenauer, "Age Determination of Wine Sediments by Thermoluminescence Method" (GSF-Forschungszentrum für Umwelt und Gesundheit, Neuherberg); and Manfred Wolf, "Datierung des Bordeaux '1787 Lafitte Th. J.' durch Kohlenstoff-14-und Tritiumanalysen" (GSF-HY 1/93 Neuherberg [1993]).

173　*Broadbent had flown in*　　December 7, 1991, letter from Broadbent to *Rarities* 1, no. 3.

173　*"I am not particularly impressed"*　　"'Vintage' wine," *Times* (of London), December 15, 1990.

174 Wine Spectator *had run a cover story*   March 15, 1991.

174 *he insisted that he had sold*   "400 000 Mark—beim teuersten . . . ," *MAZ*, February 28, 1991.

174 *"friendship price"*   "Rodenstocks 1787er Lafite," *VIF-Gourmet Journal*, no. 3, 1993.

174 *Frericks responded by obtaining a court order*   "400 000 Mark—beim teuersten . . . ," *MAZ*, February 28, 1991.

174 *withdrew his appeal*   "400 000-Mark-Wein wird entkorkt: Leider fürs Labor," *MAZ*, May 18, 1991.

174 *pulled his bottles from Christie's*   "400 000 Mark—beim teuersten . . . ," *MAZ*, February 28, 1991.

175 *before-and-after photos*   "Der Fall Lafitte 1787 und die Folgen," *Alles über Wein*, no. 4 (1992); "Ein edler Tropfen machte aus zwei Freunden Feinde," *MAZ*, July 13, 1991; "The Mystery of the Lafite 1787," *Decanter*, October 1992.

175 *"I never had the bottles resealed or sealed"*   *Bunte*, date unknown, p. 219.

175 It tasted, Broadbent said, like the Mouton   "1787 Rodenstock Lafite Fails a Test," *WS*, August 31, 1992.

176 *"one thousand wines"*   JMB, *New Great Vintage Wine Book*, 436.

176 *"was not aware of the significance"*   Ibid., 437.

181 *"ambitions to rank among"*   Hans-Peter Frericks, "Presseerklärung," June 23, 1992.

181 *"the Konrad Kujau of the grapevine"*   "Der teuerste Wein der Welt ist gepanscht," *Münchner tageszeitung*, June 24, 1992.

181 *sometimes claiming tax reasons*   "Authentic Old Bottles, But Were They Jefferson's?" *WS*, March 15, 1991.

182 *he wanted to write about it himself*   "400 000 Mark—beim teuersten . . . ," *MAZ*, February 28, 1991.

182 *publicly called on Rodenstock*   "Th.J., Fighting Words, and Tangled Vines," *WS*, September 30, 1992.

182 *Switzerland . . . severe disruptions in the old-wine market*   Rudolf Knoll, *Vinum*, no. 9 (1992).

182 *"There is almost no interest"*   "New Tests on Jefferson Bottle Support Rodenstock," *WS*, February 28, 1993.

182 *"I just wish Hardy Rodenstock"*   "A wine market as soft as Mr. Whippy," *The Independent* (London), August 29, 1992.

14. LETTERS FROM HUBSI

183   *"the renowned Jefferson Institute"*   "Statements der Betroffenen,"
      Alles über Wein, no. 5 (1992).

183   *the "assumption of many wine experts"*   Rudolf Knoll, *Vinum,* no. 9
      (1992).

183   *"making a false public oath"*   "Das Ende eines engewöhnlichen
      Weinkrimis," *Falstaff,* no. 1 (1993).

183   *Rodenstock sought to cast suspicion on GSF*   "Statements der
      Betroffenen," *Alles über Wein,* no. 5 (1992).

183   *GSF responded that Broadbent*   "Das Ende eines . . . ," *Falstaff,* no.
      1 (1993).

183   *The lead in the wine*   *gsf aktuell,* June/July 1992.

184   *thus evidence of tampering*   "Das Ende eines . . . ," *Falstaff,* no. 1
      (1993).

184   *a police raid on GSF*   "Der Wahrheit ein Stück näher," *Alles über
      Wein,* no. 1 (1993).

184   *"A reliable dealer"*   "1787er Gepanscht," *Weinwirtschaft Markt,*
      July 10, 1992.

184   *"a photo montage" or "an optical trick"*   "1787 Rodenstock Lafite
      Fails a Test," *WS,* August 31, 1992.

184   *a Bad Marienberg photo studio*   "The Mystery of the Lafite 1787,"
      Decanter, October 1992; "Statements der Betroffenen," *Alles über
      Wein,* no. 5, 1992.

184   *Frericks's lawyer retorted*   Ibid.

184   *"[Clearly] Mr. Frericks didn't expect"*   Ibid.

184   *"I have sealed all the bottles"*   "Jefferson's Paris Wines Found,"
      VWGJ, Fall 1985.

185   *Scheuermann then wrote an article*   "Ein Weinstreit mit Nach-
      spiel," *Welt am Sonntag,* no. 26 (1992).

185   *"Somebody is carrying out active protection"*   Knoll, *Vinum,* no. 9
      (1992).

186   *It is extremely important for the determination*   "Verborgene
      Keller," *Der Spiegel,* October 28, 1991.

186   *Rodenstock had earlier suggested to* Der Spiegel   Ibid.

186   *"in case the scientists were to reveal"*   Knoll, *Vinum,* no. 9 (1992).

186 *"steaming turds"* "Verborgene Keller," *Der Spiegel,* October 28, 1991.

186 *Hubert Meier* Knoll, *Vinum,* no. 9 (1992).

187 *"Hubsi"* "Nach den Umarmung die Schelt," *Vinum,* no. 3 (1992).

187 *"Little Darling"* *Vinum,* no. 7 (1991).

187 *"Uschi Berthold"* "Hubsi und Usch," *Vinum,* no. 7 (1991).

189 *"a very keen wine man"*... *Hall was going to test* "Response from Michael Broadbent," August 12, 1992, letter to *Rarities* 1, no. 4.

190 *Eschnauer ... rejected Rodenstock's contention* "Verborgene Keller," *Der Spiegel,* October 28, 1991.

190 *"adulterated the wine or knowingly offered adulterated wine"* "Wine Lover's Nose for Fakery Leads to Famous Bottles," *Wall Street Journal,* September 1, 2006.

191 *"wine couldn't be younger than 1795"* "The Results of the New Tests," December 15, 1992, letter from Rodenstock to Foley, published in *Rarities* 2, no. 1.

192 *Rodenstock gloated* Rodenstock's January 21 and February 15, 1993, letters, and Broadbent's February 23, 1993, letter, to Foley, published in *Rarities* 2, no. 1.

192 *Rodenstock and Frericks tentatively agreed* "Rodenstocks 1787er Lafite," *VIF-Gourmet Journal,* no. 3 (1993).

192 *"Churchill always said"* "Das Ende eines...," *Falstaff,* no. 1 (1993).

192 *an entirely personal tangent* "The Final Word on Hardy Rodenstock," *Rarities* 2, no. 1.

192 *wouldn't reach a final settlement until 1995* "Wine Lover's Nose for Fakery...," *Wall Street Journal,* September 1, 2006.

193 *Rodenstock claimed that his business* "The Final Word on Hardy Rodenstock," *Rarities* 2, no. 1.

194 *"the awe-inspiring vulgarity"* "Les Cinq À Tokyo," *Decanter,* July 1993.

194 *"extraordinary charm and graciousness"* "What About Now?" *The Wine Advocate,* issue 103.

195 *captured him and Rodenstock* "Das Münchener Weinwochenende" (photo), *Falstaff,* no. 1, 1996.

15. "Awash in Fakes"

197   *auction totals in the United States*   "Grand Totals," *WS*, February 28, 1997.

197   *In 1996, worldwide wine auction sales*   Ibid.

198   *a case of six magnums of '82 Le Pin*   Ibid.

198   *a case of '45 Mouton*   Ibid.

199   *"If the trail goes dead"*   "Compared with bank notes, faking a Le Pin label is a doddle," *Daily Telegraph*, April 19, 1997.

199   *"awash in fakes"*   "A Taste of Deception," *WS*, May 31, 1998.

199   *an essay titled "In Vino Veritas?"*   *The Wine Advocate*, issue 105.

200   *French police arrested*   "Cru Bogus," *Decanter*, 1986(?).

200   *seventy cases*   "How Château Pétrus Became Bordeaux's Most Coveted Wine," *WS*, February 15, 1991.

200   *five cases of 1986 DRC Montrachet*   "A Wine Whodunit with DRC," *WS*, October 30, 1990.

200   *In 1995, at a dinner in Hong Kong*   "Compared with bank notes . . . ," *Daily Telegraph*, April 19, 1997.

200   *In 1996 an attempt to sell fake*   Ibid.

200   *In the late 1990s a London customer*   "A Taste of Deception," *WS*, May 31, 1998.

201   *In March of 1998, Langton's*   "Australian police investigate fake wine racket," BBC News, March 18, 1998; "Fighting forgery," *Wine International*, December 22, 2004.

201   *In 1985 two American businessmen*   "Reducing the Old-Wine Risk," *WS*, June 30, 1992.

201   *a bottle of 1947 Romanée-Conti*   "Beware of Bogus DRC Bottles," *WS*, November 30, 1990; John Tilson, "Another View," *Rarities* 1, no. 1 (First Quarter, 1991).

201   *Impériale of 1947 Cheval Blanc . . . 1908 Port*   "A Taste of Deception," *WS*, May 31, 1998.

202   *A German restaurant was reported*   Ibid.

202   *Serena Sutcliffe was convinced*   Ibid.

202   *Colin Lutman, an English forger of Port*   "The Case of the Exploding Bottle," *Decanter*, September 1987.

202   *At the molecular level*   "'Vintage' wine," *Times* (of London), December 15, 1990.

203 *Émile Peynaud . . . once conducted an experiment*   Author interview with Alexandre de Lur Saluces, February 16, 2006.

203 *"German sommelier with a vast knowledge"*   "A Taste of Deception," *WS*, May 31, 1998.

204 *In the Mouton episode in 1982*   "Counterfeit Wine," *Vintage Wine*, October 1982.

204 *The 1981 and 1982 Pétrus*   "How Château Pétrus Became Bordeaux's Most Coveted Wine," *WS*, February 15, 1991.

204 *The fraudsters behind*   "Fighting Forgery," *Wine International*, December 22, 2004.

204 *cases, packing tissue, and corks*   "Security Packaging Offers Brand Protection," *Wines &Vines*, May 2006.

204 *incorrectly colored bar codes*   "In Vino Falsitas," forbes.com, May 26, 2003.

204 *the Japanese customer noticed*   John Tilson, "Another View," *Rarities* 1, no. 1 (First Quarter, 1991).

205 *a Jéroboam of 1869 Mouton*   This is according to Littler; JMB recalls it as a 1920s vintage.

206 *When the police arrived*   "'Vintage' wine," *Times* (of London), December 15, 1990.

206 *"a shipment of sardines"*   Simon Loftus, *Anatomy of the Wine Trade* (Harper & Row, 1985), 77.

206 *nuclear magnetic resonance*   "'Vintage' wine," *Times* (of London), December 15, 1990.

207 *leading châteaux had become suspicious*   Ibid.

208 *FBI and New Scotland Yard*   "A Taste of Deception," May 31, 1998.

210 *Baltimore Sun article*   "Toasted in Old Madeira," October 11, 1904.

210 *oversaw a $6-million collection*   "Wine Cellar at the Rio Suite Hotel & Casino Now Exceeds 100,000 Bottles," hotel-online.com, August 24, 1998.

210 *largest bottle in the world*   Ibid.

210 Wine Spectator *identified these bottles*   "Jefferson's Madeira and More Recent Wines Lead Strong New York Sale," *WS*, July 31, 1997.

211 *"The bouquet was extremely powerful"*   Ben Killerby and Barrie Larvin, "A 200-year-old treat," Robin Garr's Wine Lovers Page, January 4, 2000.

211   *"research involved our book experts"*   E-mail from Sutcliffe to author, October 17, 2005.

211   *"The origin of the Madeira was solid"*   E-mail from Sutcliffe to author, October 19, 2005.

16. THE LAST VERTICAL

My main textual sources for reconstructing the Yquem vertical were Per-Henrik Mansson, "Three Centuries of Château d'Yquem," *WS,* May 15, 1999; Dennis Foley, "Hardy Rodenstock's Château d'Yquem Tasting," *Underground Wine Journal* 17, no. 6; Jancis Robinson, "A Taste of Thomas Jefferson's Wine," *Los Angeles Times,* December 30, 1998; and Peter Moser, "Ein stück vom Paradies," *Falstaff,* no. 6, 1998.

213   *"than anyone else in the world"*   "A Taste of Thomas Jefferson's Wine," *Los Angeles Times,* December 30, 1998.

215   *"I was an excellent heathen"*   "Famed Collector Dismantles Huge Cellar," *WS,* January 31, 1994; "Born Again Surgeon Is at One with God, But Not with Peers," *Wall Street Journal,* June 6, 1994.

215   *Tawfiq Khoury*   "Lots Left," *WS,* May 15, 1997.

215   *Lloyd Flatt*   "Celebrated Collector Lloyd Flatt Rebuilds His Cellar . . . ," *WS,* March 31, 1995.

215   *18,000-bottle cellar*   "From the Estate of Lord Andrew Lloyd Webber," Slate.com, June 19, 1997.

215   *from the cellar of Norwegian investor*   "Best wine sale ever . . . part II," *Times* (of London), November 17, 1999.

215   *$14.4 million*   "2006 Consolidated Results for Sotheby's International Wine Department," finewinepress.com.

215   *"the world's most exclusive private wine cellar"*   "Wine sale of the century," *Evening Standard* (London), August 14, 1997.

215   *"jammy wonder"; "the Cairo spice bazaar"*   "Pretentiousness? It's poetic license," *The Independent* (London), September 30, 1998.

216   *"I find that there is a chemistry"*   "A cheeky little whine from Christie's," *Daily Telegraph,* September 29, 1998.

216   *"pre-revolutionary bouquet"*   Jancis Robinson, *Tasting Pleasure* (New York: Viking Penguin, 1997), 177.

217   *definitive studies*   Richard Olney, *Yquem* (Boston: Godine, 1986); Nicholas Faith, *Château Margaux* (New York: Vendome Press, 1991).

217   *held forth in Cantonese*   "Restrainers cut loose with vintage display," *South China Morning Post* (Hong Kong), November 19, 1998.

219   *"[I]t is crazy, really"*   "A Taste of Thomas Jefferson's Wine," *Los Angeles Times,* December 30, 1998.

219   *"the deepest of deep browns"*   Ibid.

220   *Moise Pe'er*   "What's an inauguration party without a little nosh?" *Jerusalem Post,* January 20, 1997.

220   *"one or two" left*   "A Taste of Thomas Jefferson's Wine," *Los Angeles Times,* December 30, 1998.

220   *"The journalists have written so much nonsense"*   Fax from Rodenstock to author, July 22, 2005.

221   *"a couple of half bottles"*   "The World's Wildest Collector," *WS,* December 15, 1988.

221   *a late-1992 interview*   "The Mystery of the 1787 Lafite," *Decanter,* October 1992.

17. KOCH BOTTLES

I was helped, in telling Bill Koch's story, by three articles in particular: Bryan Burrough, "Wild Bill Koch," *Vanity Fair,* June 1994; Ryan Isaac, "Oil, Water, and Wine," *WS,* November 15, 2005; and Ted Loos, "Raising America's Cup," *WS,* August 31, 1996.

225   *to Steve Martin, the actor*   "A Pedigree with Pull," *NYT,* November 9, 2001.

225   *"given the Forbes provenance"*   Ibid.

226   *over the objections of Kip*   "Forbes Dynasty Split by £25M Art Sale," *Sunday Times* (United Kingdom), January 26, 2003; "Forbes Unloads Treasures," *New York Daily News,* February 19, 2003. Forbes denies that he objected to the sale.

226   *"Spotting Fakes"*   *Forbes,* December 24, 2001.

226   *"In Vino Falsitas"*   forbes.com, May 26, 2003.

226   *"Château Faux"*   forbes.com, June 19, 2006.

226   *had turned out to be a forgery*   "Fake Art Moves from Gallery to Internet," *Maine Antique Digest,* July 2000.

226   *"Blunders of the World"*   *Times* (of London), August 20, 2005.

228   *"We are ready to set the record"*   "Auctions," *NYT,* January 11, 1991.

229   *which had gotten its estimate*   "The Adventures of an Incorrigible Hypemeister in the Wine Trade," *New York Observer,* November 21, 1994.

229   *he had lowered its valuation*   "We Hear . . . ," *New York Post,* September 11, 2002.

229   *"to help raise money for tsunami relief"*   "1787 Bordeaux Reserve Up for Bid to Aid Tsunami Relief," AScribe Newswire, January 28, 2005.

230   *red outsold white*   A.C. Nielsen data, cited by the Wine Institute, April 5, 2005.

230   Wine Spectator's *paid circulation*   "Wine Spectator Celebrates 30 Years," *WS,* April 30, 2006.

230   *a circulation of 250,000*   "Cigar Aficionado Rolls Blunt Jordan Interview," *Folio,* July 13, 2005.

232   *Despite having pruned his cellar*   "Unlocking the Cellar, Quenching the Thirst," *NYT,* May 2, 1999.

232   *Latour at his third wedding*   "28-Story Mast to Be Visible for Miles," *Palm Beach Post,* February 20, 2005.

232   *while admitting he hadn't read many*   "Unlocking the Cellar . . . ," *NYT,* May 2, 1999.

233   *saw a couples therapist*   "Lowlife Behavior Alleged in Palm Beach Divorce," *Palm Beach Post,* October 24, 2000.

233   *checking into rehab*   "How Angela Outslicked Oilman Ex," *New York Post,* February 20, 2001.

233   *hired a team of MIT scientists*   "Captain America 3," *Sports Illustrated,* April 20, 1992.

234   *promised to include at least one*   "Koch at the MFA," Greater Boston TV, August 9, 2005.

234   *"My brother Charles collects money"*   "Shopping with William I. Koch," *NYT,* February 5, 2004.

18. Ghost Particles

237 *thirteen silver decadrachms* "Turkey, Investors Fighting Over Ancient Coins," AP Worldstream, February 14, 1994.

237 *"bought a Mercedes"* "The Case of the Contested Coins," *NYT,* September 24, 1998.

238 *in exchange for a plaque* "People," *International Herald Tribune,* March 6, 1999.

238 *subpoenaed his eighty-two-year-old mother* "The Curse on the Koch Brothers," *Fortune,* February 17, 1997.

238 *When he had expelled his mistress* "Koch Kiss-Off: Hi, I love you—you're evicted," *Boston Globe,* October 18, 1995.

239 *"[threatening] to beat his whole family"* "Lowlife Behavior Alleged in Palm Beach Divorce," *Palm Beach Post,* October 24, 2000; "The Things Bill Koch Really Loves," *Boston Globe,* August 9, 2005.

239 *restraining order* Ibid.

239 *willingness to introspect in public* "Wild Bill Koch," *Vanity Fair,* June 1994.

239 *"X-rated Protestant princess"* "Eviction Style of Very Rich Titillates Boston," *Philadelphia Inquirer,* November 23, 1995.

239 *"My body parts are like moist orchids"* "Look who's talking dirty," *Sunday Times* (London), December 3, 1995.

239 *Alex Beam was especially caustic* "The Things Bill Koch Really Loves," *Boston Globe,* August 9, 2005; "Koch Kiss-Off: Hi, I love you—you're evicted," *Boston Globe,* October 18, 1995.

239 *With Koch talking about a lawsuit* "Libel in the Air?" *Boston Phoenix,* September 13, 2005.

239 *groveling editor's note* *Boston Globe,* September 22, 2005.

240 *"would make Dallas and Dynasty"* "Build Your Own Playpen," *New England Business,* September 1988.

240 *private detectives and wiretaps* "Wild Bill Koch," *Vanity Fair,* June 1994.

240 *stolen garbage bags* "Captain America 3," *Sports Illustrated,* April 20, 1992.

240 *"perhaps the nastiest family feud"* "The Curse on the Koch Brothers," *Fortune,* February 17, 1997.

240   *blew the whistle on their alleged theft*   Ibid.

246   *"You just can't get a good bottle of wine"*   "The Jefferson Bottles,"
The New Yorker, September 3 & 10, 2007.

247   *had programmed his cell phone to ring*   Ibid.

250   *A lower-tech exam*   "Wine Lover's Nose for Fakery . . . ," *Wall
Street Journal,* September 1, 2006; "Entkorkt! Der grosse Wein-
schwindel," *Stern,* no. 12 (2007).

250   *Elroy had been running his fingers*   "The Jefferson Bottles," *The
New Yorker,* September 3 & 10, 2007.

19. TAILING MEINHARD

254   *a ham-fisted play*   "Wild Bill Koch," *Vanity Fair,* June 1994.

256   *"a very impressive fake"*   Complaint, *William I. Koch vs. Hardy
Rodenstock,* United States District Court, Southern District of
New York, 11.

263   *although Forbes wanted to*   Author interview with Brad Goldstein, September 1, 2006.

20. THE FINISH

266   *Gisbert appeared to share*   *Welt am Sonntag,* May 21, 2000;
"Jahrgang gehört auf Kapsel," *Vinum,* no. 9 (2004).

266   *Koch's investigators interviewed . . . Tina York*   "The Jefferson
Bottles," *The New Yorker,* September 3 & 10, 2007.

270   *spent more than $1 million*   "Wine Lover's Nose for Fakery . . . ,"
Wall Street Journal, September 1, 2006.

271   *Rodenstock said that even if the bottles were fake*   Ibid.

271   *He said he had bought the bottles without*   "World's most expensive bottle claimed fake as renowned collector sued," decanter
.com, September 6, 2006.

271   *Rodenstock bought one*   E-mail from Ulrich Sautter to author,
October 10, 2006.

271   *"a neurotic maniac"*   E-mail from Mario Scheuermann to author,
September 4, 2006.

272   *"The oak tree is not concerned"*   "Wer ist die Flasche" (caption),
Bunte, no. 40 (2006).

272 *"I should perhaps have smelled a rat"* "Rodenstock accused," jancisrobinson.com, September 6, 2006.

272 *now stated that he had always been skeptical* "Wine Lover's Nose for Fakery . . . ," *Wall Street Journal,* September 1, 2006.

272 *"Our position . . . is that we made it clear"* E-mail from Browett to author, September 6, 2006.

273 *"I don't think that anyone would have bought"* E-mail from Browett to author, December 7, 2005.

273 *"Looking back, more questions"* "Wine Lover's Nose for Fakery . . . ," *Wall Street Journal,* September 1, 2006.

273 *"among whose number I am lucky to count myself"* JMB, *Vintage Wine,* 110.

274 *"we can confirm that the engraving"* Fax from JMB to author, November 14, 2006.

274 *a Christie's spokesman disavowed* E-mail from Toby Usnik to author, November 14, 2006.

276 *"cathartic"* "Comments on the Rodenstock Affair," jancis robinson.com, September 7, 2006.

277 *"fortune and some visionary wine men"* "The power of one," *Decanter,* May 1, 2001.

277 *Sotheby's had pulled ahead* "2005 Wine Auctions Exceed $166 Million," winespectator.com, December 22, 2005.

280 *"molecular" and "chemical" analysis* "Most extensive collection of Chateau Lafite to be tested prior to sale," decanter.com, April 23, 2007.

281 *A University of Bordeaux study* Frédéric Brochet, "Tasting: Chemical Object Representation in the Field of Consciousness," 2002.

282 *whom Koch misidentified* "Wine Lover's Nose for Fakery . . . ," *Wall Street Journal,* September 1, 2006.

EPILOGUE

283 *The FBI was reported to be continuing* "In Vino Veritas?" *Manhattan,* September 2008.

284 *the auction house had to interrupt a sale* "Bogus Burgundies Uncovered," *WS,* July 31, 2008.

285 *"an embarrassing farce"*   Letter from JMB to author, June 30, 2008.

286 *a Stanford / Caltech study*   "Marketing actions can modulate neural representations of experienced pleasantness," Plassman, et al. Proceedings of the National Academy of Sciences, 2008.

Acknowledgments

I could not have written this book without the help of the small club of men who have bought or sold Jefferson bottles. Kip Forbes gamely brought the 1985 auction back to life for me and provided access to the Forbes curatorial files on the 1787 Lafite. Michael Broadbent gave indispensable and charming assistance over several years, answering and reanswering questions he tired of long ago and forthrightly opening his files to me. Bill Sokolin was candid, good-humored, and always receptive. Marvin Shanken, amid an audacious cigar-smoke haze in his Manhattan office, obliged me by sharing his auction war stories. Bill Koch provided enlightenment over lunch in Palm Beach, and I am especially thankful to Brad Goldstein, in his office, who was a worthy notes-trader as we pursued parallel investigations. Hardy Rodenstock, an elusive and enigmatic subject, kept things interesting; I never knew where his next fax would come from, and he always kept me guessing with his spirited correspondence.

Pursuing the story of the Jefferson bottles was a pleasurably far-flung endeavor, and so is acknowledging the many other people who aided my quest:

IN GERMANY: Many thanks to Mario Scheuermann in Hamburg, for opening doors and wines, and to Walter Eigensatz in Wiesbaden, for his hospitality and candor. In Munich, Yeter Göksu, Norbert Menzel, and Manfred Wolf explained the complexities of radiometric dating. From

Berlin, Hans-Horst Bethge assisted with legwork. I also thank Fedor Brunner, Ralf Frenzel, Hans-Peter Frericks, Madeleine Jakits, Hanns O. Janssen, Otto Jung, Petra and Andreas Klein, Monika Krupski, Ulrich Sautter, Emmy Scherrer, Jack Schiffer, Bodo Schlosshan, Toni Viehhauser, Karl-Heinz Wolf, Heinz-Gert Woschek, and Andreas Zielcke.

In England: Simon Woodroffe, a true wine lover, generously shared his home, company, cooking, cellar, and *Decanter* subscription during a two-month research stay in London. For interviews and other help, I owe thanks to Stephen Brook, Stephen Browett, Jim Budd, Patrick Grubb, Tom Higham, Ben Howkins, Malcolm Kimmins, Tim Littler, David Molyneux-Berry, Adrian Monck, Stephen Mould, Jancis Robinson, Maggie Rosen, Sam Sandbach, Steven Spurrier, Serena Sutcliffe, Jess White, and Amy Wislocki. Other people who helped me feel at home in England include Belinda Carruthers, Michael and Sheila Furth, Bridgie and Richard Griffiths, Linda Gummery, Maureen and Walter Marlowe, and Christopher Wickham and Diego Choi.

In Bordeaux: Christian Moueix and Paul Pontallier graciously had me to lunch in the middle of the harvest, and Alexandre de Lur Saluces did the same on a bleakly beautiful January day in Sauternes. Philippe Hubert and Bernard Medina let me into their "garage" and, with great patience and good humor, showed me their high-tech wine-dating tools. Thanks also to Murielle Andraud, Laurent Barbier, Martin Both, René Lambert, Alain Puginier, and Jean-Luc Thunevin. Elsewhere in France, Fabian Cobb was warmly encouraging.

In Switzerland: Wolfgang Grünewald was especially hospitable and helpful, as was Franz Wermuth. Thanks also to Rudolf Knoll, Bruno Künzle, and Raphael Mullis.

In Austria: Georg Riedel in Kufstein, Klaus Wagner in the Wachau, and Adi Werner in the Arlberg showed me by their hospitable examples why Hardy Rodenstock has thrown so many of his tastings in their beautiful country. August Winkler was an obliging interviewee.

Elsewhere: I received help, remotely, from Jeannie Cho Lee in Hong Kong, Nachshon Sneh in Israel, and Ben Ami Fihman in Venezuela.

In the United States: Dan Jordan welcomed me to Monticello, and Cinder Stanton was good natured in explicating her 1985 investigation. I am grateful to Dennis Foley for sending me a very rare complete set of the handsome, short-lived newsletter *Rarities*. At the University of California at Davis, Vernon Singleton and Andrew Waterhouse helped me to understand how wine ages. I owe thanks to Salma Abdelnour and Dana Cowin, at *Food & Wine*, for some timely assignments that helped broaden my knowledge of wine. David Black and Gary Morris provided early encouragement and advice. A number of other people, many of them wine merchants, auctioneers, collectors, and journalists, gave me essential interviews and other help. They include Michael Aaron, Mark Bravin, John Brincko, Bartholomew Broadbent, Alyson Careaga, James Climan, Chris Coover, Bipin Desai, Jim Elroy, Russell Frye, Eric Greenberg, Robert W. Hutton, Wilf Jaeger, Richard Johnson, John Kapon, Bonnie Kirschstein, Frank Komorowski, Andy Lawlor, Edward Lazarus, Edward Lollis, Russell Martin, Tom Matthews, Elin McCoy, Janice McManus, Peter Meltzer, Peter and Roberta Morrell, Julian Niccolini, Robert M. Parker Jr., Frank Prial, Sam Santarelli, Peter M. F. Sichel, Dave Sokolin, Gloria Sokolin, John Tilson, Margaret Kelly Trombly, Geoffrey Troy, Toby Usnik, Len Yablon, Jeff Zacharia, and, in Vancouver, Albert Givton.

Many thanks to the staffs of the British Library, the Cambridge University Library, the Hauptbibliothek Geisenheim, the Jefferson Library of the Thomas Jefferson Memorial Foundation, the Peter J. Shields Library at the University of California at Davis, the New York Public Library, the Free Library of Philadelphia, the American Philosophical Society, and the Van Pelt Library at the University of Pennsylvania, and to Fritz Blank, whose remarkable culinary collection is now part of Penn's Rare Book and Manuscript Library.

I am lucky to have found, in Larry Weissman, a literary agent who is a passionate reader, fierce advocate, and steadfast advisor. He was a true partner in the making of this book. Many thanks also to Sascha Alper, for her enthusiasm, good judgment, and hard work.

At Crown, I am grateful especially to the three talented editors I was privileged to work with, each of whom made the book better: Annik LaFarge, whose enthusiasm was inspiring, and who very generously read the manuscript and gave valuable criticism; Luke Dempsey, who provided sound counsel during much of the reporting and writing; and Rachel Klayman, who saw the book through to completion with a rare mix of intelligence, rigor, and restraint. Many thanks also for the warmth, attention, and support of Steve Ross, Kristin Kiser, Tina Constable, Jenny Frost, and the whole team at Crown, including Christine Aronson, Mary Choteborsky, Whitney Cookman, Lauren Dong, Linda Kaplan, Min Lee, Courtney Morrow, Donna Passannante, Philip Patrick, Robert Siek, and David Wade Smith.

Several other people who helped bring this book to fruition are: Jennie Dorris, who checked facts with admirable professionalism and persistence; Lawrence Schofer, who eloquently and efficiently translated German-language documents; Jamie Pastor Bolnick, who transcribed some interviews; Victor Fiorillo, a skilled computer researcher; Dan Shimberg, who came to the occasional technological rescue; and Peter Jones, who keeps Fear the Fro, Inc., solvent.

In Philadelphia, the multitalented David Fields is a treasured friend and advisor, who has taught me a lot about wine, among other things. Cary Borish and his family generously gave me a place to write. I received encouragement, tutorials, collegial support, and other help from Buzz Bissinger, Michael Bloom, Joanne Buzzetta, Amy Donohue, Jason Fagone, Bob Huber, David Lipson, Herb Lipson, Chris McDougall, Pat McGovern, Marnie Old, Shola Olunloyo, Michael and Jenny Raphael, Dan Rubin, Rich Rys, Deborah Scoblionkov, Mark Squires, and Amy Strauss. Thanks also to everyone at La Colombe, one of the world's best coffee shops and my second office for many years.

Larry Platt, a great friend, generous colleague, and early believer in this project, read the manuscript and gave helpful criticism, as did Sasha Issenberg, to whom I also owe my agent and who was the closest thing to a coworker as I labored on this book. Two other gifted friends and colleagues who made the considerable effort to read a draft of the manuscript and helped improve it are Max Potter and Mike Steinberger.

I am grateful to Lois Wallace and Tom Wallace, who have both been longtime supporters.

Many thanks to my parents, Daphne and Don Wallace, and my sisters Alexandra and Sarah, for their enduring love and support.

Jessica Pressler lived with this project for more than two years. She was understanding of its demands, gave constant support, and with her unerring nose for the fraudulent was an invaluable reader of the manuscript. I am so grateful for her love.

ABOUT THE AUTHOR

BENJAMIN WALLACE has written for *GQ, Food & Wine,*
and *Philadelphia,* where he was the executive editor. He
lives in Brooklyn, New York, and can be reached on the
Web at www.benjaminwallace.net.